SO-BYT-260

THEOLOGY IN THE SERVICE
OF THE CHURCH

Thomas W. Gillespie

THEOLOGY *in the* SERVICE *of the* CHURCH

• •

Essays in Honor of
THOMAS W. GILLESPIE

Edited by

Wallace M. Alston, Jr.

WILLIAM B. EERDMANS PUBLISHING COMPANY
GRAND RAPIDS, MICHIGAN / CAMBRIDGE, U.K.

© 2000 Wm. B. Eerdmans Publishing Co.
255 Jefferson Ave. S.E., Grand Rapids, Michigan 49503 /
P.O. Box 163, Cambridge CB3 9PU U.K.
All rights reserved

Printed in the United States of America

05 04 03 02 01 00   7 6 5 4 3 2 1

Library of Congress Cataloging-in-Publication Data

Theology in the service of the church:
essays in honor of Thomas W. Gillespie /
edited by Wallace M. Alston, Jr.
p.   cm.
ISBN 0-8028-3881-2 (cloth: alk. paper)
1. Theology.
I. Gillespie, Thomas W., 1928-
II. Alston, Wallace M., 1934-
BR118.T483   2000
230 — dc21

99-051587

Contents

Contents

Contents

Preface

This volume is an expression of appreciation and gratitude from a mere portion of those who count Thomas W. Gillespie as colleague and friend. To have included everyone who desired and deserved to be a part of it would have required a volume too large to print. What we have here is but a representative sample of those from near and far, whose respect and admiration for Tom Gillespie transcend all differences of position, place, doctrine, and perspective, and testify to the practical power of the tie that binds our hearts in Christian love.

Locating contributors to this volume, receiving their essays on time, and preparing them for publication has amounted to one of the easiest projects I have ever undertaken. This is due in large part to the skill and effectiveness of Kathi Morley and Mary McCormack, who spent many hours gathering and editing these essays, and to Laine Alston and Oman Oetiz, whose facility in Spanish was of immense assistance with translation. Likewise, those invited to author essays for this volume responded promptly and enthusiastically. Some commented that they would gladly put aside other projects in order to be included in a volume honoring the person, life, and work of Tom Gillespie. Even the few who were forced to decline on the basis of prior commitments asked to be included among the company of well-wishers.

It is obvious to anyone who knows him that Tom Gillespie is a pastor with a pastor's heart. He is determined to stand for his convictions, and can be counted on to represent them well even before those who believe him to be wrong. But there is a grace about the man that confounds the critic, compels the doubter to take him seriously, and shames the one who would characterize him unfairly.

Tom Gillespie is also an able pastor-theologian, who incarnates the very best of the Reformed tradition of a learned ministry. He is committed to the life of the mind as service to God and has spent his vocational life in pursuit of theology as the servant of the church. "Theology in the service of the church," therefore, seemed to be an appropriate rubric for this volume, and each author was invited to write with that theme in mind. The subjects of these essays are as varied and different as the people who wrote them and the places from which they come. One of the greatest tributes offered by this volume is its pluralism and diversity of author and subject, of position and perspective, and the manner in which it bears witness to the catholic character of the respect accorded this man. The essays suggest no thematic grouping and defy any attempt at logical consensus. Therefore, except for the biographical essay by which the volume is introduced, all authors are placed in alphabetical order and each essay stands on its own.

No honor could be honestly accorded Tom that did not also include Barbara. She scolded me once for introducing them as "Tom Gillespie and spouse," and I would never do so again, for she is equally deserving of honor and has her own proper name! Barbara Gillespie is wife, mother, and grandmother to this family in a particularly profound and creative way, such that Tom's life and work cannot possibly be separated from hers, nor would they want it any other way. Had the one of them not been two, and the two of them one, I cannot imagine that either of them would have been nearly as human, or as gracious, or as effective in their service to Christ and his church. They are my dear friends. I am grateful to God for them and pleased beyond words to have the privilege of saying so by way of this volume.

WALLACE M. ALSTON, JR.
Center of Theological Inquiry
Princeton, New Jersey

Thomas William Gillespie:
A Biographical Essay

WILLIAM O. HARRIS

Thomas William Gillespie was born in southwest Los Angeles, California, on July 18, 1928, the only child of William A. and Estella (Beers) Gillespie.

About 1910 Thomas Gillespie's grandparents, Thomas and Agnes Storey Gillespie, came from the Scottish mining town of Shotts, located midway between Glasgow and Edinburgh, to western Pennsylvania. The couple brought with them a family of eleven children, settling in Turtle Creek, a community near Pittsburgh. The father found work there in the coal mines along with other Scottish-born miners. While in Turtle Creek they had another son, William A. Gillespie, who would become the father of Thomas W. Gillespie. Within a few years of arriving in America, the grandfather died of black lung disease, a malady that continues to afflict many coal miners. His widow took their younger children to Venice, California, to join several of their adult children who had previously moved there.

Gillespie's mother, Estella Beers, was born in Dallas, Texas, but moved as a child with her parents to Los Angeles. There she later met and married William Gillespie, a printer and a talented carpenter. When their son was born in 1928, Bill and Estella became active members of the Florence Avenue United Presbyterian Church.

When Gillespie was nine years old, his parents became members of the Vermont Avenue Presbyterian Church. It would be difficult to overstate the influence of that church, its pastors and its people, in his faith formation and in setting the agenda for his life. The church was a large, warm-hearted, and active evangelical congregation where the young man was solidly nurtured in the Christian faith. The church's pastors, especially Edward Caldwell, became role models for Gillespie when he himself entered the ministry. A college classmate of Gillespie, who attended the Vermont Avenue Presbyterian Church with him and later spent forty years teaching religion in various colleges, made the following comment about Caldwell:

> Edward Caldwell had a powerful and enduring influence on Tom, and it was clear even during Tom's freshman days that Ed Caldwell had his eye on him as a future Presbyterian minister. Caldwell was a rare sort of evangelical in those days, a truly scholarly man who understood and accepted biblical criticism, and who found that a critical understanding of the Bible buttressed rather than hindered his faith. Tom maintained a friendship with Caldwell until he died just a few years ago.

In high school, however, Gillespie was not headed for the ministry. He was a budding architect who enjoyed drawing up plans for buildings and constructing such things as tree houses, soapbox-derby racers, and model airplanes.

In the spring of his senior year in high school, Gillespie enlisted in the United States Marine Corps. World War II had just ended, and the call had gone out for new recruits to replace Marines being discharged from active duty. The rigor and discipline of Marine boot camp fulfilled the requirements for his high school graduation, so Gillespie exchanged high school for the Marine Recruit Base at Camp Pendleton, near San Diego. Following his basic training he was assigned to be a chaplain's assistant and spent the remainder of his service time in that capacity. While serving as a chaplain's assistant, Gillespie experienced God's call to the ministry, a call he resisted for some time. Later he described his resistance in the form of a protest to the Almighty: "You have to be kidding! The ministry? That would mean studying Greek and Hebrew, and you know me and languages. The only 'D' I got in high school was in first-year Spanish. You've got the wrong Gillespie!" This initial reluctance was overcome and his resistance changed to an acceptance of God's call. Gillespie went on to minor in Greek in college, successfully to master Hebrew in seminary, and to pass qualifying examinations in Aramaic, German, and French on his way to earning his Ph.D. God, it seems, had the right Gillespie all along.

Upon his discharge from the Marine Corps, Gillespie entered George Pepperdine College (now Pepperdine University), which was located near his home in Los Angeles. On Sunday nights, the college group at Vermont Avenue Presbyterian Church, mostly Pepperdine students, met for study and worship. This provided fellowship for Gillespie and many of his closest friends throughout college. In this setting he met a high school student named Barbara Lugenbill, whom he would later marry. Gillespie and this group of church friends were instrumental in starting a new fraternity at Pepperdine, Sigma Phi Chi (Greek letters which are the initials for the English words, *Service for Christ*).

In college Gillespie majored in history and minored in religion and Greek. He was especially influenced by Professor Ralph Wilburn, a religion professor and an authentic scholar who had broad Christian interests beyond the limits of his own denomination, the Church of Christ. Gillespie took all the courses that Dr. Wilburn offered, including a course on "The Living World Religions." It was in this course that Gillespie experienced his "crisis of faith." Having heard Dr. Wilburn forcefully and intelligently present the case for each of the world's living religions and having read extensively about each of them, Gillespie went to Dr. Wilburn's office one afternoon, slumped down in a chair and said, "I don't have a clue why I'm a Christian." Dr. Wilburn threw back his head, laughed, and said, "Good! Now read this." He handed Gillespie a copy of H. Richard Niebuhr's book, *The Meaning of Revelation*. Later Dr. Wilburn commented that Gillespie was far beyond his other students in grasping theological issues, and Gillespie has often remarked that "Dr. Wilburn really opened up the subject of theology for me."

When college graduation approached, it was time to plan for seminary. Gillespie had always — really, *only* — thought of going to Princeton Theological Seminary. The pastors he had known at the Vermont Avenue Church were all Princeton Theological Seminary alumni. There was, however, a definite feeling on the part of many of the pastors in California at that time that ministerial candidates should remain in the West for their theological education. When Gillespie appeared before the Los Angeles Presbytery's Committee on Candidates, one of the members asked where he planned to go to seminary, and he replied, "I'd like to go to Princeton." A deep voice from the corner of the room boomed out, "That's no heresy!"

The discussion was closed. That voice belonged to Dr. Eugene Carson Blake, PTS '32, then the pastor of the Pasadena Presbyterian Church and later to become the Stated Clerk of the General Assembly of the Presbyterian Church.

Gillespie entered Princeton Theological Seminary in September 1951 and was soon attracted to the lectures of Professor George S. Hendry, the Charles Hodge Professor of Systematic Theology. Dr. Hendry was a precise and deeply thoughtful Scot, one of the few theologians in America who had mastered the work of Karl Barth in the original German. He inspired Gillespie throughout his three years at Princeton Seminary with his respect for Biblical authority, for the dignity of reason, and for the necessity of personal spiritual commitment. Another professor who deeply influenced Gillespie during his seminary days was Professor Otto A. Piper, the Helen H. P. Manson Professor of New Testament. Because of his appreciation for Dr. Piper's vast learning and his unabashed originality, Gillespie assumed an unusually heavy academic load in order to participate in several of Dr. Piper's doctoral seminars on Paul's epistles. These seminars focused on the Greek text of the epistles. It was this work with Dr. Piper that guided his academic attention beyond systematic theology to its source in the Scriptures.

The young Gillespie was both stimulated and challenged by Dr. Paul L. Lehmann, the Stephen Colwell Professor of Christian Ethics. Lehmann's unique and exciting treatment of Christian ethics at first threatened but later intrigued Gillespie. The idea of ethics being derived from one's function in building up the community rather than from a prescriptive norm was strong meat for this Southern California evangelical. He was richly nourished by his encounter with Dr. Lehmann, and while retaining his independence, the insights and bold applications of Paul Lehmann's *koinonia* ethics have always been just below the surface of Gillespie's spirit.

The Seminary president, Dr. John A. Mackay, also had a profound effect on him. Mackay's winsome and passionate spirituality, his abiding loyalty to the Reformed heritage, his eager response to the God "who makes all things new," and his devotion to both "the majesty of truth" and the unity of the whole people of God, provided Gillespie with a vision that has never left him. Both of these sons of Princeton Seminary, Mackay and Gillespie, have demonstrated in their lives the purpose for which the Seminary was established, the cultivation of "sound learning and vital piety" (*The Plan of Princeton Theological Seminary,* 1811).

4

During the summer following the completion of his second year at Princeton Theological Seminary, Gillespie married his fiancée, Barbara A. Lugenbill. The wedding took place on July 31, 1953, at their home church, the Vermont Avenue Presbyterian Church in Los Angeles. Barbara was a native of Los Angeles, the daughter of a Swiss father and a German mother who had met and married in that city. Barbara attended Pepperdine College and graduated with a degree in education. She later taught in the schools of Monmouth Junction, New Jersey and then in Garden Grove, California. When the newly wed couple came to Princeton, the attic of a large frame house at #86 Stockton Street became home. Barbara taught school that winter and was an enthusiastic member of the Seminary Students' Wives' Club, a club sponsored by the president's wife, Mrs. Jane Logan Mackay, at her home, Springdale. Barbara recalls that on the day following commencement in June 1954, when she and Tom were packing to start their trip back to California, she paused to take her camera and to walk down to Mercer Street because "I wanted to get a picture of Springdale, since I thought that I would never see it again."

Towards the end of Gillespie's senior year, Professor Hendry made the unusual gesture of personally inviting Gillespie to continue his studies at Princeton Seminary by undertaking the pursuit of the Doctor of Theology degree in systematic theology. He declined Dr. Hendry's invitation on the grounds that he felt called to serve as a pastor in a local congregation in California. Desiring to be a pastor in Southern California and knowing that he should be present there for consideration by local churches, the couple moved to Gillespie's parents' home in Los Angeles. After some months, he was approached by the National Missions Committee of the Los Angeles Presbytery with an invitation to organize a Presbyterian church in what was at that time the village of Garden Grove in Orange County, California. The invitation in itself was highly unusual. The National Missions Committee had a rule that no minister without previous pastoral experience would be considered for the delicate work of organizing a new congregation. Gillespie's natural talents as a leader and a preacher caused the committee to suspend its rule and to entrust him with this challenging and responsible opportunity.

Shortly thereafter, Gillespie was able to rent the facilities of a small Seventh Day Adventist congregation in Garden Grove for use on Sundays. In the Fall of 1954, the First Presbyterian Church of Garden Grove began services and from the beginning grew rapidly. Gillespie has often modestly dismissed his role in the success of the Garden Grove Church by remarking "in those days all you had to do was open the door, step out of the way, and the people would just flock in." Gillespie was pastor of that church for twelve years, and when he left, he had received over eighteen hundred members into the congregation, and a sanctuary together with an education and administration complex had been constructed. While he served there, all three of the Gillespie children — Robyn C., William T., and Dayle E. — were born.

In 1966, Gillespie became pastor of the influential First Presbyterian Church of Burlingame, California, near Stanford University, where he served for the next seventeen years. When a business executive who was a member of that church during Gillespie's pastorate was asked what he considered Gillespie's major contribution to that congregation to have been, he replied with enthusiasm, "His sermons. He had something for me personally every week, and I got it, hung onto and remembered it. Fifteen years later I can still remember some of those sermons. He was a most effective pastor in all ways but especially through his preaching. Many friends have mentioned this." Gillespie was also an adroit administrator who quietly and carefully brought about significant changes in this congregation, among which was the calling of a woman assistant pastor. He was one of the first pastors in Northern California to employ a woman assistant, and he repeated these invitations several times while he was there.

While he was at Burlingame he completed the requirements for a Doctor of Philosophy degree in the New Testament at Claremont Graduate School in Claremont, California and received that degree in 1971. His dissertation was entitled, "Prophecy and Tongues: The Concept of Christian Prophecy in the Pauline Theology." An extensive revision of this work was published by Eerdmans in 1994 with the title *The First Theologians: A Study in Early Christian Prophecy.*

In 1983 the Trustees of Princeton Theological Seminary, following a long and thorough search, called Thomas W. Gillespie to be President of the Seminary and Professor of New Testament. The visible signs of his leadership of the Seminary during the past fifteen years are obvious with a look around the campus. Three new buildings have been built. Templeton Hall, which provides space for classrooms, recording and television studios, and administrative offices, was completed in 1989. A spacious additional library building, the Henry Luce III Library, was built adjacent to Speer Library and completed in 1994. In 1998, a long-time dream of

Gillespie, the Witherspoon Apartments, providing housing for fifty single, second-career students, was dedicated on the grounds of the Charlotte Rachel Wilson complex. Under his leadership every major building on the campus with the exception of Miller Chapel and Speer Library has undergone significant and esthetically pleasing renovation. The extensive renovation of Miller Chapel together with the installation of a new pipe organ and the construction of a separate chapel office building has recently begun. The rededication of Miller Chapel will be part of the Seminary's celebration of the millennium. Plans for the renovation of Speer Library are in the early stages.

Other obvious indications of the success of Gillespie's administration include eleven newly endowed professorships and the growth of the full-time faculty from thirty-seven to forty-nine. It can be said of few presidents of any institution what is true of Gillespie, that he has presided over a 500 percent increase in the Seminary's endowment. With these additional resources he has encouraged the development of a larger and more vigorous Ph.D. program in biblical, historical, and theological studies, a reflection of his concern about the future teachers in the universities and seminaries of the world. He has also greatly expanded the program of continuing education, both in program and in facilities. Under his leadership the Seminary has developed a closer relationship with the Center of Theological Inquiry, a world-class theological research center located adjacent to the Seminary campus. Gillespie has served as the chairman of its board of trustees for the past several years.

Gillespie's active participation in the affairs of the world church and its theological enterprise has been recognized by colleges and universities around the world. This recognition has been expressed, among other ways, by his being awarded the following honorary degrees: Doctor of Divinity, Grove City College, 1984; Doctor of Theology, The Theological Academy, Debrecen, Hungary, 1988; Doctor of Theology, Karoli Gaspar Reformed University, Budapest, Hungary, 1994; Doctor of Philosophy, Soong Sil University, Seoul, Korea, 1994; and Doctor of Divinity, University of St. Andrews, Scotland, 1996.

For an in-depth and comprehensive analysis of President Gillespie's administration of the Seminary and his impact upon it and its future, we have turned to a thoughtful, distinguished scholar who has been intimately involved in the affairs of the Seminary both during the administration of President James I. McCord as well as throughout Gillespie's tenure.

7

Following are his reflections on Gillespie as president at Princeton Seminary:

> When President Gillespie began his term of office his first task was the completion of initiatives conceived during the era of his predecessor, President James I. McCord: ambitious renovation and building programs, bold plans for capital campaigns to endow faculty positions and program extensions, far-reaching commitments to improve housing conditions and financial aid for students, and cherished dreams to make Princeton a global center of theological scholarship. There was also a task of leading the Seminary through major transitions the magnitude of which had only begun to dawn on the previous leadership: the integration of women and second-career students into the life of the community; the emergence of pluralistic forms of ministry; and last but not least, the computer revolution. Looking back at fifteen years of the Gillespie presidency one realizes with amazement that all these tasks have been carried out, fully and beyond expectations. The ecumenical composition of the student body and faculty has increased considerably and international ties have deepened — a Korean-American program is firmly in place, overseas seminars and exchanges are being conducted, and once again the current president of the World Alliance of Reformed Churches is a member of the faculty. Practically all campus buildings have undergone total renovation; magnificent new buildings have gone up or are planned. All existing professorial chairs are endowed and several new ones have been created. Student housing has improved dramatically and the endowment for financial aid has doubled. The number of applications for the school's doctoral degrees is at record levels and the Center for Theological Inquiry which Dr. McCord founded attracts the best minds among theological scholars in the world.
>
> From the beginning, Dr. Gillespie's presidency has introduced a different style of communication into the hierarchical structures of the venerable academic institution. He returned to the school of his student years not as a professional administrator but as an experienced pastor, formed and nourished by the congregational life of the Presbyterian Church. The pastor at the head of the Seminary made a difference in every facet of life on campus. He added a personal touch to the professional world of graduate education. Pastors are concerned with people. Dr. Gillespie listened to his colleagues on the board, on the faculty,

among alumni/ae and students. He was not in the habit of making lonely decisions but sought dialogue, advice, and common ground among the people responsible for the well-being of the school. Pastors know that efficient organization matters in an ecclesiastical institution. Dr. Gillespie reorganized the structure of the Seminary's internal operations, delegating responsibility freely and trustingly and paying attention to the human needs surfacing with every major change. His goal, it seems, was to create a new spirit of team work and accountability as the most desirable form of day-to-day cooperation between president, faculty, and staff. Pastors also know that good facilities are a major asset for successful work in a church. Dr. Gillespie made it an early priority to upgrade the older buildings on campus so that life would be easier for everyone. He did so without a grim determination to change everything but showed a consistent regard for the integrity of the architectural setting.

While his pastoral experience prepared the new seminary president to deal with unexpected challenges, it did not prepare him for challenges of the magnitude he had to deal with. In the Presbyterian Church as in other churches, the past twenty years have been a time of escalating crisis. Dwindling membership is not just a sociological phenomenon but an indication of deeper doubts, not so much about the faith itself but about the institutional church and its leadership. While continuing the tradition of not officially committing the seminary to taking sides in the raging controversies, Dr. Gillespie found it necessary to take sides himself, standing up for deeply held convictions at times when divisiveness threatened the church and even the campus. In the midst of controversy, however, he always tried to make peace and retain an open mind, allowing the Seminary to be a place where different convictions and opinions could be heard without reprisal and could be voiced, heard, and discussed.

In theological education as well as in the church, Princeton Seminary continues its leadership role. Many of the seminary's graduates are in educational positions of considerable influence around the world; four of the nine presidents of Presbyterian seminaries in this country are Princeton alumni. Top students from the best schools apply for admission to the academic programs in record numbers. The Center for Continuing Education offers a widely respected slate of professional training opportunities, and the latest review by the accrediting agencies in 1997 underscores the previous years' achievements. For the first time in decades, the visiting team filed its report without a single notation of criticism.

Dr. Gillespie has been an exemplary leader in keeping before the seminary community the abiding vision of a ministry which the "Plan of the Seminary" of 1811 describes as a combination of "sound learning" and genuine "piety of the heart." He still preaches in Miller Chapel once every week. His messages at the opening of school and commencement every year do not cease to impress upon vast audiences the challenges and rewards of this ministry which he himself exemplifies so well. At the same time, he has given outstanding leadership to the wide-ranging scholarly work which is so much a part of the Princeton tradition. Dr. Gillespie not only teaches a course in the Biblical Department regularly but has managed to publish a major book in his field during his tenure as president. A scholar himself, he has given strong encouragement to scholarly endeavors of his faculty colleagues. A liberal sabbatical policy, institutional involvement in major scholarly projects, and the support of publications such as *Theology Today*, the *Seminary Bulletin, Koinonia*, and the series *Studies in Reformed Theology* continue to affirm the Seminary's long-standing commitment to serious theological scholarship.

With all his interest in the contemporary church and its situation, Dr. Gillespie exhibits a vivid sense of history and tradition. He has tried to insure that the task of preserving what is left of the past is taken seriously. Anyone who visits the campus these days is able to experience the power of historic memory, the recollection of roots actualized by a spirit of respect and loving care. If one thing is clear, however, it is that President Gillespie does not live in the past. His orientation as a pastoral leader is toward present and future needs of people in the church and the world who are looking for reliable guidance and serious nourishment in the midst of confusion and uncertainty. For the sake of this task, he seems less interested in novelty than in continuity. His navigation of uncharted waters has been gentle and unaggressive, avoiding risk rather than seeking it. Care, not expansion, seems to be foremost in his mind. Dr. Gillespie's presidency has steered Princeton Theological Seminary to the edge of a new millennium as an institution stronger and more capable than it has ever been to honor its commitments and to be a shining light in the great house of the church with its many mansions.

There is no better way to conclude this brief biography of President Gillespie than to repeat his vision for Princeton Seminary, which he expressed on the occasion of his tenth anniversary as president in 1993:

> Our task is to reclaim the tradition and to strengthen and advance it; not to chase after fads and theological shadows, but to remain faithful to the substance of the gospel that has been handed down to us. Our mission is to continue to prepare the best preacher-pastors and the best teachers of the next generation of preachers we possibly can. We have a great responsibility, and we intend with all the energy we have and through every resource we possess to be faithful to that mission. [*Princeton Theological Seminary Alumni/ae News,* Fall 1993]

Stewardship or Generosity?

ROBERT M. ADAMS

I will be taking some potshots at a sacred cow. As long as I can remember (which is quite a while now), the standard terminology and model for discussing Christian giving, in the churches of which I have been a part, has been that of "stewardship." For some time I have suspected that the notion of stewardship has been overused in ways that have led, not merely to stale and tired terminology, but to impoverishment of our conception of Christian giving. There is something right about the idea that we are "stewards" of what is God's, and I will begin by discussing some strengths of that idea. Yet I fear it may in some ways work against something more important, and more deeply rooted in the liberty of the gospel — namely, the virtue of generosity.

Stewardship

A steward is an administrator — someone who administers some of the affairs, and possessions, of someone else, and who is responsible to that other person. Stewards figure prominently in some of the Gospel parables, and the concept of the steward's role (οἰκονομία — economy or in plain English, administration or management) is adapted to theological or ecclesiastical use in various passages of the New Testament. Clearly the model of the steward or administrator had considerable cultural resonance in a society in which the roles of owner and manager had begun to be separated.

12

Just as clearly it has in our society no less resonance — a resonance that is by no means countercultural. We prize the role of manager. Many members of our churches are managers, and many others wish to be. Whether or not we are managers in our gainful employment, many of us are officers of various sorts of organizations, and in that role we are responsible for administering affairs that are not simply and individually our own. Acculturation to such roles and responsibilities begins early, in associations and activities for youth; and our adult world is pervasively structured by a complex web of administrative responsibilities and prerogatives. In connecting their financial basis with stewardship, or the administrator's role, American churches have tapped into one of the most powerful organizing principles of American life.

That's not all bad — certainly not. The churches' use of the concept emphasizes the responsibility that goes with administrative control of what belongs to somebody else. That is a theme that can hardly be sounded too loudly where the power of managers is as vast as it is in our society. In the churches' primary application of the concept, everything belongs to God, and all of us who "own" anything merely administer what is God's. There is something right about that too. It has a wholesome (and now countercultural) bite. Our culture is one in which the affluent tend to feel a powerful moral entitlement to whatever they legally (if only temporarily) "own." This is often manifested in a resentment of taxation, a resentment that poisons political relations and distorts individual financial planning.

The resentment and the underlying sense of entitlement are in my opinion absurd. In the relevant cases, after all, we are not talking about potatoes we have grown with our own hands. What wealth and income, goods and services, we enjoy come to us through a complex social, political, and economic system of production and distribution in which vast numbers of people play a part and the effects of individual contributions are difficult to distinguish. The scale of the rewards we reap depends as much on power relationships and on what other people happen to desire and esteem as on our own creativity and effort. Government and the taxes that support it are an integral part of the system. If the share allotted to us, after taxes, by the system is much larger than that received by many others who work as hard as we do (or who do so whenever they get the chance), our predominant attitude toward the system as it affects us ought not to be resentment but gratitude and a sense of responsibility.

13

Viewing our situation theologically in terms of stewardship attacks our sense of entitlement on a deeper level. At bottom everything belongs to God, as everything comes from God and everything has been redeemed by God in Christ. The truest entitlement is God's, and belongs derivatively to the world, the church, and the persons that God loves — and to us not as legal owners but only as objects of God's love. The question "What am I entitled to?" pales into insignificance (or should) beside the question "What is my place in the divine plan (the divine οἰκονομία)?"

The message of stewardship also rebukes our pride in giving, and rightly so. If we are affluent and manage (with the aid and encouragement of tax deductions) to give 10 percent or so of our income to churches and charities, we may be tempted to think that's a big deal, especially when disclosure laws make us aware of affluent political leaders who don't do as well as that. In fact, however, it's merely decent behavior, as we can see if we manage to set aside our false sense of entitlement.

The model of the steward or administrator applies more aptly, I believe, to some of our economic roles and relationships than to others. It is maximally appropriate in our relation to the earth, its nonrenewable resources, and its wealth of plant and animal species. It is monstrous to think that we can own such things in such a way as to be entitled to use them for our own advantage without regard for their own wonder and beauty or for those who will come after us. Much the same is true of political institutions, universities, and churches, which we did not create and whose importance for other people we should expect (and hope) will outlive us.

Something similar can be true of a large business, which may be legally owned by an individual or a family though the prosperity of many persons and even communities may depend on it. When the factory in Massachusetts that produces Polartec suffered a disastrous fire recently, the family who own the business were widely and rightly praised for their sense of responsibility, grounded in their Jewish faith, in rebuilding the plant and retaining their employees rather than taking the occasion to move their production to a cheaper labor market. This is not to say that the proprietors in such a case should think of themselves, ethically, as mere administrators rather than owners; it is rather that they should see their role less in terms of entitlement than of solidarity or, in biblical terms (as I will explain it in the second part of this paper), of *hesed*.

The model of the steward is less evidently appropriate in relation to more perishable resources. Do we merely administer the food that we eat, the services we render, and the labor that we do or do not perform — all of which will perish unused if they are not given or consumed? Members of the Franciscan order sometimes write their names in books, for some of the same reasons that the rest of us do, but preceded by the initials "A.U.S," signifying that the books are not strictly owned but possessed by them *ad usum solum* — "only for use." Without wishing to interject myself into the centuries-long debate over the appropriate nature of Franciscan poverty, I think there is something beautiful about the idea of possession *ad usum solum;* but when we are talking about the food that one eats, surely the distinction between ownership and possession only for use wears very thin.

What principally concerns us here, however, is the application of the model of the steward in relation to giving. And precisely here is a problem — I think a glaring problem. For stewards, as such, don't give — stewards administer. Giving, strictly speaking, is not something you do with someone else's resources.

Generosity

Is there another conception that might supplement, if not wholly supplant, the idea of stewardship, and that might perhaps fit better with the idea of giving? My candidate is the virtue of generosity. A generous person is one who gives of herself and her resources, and who does so freely and not out of a sense of compulsion. She does not think that giving makes her special, but she does see it as a meaningful expression of who she is and wants to be, and of what (and whom) she cares about. Usually she enjoys giving. She does not think it would be outrageous for her to have less than she has, and she is likely to be skeptical of advertisers' claims about what she "owes herself." But she does assume that what she gives is hers to give, and therefore that it is hers. Christian generosity is an expression of Christian liberty. Generosity is possible for Christians because the freedom of the gospel makes a space for love in which there are good things to do that we don't have to do.

The stress on stewardship may be in tension with the virtue of generosity. One way in which this may show itself is in a contrast between carefulness and liberality. Stewards, who administer what belongs to others, have a special obligation to be careful with it. And no doubt it is good to be careful — up to a certain point — with things that are valuable. The ethos of North European Protestantism cannot be said to have underrated the virtues of carefulness; in that respect the model of the steward suits us well. Excessive or anxious carefulness, however, is contrary to the virtue of generosity. Generosity involves liberality, or freedom in using as well as in giving. The generous person not only spends on and for others as well as himself, but also spends freely on good projects without worrying too much about whether they are the best possible use of the resources. The thought that one might possibly do something better instead is more characteristic of responsibility than of generosity, and the generous person is often not inhibited by it. Such generosity can have various sources, but it springs naturally from faith in a God whose goodness overflows and is not in short supply.

I believe that excessive and ungenerous carefulness does sometimes affect thinking about stewardship in churches. People who are not excessively careful with money in their own lives sometimes fixate on issues of best possible use when there is a question of spending money given to the church, or of giving to the church for certain purposes. Is it right, is it unselfish enough, to spend money beautifying our worship, we wonder, when there are so many urgent needs in the world? Well, perhaps we should indeed be giving more to meet those urgent needs, but if this thought inhibits us from beautifying our worship (within the bounds of reason), we are not approaching the worship of God with a generous spirit.

Theologically this is still not the deepest level of concern about the relation between stewardship and generosity, or between stewardship and giving. Theologically we must ask whether we are most fundamentally administrators or givers. That depends on whether we have much that is ours to give, and at bottom that is a question about God's grace. Does God only lend to us or employ us, or does God actually give to us?

I think we must ascribe considerable validity to both models of our relationship to God. Certainly the Bible makes use of both. We are God's servants; Christ is our Lord. We are to think of ourselves as stewards responsible to God. Nonetheless I believe that the center of the New Testament message is closer to the other model, the one in which we have something that is ours to give because it has actually been given to us by God. We are not only servants. Jesus says to his disciples, "I no longer call you servants [or slaves, δούλους], . . . but I have called you friends" (John 15:15). And according to Paul, the Christian is no longer a slave [δοῦλος] but a child of God, and hence an heir (Galatians 3:26–4:7).

16

The thought may arise at this point that if we have something that is ours to give because it has really been given to us by God, then perhaps I was wrong to criticize the sense of entitlement that our culture encourages us to have regarding our possessions. I do not think this follows. What is given me by the bountiful Giver is not given to me to defend against others in the way suggested by the sense of entitlement. It is given me that I might be free with it in using it, sharing it, and giving it (though some things may indeed be mine in such a special way, so connected with my vocation and my selfhood, that I should not easily let go of them). God's gift to me is part of God's gift to us. Indeed, I, and you, are part of God's gift to us. What is given to you is given so that your life might the better be a gift to all of us — including you, of course. For if your life is to be a gift, it is important that you should have much that you are free to give.

If God's gift to you or to me is a part of God's gift to us, the virtue of generosity can be seen as an aspect of an even more central biblical virtue, the virtue of *hesed* (חֶסֶד). חֶסֶד is one of the most famously untranslatable words in the Hebrew Bible. It is one of the biblical words for grace. In the King James Version it is often translated as "mercy," and often as "lovingkindness," a lovely, if not altogether accurate, coinage. A note of reliability is rightly added in the Revised Standard Version rendering, "steadfast love." Yet all these translations leave out much of the meaning of the Hebrew word. My favorite English equivalent is the early modern phrase, "covenant mercies." It captures to a considerable extent the two main aspects of the meaning of "*hesed.*"[1]

"Covenant" rightly suggests that *hesed* has its home in the context of an ongoing and significant social relationship. It would narrow the meaning too much to insist that the relationship must be contractual or involve an explicit covenant, but *hesed* does involve a commitment or loyalty to another person or persons — hence its "steadfastness." The relationship need not be a particularly close one. There is a *hesed* that is appropriate for us to have toward persons merely as fellow citizens, for instance — or, indeed, in Christian perspective, merely as children, with us, of the same God.

---

1. Which I use from this point on as an English word, acknowledging that I am abstracting from some of the untidy diversity of use and meaning that the Hebrew word has as a word in a natural language.

At the same time *hesed* is mercy or grace or gratuitous in the sense that it goes beyond any specific obligation one has in the relationship. *Hesed* is "kindness" that is generous and forgiving. It is a commitment to the other person or persons rather than to specific duties toward them. It is rather open-endedly disposed to respond to the partner's needs and opportunities. It will not abandon the partner.

If we want a single ordinary English word for it, "solidarity" will often be a good choice. *Hesed*, or solidarity, is something that any healthy society must have. It is often claimed that the sense of community is being lost in our culture, and many of those who make the claim attribute the loss to a lack of respect for authority. A much more plausible account, in my opinion, is that the defensive sense of individual entitlement of the affluent is an acid that is eating away at the solidarity or *hesed* that sustains community.

Christian generosity is an aspect of *hesed*. It is a stance in which one gives freely, out of love rather than compulsion, out of personal commitment rather than strict obligation. Yet it springs from a vision of personal and social relationships in which solidarity is more fundamental than individual entitlement — a vision grounded in God's *hesed* and God's giving, in which much can be yours, not in the sense that it is only for you, but in the sense that you can be free with it. This is doubtless an ideal that we are often too vulnerable to dare to realize very fully; but we have before us the example and the gift of the generosity and *hesed* of Christ, who did not regard equality with God as something to be grasped as an individual entitlement (Philippians 2:6), but gave himself freely to have solidarity with us.

The Ministry of Christian Theology

WALLACE M. ALSTON, JR.

Theology is thinking God. Christian theology is thinking God in the light of Jesus Christ. Ministry is serving people in his name. Theology as a purely academic discipline may be interesting, provocative, and deserving of the scholar's time and attention. But Christian theology without ministerial motivation simply does not exist and is found in the form of a pretender. The church, and particularly the congregation, is the locus of the ministry of Christian theology, and pastoral occasions test and evaluate its reality. The ministry of Christian theology does not end with the church. It has a public as well as an ecclesial calling. But when Christian theology is pursued without reference to the church, as so often happens today, the result is cut-flower God-thought. The claim registered here is that the reformation of the church, if and when it is granted, will require and include the recovery of the church as a theological community, and the ministry of the church as a theological vocation.

Statistics often quoted tend to be boring, except when they sound an alarm that the sleeper fails to hear. If one is permitted to use one denomination as symptomatic of mainline American Protestantism in general, the thing to note is how calm and composed the church has been upon hearing these statistical "maydays." In fact, there seems to be little embarrassment about the situation in high places and even less concern to identify and remedy the problem. In 1966, the combined United Presbyterian Church in the United States of America and the Presbyterian Church in the United States numbered 4,250,000 members; in 1996, the figure was 2,665,276. The two major Presbyterian bodies in this country, which merged in 1983, have "succeeded" in losing 1,584,724 members in just thirty years, and that without even trying! If the Presbyterian Church had wanted to downsize or sought a strategy for going out of business, it could not have done so more effectively. In that regard, perhaps, the Presbyterian Church (USA) is more typical than unique.

I

Does this mean that the church is in trouble? No, of course not, at least not in any ultimate sense of the word. The church is God's creation, not our own. We did not make it and we will not destroy it. The church is part of God's plan and purpose to renovate the fallen world, and its future is in God's hands. That is what we affirm in the third article of the Apostles' Creed. We say, or at least mean to say, not "I believe *in* the church," but "I believe the church." According to John Calvin, the word "believe" is used to indicate that the existence of the real and true church is not an empirical fact, but rather that it is known only to God. "We testify that we believe in God," said Calvin, "because our mind reposes in him as truthful, and our trust rests in him. To say 'in the church' would be as inappropriate as 'in the forgiveness of sins' or 'in the resurrection of the body.'"[1] Calvin's point is that we believe, repose, rest, and trust solely in God, in whom and by whose grace we confidently affirm his benefits.

When we say, "I believe the church," what we mean to say is, "Regardless of how it appears, dire statistics to the contrary notwithstanding, I believe the church exists, that its location and constituency are known to God, and that it has a future in God's unfolding plan and purpose for the world." Calvin's confidence in the church was well expressed as a resounding "therefore." . . . "Therefore, though the melancholy desolation which surrounds us seems to proclaim that there is nothing left of the church, let us remember that the death of Christ is fruitful, and that God wonderfully preserves his church as it were in hiding-places."[2]

1. John Calvin, *The Institutes of the Christian Religion*, IV.1.2, ed. John T. McNeill (Philadelphia: The Westminster Press, 1960), p. 1013.
2. John Calvin, *The Institutes of the Christian Religion*, ed. John Allen (Philadelphia: The Presbyterian Board of Christian Education, 1928), p. 222.

In the same vein, Karl Barth warned against two dangers:

> One consists in despising the church . . . by comparing her with the kingdom of God and getting rid of her under the pretext that she is not the kingdom; if we do so we betray the very kingdom which wants to be announced through the weakness of the church; one becomes incapable of really laboring for this kingdom. The other danger consists in exalting the church, in forgetting that she is not the kingdom, that she lives under the sign of the "Not yet." . . . The consequence for us of the real situation of the church within this "short" time, between the Resurrection and the Return, is what I should like to call a hope brought under discipline. Discipline for the church and hope for the kingdom of God.[3]

The trouble of the church is not trouble at all if one means by that a harbinger of its demise. Its trouble is the weakness in which God's power is to be made perfect. Reformation, if and when it comes, will make its way in the church through hope brought under discipline. It is this disciplined hope expressed in hopeful discipline of heart and mind within the community of faith that both nourishes and is nourished by the ministry of Christian theology.

II

The trouble of the church in and through which God would announce the kingdom consists of at least three dimensions of causation, no one of which is its sole cause, and all of which share its constitution.

First, the desacralization of the world. Theologians of the late 1950s and 1960s welcomed the desacralization of the world, celebrating the secular city as liberating and humanizing. They viewed it as cultural obedience to the First Commandment, i.e., the willingness of culture to "wait without idols," although it was not at all clear what culture was waiting for. Desacralization was touted as empirical evidence of the freedom of nature and history from divine manipulation. We were told to rejoice in the emancipation of the human creature and cultural institutions from the narrow strictures and oppressive structures of the church. Education, poli-

---

3. Karl Barth, *The Faith of the Church* (London: Fontana Books, 1960), p. 126.

tics, medicine, the arts, and science were now supposed to be free from all metaphysical assumptions and constraints, and free for the creation of self-organizing, self-governing, self-justifying institutions with processes and histories evolving from within, not above or beyond themselves.

The desacralization of the world was not all bad by any means. It issued in a measure of confidence in the human capacity for social reform, granting to many dispossessed and marginalized peoples the freedom and opportunity that had been denied them for centuries. It rewarded ventures and experiments in science and technology that resulted in an unparalleled explosion of knowledge and know-how. But there was a downside to the process of ridding public life of all vestiges of the divine. The desacralization of the world amounted to a wholesale invitation to individuals and entire cultures to live as if there were no God, and so they did. As a result, individuals became strangers to the mystery of life, and the culture experienced a general numbing down. Nor, needless to say, has desacralization left the church untouched.

Second, the disestablishment of the church. The death of Christendom is old news, yet there is scant evidence that the church has heard it or reacted to its consequences. Theologians, cultural critics, novelists, musicians, and our own children have been telling us for decades that the imperial church . . . that process inaugurated in the fourth century A.D. by the Emperors Constantine and Theodosius I, whereby the faith and values of the church were normative for the culture . . . is no more. Yet pastors and congregations continue on their merry way of promoting and promulgating ideas, structures, and programs with little attention given to the fact that these former ways of being and doing the church may be inadequate for "the equipment of the saints" for life and witness in an alien and often inhospitable world. They are entertaining their people, not equipping them to meet the challenges posed by a disestablished church.

Douglas John Hall has been trying to get the attention of the church for some time. He writes,

> Although there are exceptions, it seems to me that most Christian denominations and congregations in our context are trying to behave as if nothing has happened . . . as if we were still living in a basically Christian civilization; as if the Christian religion were still quite obviously the official religion of the official culture; as if we could carry on baptizing, marrying and burying everybody as we have always done; as if govern-

ments would listen to us and educational institutions would respect us, and the general public would (perhaps begrudgingly) heed our moral and other pronouncements, and so on, and so on, "world without end." Many denominations mount specific programs to deal with this or that "new" issue; but few want to pay attention to the big issue, which is whether this imperial form of the Christian religion can even survive . . . or should! A sort of repressed or suppressed sense of failure eats away at denominations, often manifesting itself openly in economic and leadership crises.[4]

Instead of addressing the issue forthrightly, ministers and churches tend to live with it subconsciously, while wearing each other out with bitter controversies over sex, money, and power.

The big issue before the church is how to live faithfully as a minority community in a culture in which the cards are no longer stacked in its favor. In dealing with this issue, the Christian community has much to learn from the Jewish community about what a diasporatic existence requires. At the very least, membership requirements and procedures, education methods and goals, preaching and worship, diaconic and social action strategies, stewardship development, and those fellowship-creating processes that hold and keep a community together against all odds, will have to be rethought and changed. A large portion of church membership in the near future may well be first-generation Christians, children of families who bought into the slogans and false securities of the secular city. In that regard, conversion and adult baptism may overtake infant baptism and confirmation as the primary means of entry into membership. Traditioning the membership, i.e., handing over the Bible and the creeds of the church, as well as the hymns, prayers, and various liturgical seasons and practices, to people who possess no prior knowledge of any of these things, will make demands far beyond current expectation on the church's leadership.

Third, the confusion of the church. In 1969, Jeffrey Haddon published his analysis of "the gathering storm in the churches" and it has proved to be clinically correct.[5] The crisis of the church is threefold, ac-

4. Douglas John Hall, *The End of Christendom and the Future of Christianity* (Valley Forge, Pa.: Trinity Press International, 1997), pp. 20-21.

5. Jeffrey Haddon, *The Gathering Storm in the Churches* (Garden City, N.Y.: Doubleday & Co., 1969).

cording to Haddon. First, it is a crisis of meaning and purpose. There is no longer a consensus within the church as to what its meaning and purpose are. Second, it is a crisis of belief. There is profound disagreement within the church concerning what the Christian faith is, what its claims are, and what significance these claims have for personal and corporate life. Third, it is a crisis of leadership identity. When a community is confused as to what it is and ought to do, when it is of a divided mind as to what its constituting traditions and central convictions are, it is no wonder that its leaders are divided and confused about what leadership requires if that community is to manifest its true identity.

This confusion, I would argue, is the inevitable consequence of the absence of theological passion, knowledge, and skill on the part of the minister, and of the depreciation of the minister as theologian in the life of the church. The word "minister," when used by the church, means *"minister verbi divini,"* servant of the Word of God, and makes no sense apart from the assumption that ministry has to do with the work of theology. "Instead of catering so exclusively to what are usually described as 'pastoral needs' (though the term often cloaks institutional busywork)," writes Douglas John Hall, "ministers today are recalled to the teaching office. If the minister of the congregation is not herself or himself in some genuine sense a theologian, we cannot expect lay persons to reflect some measure of the sort of informed thoughtfulness that is needed if we, as church, are to find a way into the future."[6] Preaching and teaching are the public occasions of a minister's theological activity. Without denigrating either, however, this essay will focus on the whole range of pastoral tasks of which preaching and teaching are but two among many, that the theological opportunities offered by the daily duties of the pastoral routine might not be forgotten.

III

The trouble in which the church finds itself today is marked by the large numbers of church members who are essentially ignorant of the contents of the Bible and unfamiliar with even the most basic affirmations of the Christian tradition. Some communions have been more concerned than

6. Haddon, *The Gathering Storm in the Churches*, pp. 48-49.

others to "tradition" their people, but chances are that none measure up to even the minimal standards of catechesis that was taken for granted by these denominations four or five decades ago. Does the ecclesial pluralism of the Reformation churches destine them to theological chaos? How does the church regain a theological consensus that legitimates its evangelistic and prophetic mission in and to the world? Having no central authority and no universally agreed-upon criteria for doctrinal standardization, what is the future of a divided church that is in danger of losing its mind? Answers to these questions are not encouraging. One thing is clear to me, however, and it is that apart from the recovery of a learned ministry that approaches preaching, teaching, pastoral care, and church administration as theological occasions, the reconstitution of the church in substantive rather than market-oriented terms is highly unlikely short of a divine miracle. The minister is always more than a theologian, to be sure, but the minister is never less. So we do well to recall what the tasks of the minister as theologian are.

The first task is to give the Bible to people, and to do so in such a way as to enable them to identify with the formative story, convictions, and language of Christian faith. This may seem obvious to some, but the fact remains that it is not happening in many so-called mainline churches today. Graduates of theological seminaries can no longer be counted on to be knowledgeable and capable interpreters of the Bible. It was a sad day for the church when theological seminaries decided to drop or de-emphasize the language requirement for graduation. Once it could be taken for granted that one who earned the basic seminary degree in preparation for ordination would possess at least a working knowledge of Hebrew and Greek. Unfortunately that is no longer the case, and the church suffers the loss. Knowledge of the Bible "from the inside," so to speak, ordinarily accompanies the study of the biblical languages and, though the languages may be later lost, the intimacy with the Bible gained by way of language study remains with a minister throughout a vocational life. The Bible as the problematic with which a minister struggles weekly, the Bible as the Word of God through the spectacles of which the minister seeks to read all else, is all too often lost in the pursuit of routine. Honor is paid it, but its content and message, brooded over, prayed over, critically studied, and devotionally read, too often recede into the background until the Bible becomes little more than a prop on the stage of a career.

It was not too long ago that a minister could take for granted a biblical frame of reference in the context of which to exercise the various tasks of ministry. The vast majority of church members had grown up in Christian homes in which the stories and language of Scripture were learned and cherished. Ministers take this for granted today, however, at their own peril. Many church members today are products of the "secular city" of the 1960s and 1970s, having grown up in homes where the Bible was seldom mentioned and never read, where the hymns and prayers of the church were not sung or said, where attendance at Sunday worship was not the thing to do. The contemporary church is increasingly constituted by people whose motivation and intention bear eloquent witness to the continuing presence and activity of the Holy Spirit in the lives of people, but whose knowledge about this faith is minimal at best.

The ministry of Christian theology requires ministers who are equipped to hand over the Bible in ways that will enable people to hear and to believe the Word of God as God's Word to them. The primary task of the minister as theologian, on which all other tasks depend, is to engage people in reading, studying, praying, singing, and confessing the Bible, until it becomes for them the story of their lives.

The second task of the minister as theologian is to communicate the faith of the church, specifically, how the church through the ages has reflected on the biblical message and tried to express it in rational, intelligible, coherent language. I have reference here to the ancient creeds of the church, such as the Nicene and Chalcedonian Creeds, the Apostles' Creed, the Reformed confessions, and those composed since that time, with which the minister as theologian has a lifelong love affair. I also have reference to the great preachers, theologians, and saintly figures of the past, people such as Origen, Augustine, Catherine of Siena, Thomas Aquinas, Julian of Norwich, Martin Luther, John Calvin, Friedrich Schleiermacher, Karl Barth, Dietrich Bonhoeffer, and many others whose life and thought should be inspirations for our own. The task of the minister as theologian is to introduce the congregation to the thinking and believing of the Christian church through the ages, as witness to the fact that people do not have to begin *de novo* in each new generation in this business of being Christian. Men and women in former times struggled with many of the same problems as we, and we are privileged to have the benefit of their faith and thought as we work through to our own.

A former teacher of mine, who first laid before me the challenge of the minister as theologian, would frequently say, "Any minister who does not have members of the congregation reading and discussing serious theology is not doing the job. A good minister will always have at least a few people in the congregation reading and discussing Barth or Tillich, Niebuhr or Brunner." The theologians read and discussed may (or may not) change from time to time, but the engagement of pastor and people in theological reflection still promises to open more avenues than can be counted for the ministry of Christian theology to shape the life of the church.

This having been said, a side glance must be given to those who write theology today, for they may well be part of the problem. Much theology being written today is unconcerned with the church and unavailable to all but the theologically sophisticated. This was not always so. In former times, theologians were primarily preachers who wrote theology for the church. They wrote on subjects that would increase the faith and understanding of the members and ministers of the church, using language that people could understand. The habit of writing for promotion to tenure or for the acclaim of the guild was not yet in vogue. One of the disturbing trends in contemporary theology is the tendency of theologians, many of whom evidence only a minimal interest in the church, to write for each other. The ministry of Christian theology will be enhanced, and the theological pursuits of the ministry encouraged, when authors and publishing houses rediscover the church as the venue of their most faithful and fruitful calling.

The third task of the minister as theologian is to help people to think theologically, to interpret the world of nature, history, and their own daily experience in the light of Jesus Christ. The Bible and the history of theology do not provide us with prescription but with description, not with facts so much as with insight and illumination, by which to understand who God is, how and where God may be known, what God has done, and what God is contemporaneously doing in the world today. They help us to discern the presence and activity of the living God, not merely as a fact of the past, but as the most influential factor of contemporary life. The task of the minister-theologian is to help people to think about politics, economics, social problems, ethical decisions, and the myriad of issues and conundrums of their own personal lives, in the light of Jesus Christ.

This is possible, with God's guidance and grace, only if the minister functions in this way when interpreting his or her own life and vocation. A congregation can soon tell if the minister's life and work have behind and beneath them a theological understanding of what is at stake in what he or she is doing. All too often a minister's low regard of the mundane, routine tasks of ministry communicates the absence of that sense of the presence of God which alone enables and encourages one to think theologically about the whole of life. On the other hand, when pastoral occasions are understood and approached as theological opportunities, not only does the church tend to grow in faith and in knowledge of God, but its members begin to see what a theological interpretation of life looks like and are more likely to claim that perspective for themselves.

Nathan Pusey, former president of Harvard, referred to the minister as "the professional of whom all other professions stand in need." One might want to rephrase his remark to include the many nonprofessionals whose need is the same, but the conviction expressed in this remark is one that ministers still need to hear. In his speech at the dedication of Speer Library on the campus of Princeton Theological Seminary, Pusey noted that

> the enduring first need of the church is for a learned ministry, for a continuing succession of those scholar-teachers who shall not need to be ashamed and shall not fail to help the churches to do their work in the world because they will have been qualified rightly to divide the word of truth. . . . Many circumstances of our lives suggest that today the informed, compassionate, understanding scholar-minister is the professional of whom all other professionals stand most in need, whether they know it yet or not, for it is (the minister's) function to speak to them of that kind of redemption or redirection which alone can give acceptable meaning to their efforts and which it is in the gospel's power, helped by a truly learned ministry, widely to mediate.[7]

Since it is primarily by means of pastoral occasions that the minister as theologian most often mediates the gospel's power to people, an appropriate conclusion to this essay will try to achieve some specificity about how pastoral occasions become theological opportunities.

7. Reprint of "The Dedication of the Robert E. Speer Library," October 8, 1977, Princeton Theological Seminary, Princeton, New Jersey. The text was made available to me by William Harris, reference librarian.

IV

We begin to understand the theological identity of the pastoral ministry, and some of the ways in which the ministry of Christian theology takes human shape in the life of the church, when we realize that every meeting between minister and people is a pastoral occasion, and every pastoral occasion a theological opportunity. Some ministers deeply resent this "fishbowl" existence where he or she is constantly and continually on the spot and, in a sense, on trial on behalf of the gospel. Some ministers go to great lengths to escape the pressure of this kind of life, by doing in excess those extraordinary or questionable things that others do only occasionally or not at all. The fact remains that whenever or wherever there is a meeting between minister and people, something happens that either positively or negatively colors his or her attempt to communicate the gospel. This is the incredible pressure with which the minister must live and for which the grace and forgiveness of God alone are adequate for sustenance and continuation. But it is also the incredible privilege and joy of a minister's life to be so situated in relation to the life of God and the lives of people that he or she is occasionally used of the Spirit in life-transforming ways.

When I was in seminary, students were counseled concerning their dress and decorum in ministry by members of the faculty, most of whom had served successfully as ministers of churches. The emphasis on conservative dress, good manners, proper speech, and exemplary behavior was a holdover from the Victorian era, to be sure, and we ridiculed those who considered such things important. But their counsel, if not always followed, was never forgotten, and after more than three decades of pastoral ministry I think back on it with considerably more respect than I gave it then. The same advice on ministerial manners, if you will, could not be given to students today as was given then, for manners do change with the times. But what my teachers were trying to say still merits our attention, namely, that every personal contact between minister and people . . . be it in a committee meeting, on the street, at a dinner party, or on a vacation trip . . . is a pastoral occasion, and every pastoral occasion is a theological opportunity. It is simply a fact of life that accompanies the laying on of hands, and anyone who is unwilling to use it for the sake of the gospel had best leave the field of play. For in every interpersonal contact the minister's heart and mind are being probed, albeit unknowingly and unwittingly, by the other's question concerning whether or not there is anything worth believing and, if so, whether or not it makes any difference in the life of one who claims it to be so. This is the awesome fact of ministerial life that daily thrusts the minister back onto the life of God, which, after all, is where the ministry of Christian theology begins.

If it be true that the ministry of Christian theology begins with the life of the minister, it is also true that it does not end there, but expresses itself in the various pastoral practices of the ministerial vocation. The importance of the relationship between ministry and theology is affirmed by the Second Helvetic Confession of 1566, written by Heinrich Bullinger and included in *The Book of Confessions* of the Presbyterian Church (USA). In this confession, which has been so influential in American Protestantism, theology is defined as the servant of the church. "The most remarkable achievement of the Confession," according to Edward A. Dowey, Jr. of Princeton Theological Seminary, "is the way in which Biblical and technical theological materials are expressed simply and always with a view to their practical significance for daily life."[8] The Second Helvetic Confession, if rescued from virtual obscurity, could assist the church and its ministry in the recovery of pastoral occasions as theological opportunities.

One pastoral occasion, often sloughed off by the busy minister, is the planning of worship, and particularly the writing of pulpit prayers. Worship is always an exercise in pastoral care. Nothing a minister does has more pastoral and theological potential than the planning of worship, for people known and unknown come to worship in anticipation that something may happen there that will make them whole. Worship in many churches these days appears to be thrown together as an afterthought of the minister's work week. These services give the impression of having been hastily and thoughtlessly planned, offering scant evidence of serious theological reflection given to their content, elements, or order. Chatty and conversational in style, conducted amidst the late comings and premature goings of the "audience," peppered with announcements, appeals for donations, and program promotions, while the minister wanders up and down the aisle or about the chancel . . . they remind one of a town meeting rather than a worship assembly.

Worship cannot be programmed in the sense of being so rightly put

8. Edward A. Dowey, Jr., *A Commentary on the Confession of 1967 and an Introduction to The Book of Confessions* (Philadelphia: Westminster, 1968), p. 203.

together that the onset of God is placed under human control and the experience of God is elicited on call. Worship is always an event of the Spirit wherein the miracle is the only thing that happens. What the minister may do through thoughtful worship planning is to remove all barriers thrown up against the miracle, so that the worshiping community may be expectant and ready to receive what the Spirit has to give. In worship planning the minister seeks to shape a liturgical experience that intensifies a people's awareness of God, nurtures a people's relationship with God, strengthens a people's faith in God, invites a people's praise of God, calls for a people's obedience to God, and encourages a people's enjoyment of God. A worship service planned with such care and insight as to draw people into the purview of the divine presence and providence is indeed a pastoral occasion fraught with theological opportunities.

A case in point is the composition of pulpit prayers. The Second Helvetic Confession acknowledges the fact that a person may pray privately in any language that he or she understands, but it goes on to say "public prayers in meetings for worship are to be made in the common language known to all" (Chap. XXIII). Some ministers regularly avail themselves of the treasury of prayers out of the liturgical history of the church, reading prayers of great beauty and profound conviction authored by others, and only rarely composing public prayers of their own. This practice is not to be denigrated, for by so doing the history of Christian devotion is chronicled and experienced anew, bearing witness to the essential catholicity of the church. When people pray in the context of their daily round, however, they generally author their own prayers. The minister has a unique opportunity from the pulpit to teach people to author their own prayers by contextualizing both the affirmations of faith and the petitions of a people, by folding their current circumstances into the theological perspective of the gospel, and by practicing in public a language of devotion that may instinctively and intuitively come to mind in those times when prayer can neither be postponed nor denied.

Another pastoral occasion that presents the minister with a great opportunity to communicate the faith of the church is the visitation of the sick. On this subject the Second Helvetic Confession is as prophetic as it is wise.

Since [individuals] are never exposed to more grievous temptations than when they are harassed by infirmities, are sick and are weakened by

31

diseases of both soul and body, surely it is never more fitting for pastors of churches to watch more carefully for the welfare of their flocks than in such diseases and infirmities. Therefore let them visit the sick soon, and let them be called in good time by the sick. . . . Let them comfort and confirm them in the true faith, and then arm them against the dangerous suggestions of Satan. (Chapter XXV)

The Confession here speaks of the ministry of Christian theology by identifying a pastoral occasion, i.e., the visitation of the sick, as a theological opportunity. It is a much needed reminder to those of us who would be pastor-theologians that illness is an occasion of intense vulnerability to feelings of helplessness and abandonment, when self-reliance seems most impossible, and when isolation from sources of meaning opens one to the invasion of those attitudes and emotions that militate against healing. Sickness is the disruption of the good life. Disease and infirmity, especially when they assume demonic proportions in the lives of children, amount to the encroachment of dissolution and death onto the land of the living in ways that are morally unacceptable to anyone with even a minimal sense of justice and love. It is an occasion of being confronted against one's will by the fact of mortality and the prospect of the end, when one realizes and must come to grips with the fact that one is up against powers and principalities hostile to physical existence in relation to which one is finally helpless.

The Confession reminds the minister that the pastoral task is to mediate the ministry of Christian theology in and to such issues and circumstances. It identifies the visitation of the sick as an occasion for communicating the gospel of God's unconditional love, unfailing presence, unparalleled power, and unbroken promise of a future. Furthermore, Jesus taught that sickness is not far removed from sin. Whatever else he may have meant, it is certainly true that physical vulnerability causes one to experience past mistakes and treacheries in particularly poignant ways, even to the point of associating the absence of physical well-being with a separation from God. Such times are prime occasions for conversations, prayers, or other forms of communication that assure the sick person of the grace of God in the forgiveness of sins. Geoffrey Preston suggests that the kinship of sickness and sin is also to be found in a person's separation from the community of faith and its celebration of the Eucharist. "The sinner may take part in the public celebration of the Eucharist but he may not receive the sacrament itself. The sick man may receive the sacrament itself but is not able to take part in the public celebration of the Eucharist. When a person is in either situation . . . the pastoral care of the Church is called for."[9]

This is not to say that sickness should provide the minister with an opportunity to "sock" a person with the gospel, or that it should call forth from the minister dogmatic dictums couched in pious and patronizing language. The minister as theologian will not use this occasion to push a favorite doctrine or to provoke a confession of faith that would not have been forthcoming in times of health. All pastoral occasions, but especially the one provided by sickness, should be approached with propriety, humility, and sensitivity to the integrity and freedom of the afflicted. In fact, it is most often the simple word that bears the most freight. Upon leaving a hospital room without having discussed anything explicitly theological, I have often said simply: "Close your eyes for a minute," and prayed the familiar benediction: "The grace of our Lord Jesus Christ, and the love of God, and the communion of the Holy Spirit, be with you now and forever. Amen," or something like that, confident that these familiar words of faith, prayed by the minister at bedside, can be used of God to make people whole.

Yet another pastoral occasion which offers tremendous theological opportunities is the sacrament of Baptism. There are few times in a minister's life that one finds such openness to conversation concerning the substantive issues of meaning, purpose, and destiny as the time of baptism. The time taken to prepare a congregation for the occasion, the time spent with the parents presenting their child for baptism, the time spent with an adult preparing for a profession of faith and baptism, are all occasions that dare not be routinized or delegated, but honored by the minister who cherishes his or her theological vocation. These are rare opportunities for the proclamation, explication, and application of the gospel.

Infant baptism in particular offers unusual theological opportunities, as the minister draws upon such theological convictions as covenant theology, the doctrine of prevenient grace, and the call to discipleship in interpreting to the parents what their child's baptism is and means. The minister may interpret the calling of the child's name as the sign that this little life is rooted and grounded in the eternal will and purposes of God,

9. Geoffrey Preston, *Faces of the Church* (Grand Rapids: Eerdmans, 1997), pp. 172-73.

that God gives to the child a name (meaning a nature or an identity), which no one dare deny or profane. The minister may go on to locate that child's identity within the circle of grace, and specifically in the church, by adding to the calling of the name the phrase "child of the covenant," reminding the parents of their covenant responsibility to raise their child "in the nurture and admonition of the Lord." In my pastoral experience, more than one couple has decided not to present their child for baptism because of their unwillingness to accept responsibility for the conviction that their child is a "child of the covenant." The minister may continue by interpreting the meaning of infant baptism "in the name of the Father, and of the Son, and of the Holy Spirit," in terms of the divine initiative, i.e., the fact that God moves toward us before we move toward God, long before we are even aware of God's presence in our lives, doing for us what we could never do for ourselves.

Finally, the presentation of the child to the church in the form of the gathered congregation provides the occasion in which people see as well as hear the gospel proclaimed in the sacrament of Baptism and are moved to ponder anew the meaning of their own baptism. With all of its ethical implications, the congregation itself, on behalf of the church catholic, takes responsibility for its own part in the child's growth in grace, promising its love and support in this process.

A Presbyterian Session in the state of Alabama once graphically defined for me the church's baptismal responsibility for its children. The integration of the public schools in that state in the 1960s was accompanied by tensions and hostilities that divided families, split churches, and elicited from people forms of mischief and violence of which they would not have considered themselves capable. One evening, as the Session meeting was about to conclude, an elder raised his hand and said, in effect:

> There is a young girl in our congregation who is being maligned by a well-known person in our town. When black students entered our high school, she was one of the courageous few who befriended them, sat with them at lunch, and invited them to her home. She is risking social rejection on the part of her peers because she is trying to do what her church taught her is right. There is a man in town who is trying to ruin her by spreading rumors that she is sleeping with black boys, which you and I know is a damn lie! Seventeen years ago, when her parents presented her for baptism, we stood and vowed to take responsibility for

her, to help her grow in grace, to be her corporate godparent, her church, if you will. Now she is in trouble. What are we going to do about the promise we made at her baptism?

After considerable discussion of the theology of baptism and the ethical responsibility of the church for her children, the Session appointed a committee to confront the man who was spreading the lies about the girl and threatened legal action against him for defamation of character if he did not cease and desist. The rumors stopped. A pastoral occasion had drawn a church into theological reflection and, upon reflection, action was taken to secure a young girl's life.

Stories like that are legion, and they all add up to the ministry of Christian theology in the life of the church. Other illustrations of pastoral occasions as theological opportunities lie close at hand. The three mentioned above are but random samples of ministerial practices that provide opportunities for the faith of the church to become a vital part of people's lives. One who spends a vocational lifetime trying to lay these occasions open to the Spirit of the living God, as Tom Gillespie has done both as pastor and as president, knows the difference between metaphysical speculation and the ministry of Christian theology, and is ever grateful for the joy of being included among those who cherish theology as the servant of the church.

Theology After Apartheid: Paradigms and Progress in South African Public Theologies

H. RUSSEL BOTMAN

The political changes in South Africa have had a direct impact on the country's theologies and specifically its public theologies. Public theologies are always sensitive to shifting political, cultural, and economic realities. There has already been talk of a crisis in contextual theology. At the same time it is being said that Reformed theologies necessarily will undergo paradigmatic changes precisely because they were so intimately related to apartheid, either in resisting or sanctioning it.

The notions of Thomas Kuhn are most helpful in describing the situation. Thomas Kuhn uses the term "paradigm"[1] as a concept that typifies scientific development. In *The Structure of Scientific Revolutions,* Kuhn likens a scientific revolution to a conversion experience. He identifies the latter as a *Gestalt* switch. South African scholars have also used Kuhn's theory. Three important publications played a formative role in this reflection in South Africa. The first, *Metodologie van die Geesteswetenskappe,* was published in 1985 and reflected broadly on changing questions of methodology in the human sciences. Wentzel van Huyssteen's publication, *Teologie*

---

1. Kuhn defines a paradigm as a disciplinary matrix, " . . . disciplinary because it refers to the common possession of the practitioners of a particular discipline; matrix because it is composed of ordered elements of various sorts, each requiring further specification" (Kuhn, *The Structure of Scientific Revolutions,* 2nd enlarged edition [Chicago: University of Chicago Press, 1970], p. 182). *Matrix,* therefore, refers to the framework of the scientific activity which seeks to acknowledge and respond to problems.

as kritiese geloofsverantwoording in 1986, focused the debate on how theory-formation happens in systematic theology. Subsequently, a conference was called by the Human Sciences Research Council of South Africa; the papers were published as *Paradigms and Progress in Theology* (1988). These papers summarized and presented the main paradigmatic issues related to the search for progress in South African theology at the time. The magnum opus of David J. Bosch, *Transforming Missions: Paradigm Shifts in Theology of Mission* (1991) paved the way for what he called "a hermeneutics of transformation." Although South African scholars reckoned with the shortcomings of Kuhn's conceptions as expressed by Feyerabend, Lakatos, Masterman, Toulmin, and Watkins, they nevertheless continued to use Kuhn's basic idea. They saw in it a powerful metaphor to explain sudden and fundamental changes in the way problems are conceptualized and the methods and strategies used to solve these problems.[2]

Therefore, when I use terms such as paradigm and progress, I mean to do so in this specifically South African way. Kuhn helped us to understand that sometimes a new paradigm is in conception, but not yet born. In that case we talk of a *pre*-paradigmatic phase in science development. In a pre-paradigmatic phase, scholars present different scientific proposals, often conflicting explanations for the same scientific problems, and even clusters of theories and worldviews.

Public Theologies and Church in Transition

It is my understanding that South African public theologies find themselves in a pre-paradigmatic mode. We are searching for the most adequate theological images, biblical metaphors, and prophetic parables capable of capturing the meaning of the present and dawning *kairos*. Subsequently, diverse proposals are being made, conflicting viewpoints held, and new questions raised.

The most vital forms of anti-apartheid public theologies in South

2. Cf. *Metodologie van die Geesteswetenskappe,* ed. J. Mouton and Marais (1985); J. Wentzel van Huyssteen, *Teologie as kritiese geloofsverantwoording: Teorievorming in die sistematiese teologie* (Pretoria: Raad vir Geestesweterskaplike Navorsing, 1986); *Paradigms and Progress in Theology,* papers delivered at a 1988 conference of the Human Sciences Research Council of South Africa, and David J. Bosch, *Transforming Missions: Paradigm Shifts in Theology of Mission* (Maryknoll, N.Y.: Orbis Books, 1991).

Africa, whether Reformed or ecumenical, were developed in direct dialogue with liberation theology and presented themselves as emancipatory theologies. Their paradigm shifts also relate to changing patterns in liberation theology. Leonardo and Clodovis Boff affirm this position when they say that

> the banner of liberation theology, firmly set in biblical ground, waves in the winds of history. Its message is that today the history of faith is embarking on its third great period, the period of, what they call, construction. In the past, faith has performed a *contestatory* function: this was in the first centuries, the times of the church of the apostles, martyrs and virgins. Then, in the post-Constantinian era, faith performed a *conservatory* function in society, *consecrating* the status quo and collaborating with the powers of the world. Today, faith has decidedly taken on a *constructive* function, contesting the existing order — thereby referring back to the early church — but also taking a longer-range view — that is, taking on its responsibility in history, which is to persuade society to conform to the utopia of the kingdom.[3]

Instead of venturing into *all* aspects of the debates, I focus on the impact of the pre-paradigmatic mode of our understanding of changes in theology as they relate to new understandings of the public role of the church. South African public theologies were always related to the identity and practices of the church. We never thought that one could do theology and not like the church. We never thought that one could hate the church, detest its public worship, and continue to do theology as a diplomatic or professional gesture to the community called "the body of God" in a world created by God. The idea of theological formation was not simply restricted to the privacy of the local congregation as Christians relate to their own story. Theological formation was understood as both personal and communal, a struggle of the community with itself as well as its context. The academic differentiation between the ideas of the church *unto itself,* the church *for the world,* and the church *of the poor* is a construction that has no African counterpart. In South African theologies, the mind served

---

3. Leonardo Boff and Clodovis Boff, *Introducing Liberation Theology: Liberation,* Liberation and Theology series 1, trans. Robert R. Barr (Kent: Burns and Oates, 1989), pp. 92-93.

the church and thus became a blessing of salvation and liberation. The relationship between the church and South African public theologies had two dimensions. On the one hand, public theologies challenged the church to change its ways and become more relevant in a world of oppression, enmity, and poverty. On the other hand, public theologies nurtured the church by stimulating its pastors and members with hopeful visions of public faithfulness without which they might have perished.

The announcement of sweeping reforms by then president F. W. de Klerk in 1990 and the subsequent release of Nelson Mandela fundamentally impacted theology and the role of the church in South Africa. A survey of the themes of annual conferences of the South African Council of Churches (SACC) is quite revealing. The Institute for Contextual Theology in South Africa published an article on *New Debates at the SACC Conference, 1992* entitled "Prophets or Mediators or Both?" The report speaks about the serious crisis caused by the situation of transition. It observes that the main theological question the SACC faced had to do with the role of the church. In the apartheid years, the quest was for a theology that was prophetic and for a church that could be a confessing community. After 1990, theologians and church representatives have begun to wonder whether to respond with a theology of prophecy or a theology of mediation. The National Conferences of the SACC in 1991 focused on the theme "From Egypt to the Wilderness," and in 1992 on "The Crucified God and the Easter God: Are We Seeing Light in the Darkness?" There was a feeling that the liberation from bondage also took South Africans theologically from Egypt to the wilderness of reconceiving the nature and task of theology and the church. These themes speak for themselves about the theological wrestling for a contextual theology that is relevant in a traumatic time of transition.

The debate about reconciliation followed these initial ecumenical discussions. Again, questions were raised about the proper role of the church and therefore the theology that could inform it. Should the church take a wait-and-see role regarding the national search for reconciliation? Should the church be seen as part of what looks like a secular act of reconciliation? Does the church have a separate and parallel responsibility to the Truth and Reconciliation Commission? The general consensus was, indeed the church has a separate calling to reconciliation, but the secular process of reconciliation would take symbolic preference. A new question arose then about the role of the church in making the memories redemptive. The controversy concerned how to effect a reconciliation that was maximum, but not cheap, and a healing of the memories.[4] For Christians in South Africa this is still a daunting task, but also a most humbling calling because the Christian religion was used to sow conflict and thus contributed to the suffering, oppression, and exploitation of millions in South Africa. This devastating realization can be sensed from the preamble of the *Declaration on the Rights and Responsibilities of Religious People,* published by the South African Council of Churches. While it laments the role the Christian faith played in legitimizing apartheid, the *Declaration* notes that our faith must, nevertheless, play a role in the creation of a just social order.

The Christian community of South Africa is a significant role player in the transition, given the number of its adherents. Recent research done for the Joint Enrichment Project[5] provides important results about the position of South African youth. The research found that less than 16 percent of the youth were card-carrying members of political parties, while more than 60 percent claimed membership in the church.

The questions we faced were whether the conditions of crisis and renewal of our country call for a historical break in the interest of a new paradigmatic vocation, and if so, what kind of discernment, and what kind of church would this require. Dirkie Smit, systematic theologian at the University of the Western Cape, appropriated Richard Niebuhr's theological constructs to present proposals for the role theology should play in the transformation of culture.[6] The legacy of David Bosch, the South African missiologist, lies in his proposal for a hermeneutic of transformation:

> The point I am making is simply that, quite literally, we live in a world fundamentally different from that of the nineteenth century, let alone earlier times. The new situation challenges us, across the board, to an appropriate response. No longer dare we, as we have often done, respond only piecemeal and ad hoc to single issues as they confront us. The contemporary world challenges us to practice a "transformational herme-

4. Cf. H. Russel Botman and Robin M. Petersen, eds., *To Remember and to Heal: Theological and Psychological Reflections on Truth and Reconciliation* (Cape Town: Human and Rousseau, 1996).

5. Cf. Joint Enrichment Project (JEP) survey of 2200 youth aged between 16 and 30, published in David Everatt and Mark Orkin, *Growing Up Tough: A National Survey of South African Youth* of CASE.

6. Dirkie J. Smit, "Theology and the Transformation of Culture — Niebuhr Revisited," in *Journal of Theology for Southern Africa* 72 (September 1990).

neutics," a theological response which transforms us first before we involve ourselves in mission to the world.[7]

Bosch claimed that, in the field of religion, a paradigm shift means both continuity and change, faithfulness to the past and engagement of the future. John de Gruchy added the claim that "the precise role of the church cannot be the same in a post-apartheid South African society as it was, of necessity, in the struggle against apartheid . . . yet certain elements must remain constant."[8] An authentic theology of politics has to be revisited as the ground shifts, but it should always enable the church to fulfill its evangelical, prophetic, and pastoral calling. He then goes into a discourse on John Calvin's political thought as a basis for developing a Reformed theology of politics. Such a theology must "enable a Christian presence and witness that contributes to the just transformation of society irrespective of who is in power."[9] De Gruchy then maintains that the church has a very important role to play in helping shape public opinion and the fabric of a nation. De Gruchy makes this argument more specific in describing the new role of the church as one of acting as a midwife to the birth of our democracy.[10]

N. Barney Pityana, the Anglican theologian, places lawmaking at the center of his proposals. He wants to see the development of an ethic of responsibility within the context of the development of a human rights culture. He takes up the point that "law" and "order" were meaningless on both sides of the apartheid divide. A culture of conspiracy protected revolutionary comrades and government officers from the real intention of law and order. In the light of these factors, he claims that the development of a human rights culture lies on the path to free responsibility. Human rights, he asserts, provide a context for our appreciation of God's work in creation and redemption.[11]

---

7. David Bosch, *Transforming Missions: Paradigm Shifts in Theology of Mission*, American Society of Missiology Series 16 (Maryknoll, N.Y.: Orbis, 1991), p. 189.

8. John DeGruchy, *Liberating Reformed Theology — A South African Contribution to an Ecumenical Debate* (Grand Rapids: Eerdmans, 1991), p. 242.

9. DeGruchy, *Liberating Reformed Theology*, p. 243.

10. "Midwife of Democracy," *Journal of Theology for Southern Africa* 86 (March 1994): 14-25.

11. Cf. N. Barney Pityana, "The Ethics of Responsibility: Human Rights in South Africa," in *Bonhoeffer for a New Day: Theology in a Time of Transition*, ed. John W. de Gruchy (Grand Rapids: Eerdmans, 1997), pp. 209-19.

A Theology of Reconstruction

Charles Villa-Vicencio's publication in 1992 is still the most comprehensive attempt at renewal theology in South Africa after 1990. His work can be regarded as a systematic attempt to deal with the concerns presented by Bosch, De Gruchy, Pityana, and others. Villa-Vicencio, professor at the University of Cape Town, founded his contribution on the Frank Chikane question[12] about the youth and the future of the rule of law. Frank Chikane felt that the most crucial question facing South Africa was: How is the rejection of laws by many black people in their resistance to apartheid to be replaced by the affirmation of renewal and good order on which the nation-building task feeds as it engages the future?[13]

Villa-Vicencio identified three ways in which theology commonly responds to historical realities. Theology, he said, has often legitimated the status quo in different parts of the world. At other times it has fueled resistance and revolution. Rarely has it taken the third option, which is to contribute seriously to the difficult program of nation-building and political reconstruction. In the interest of the third option he developed his "theology of reconstruction." His question to the church is whether it is theologically capable of contributing to the establishment of good government (in the interest of "the common good"), or whether this responsibility is better left to secular forces.

Villa-Vicencio sought to serve South African theology as it undergoes self-examination and reflection on matters ranging from content to methodology. The theology of reconstruction is in every sense a post-exilic theology.[14] The "exodus" is an outdated metaphor[15] that must be transcended by the metaphors of wilderness, exile, and homecoming. At times it appears that Villa-Vicencio viewed "a theology of reconstruction" as qualitatively different from liberation theology. He admitted that his proposal of a theology of reconstruction could mean the birth of a different

12. Charles Villa-Vicencio, *A Theology of Reconstruction: Nation-building and Human Rights* (Cape Town: David Philip, 1992). This work is dedicated to Frank Chikane, then General Secretary of the South African Council of Churches and President of the United Apostolic Faith Mission Church of South Africa.
13. Villa-Vicencio, *A Theology of Reconstruction*, pp. 49-51.
14. Villa-Vicencio, *A Theology of Reconstruction*, p. 7.
15. Villa-Vicencio, *A Theology of Reconstruction*, p. 6.

kind of liberatory theology, this time one more in line with the positive aspects of liberal thinking.[16]

The "immediate task" of this new theology is to place certain values and structures, which he called middle axioms or provisional definitions, in position.[17] Instead of focusing on ultimate goals, Villa-Vicencio proposed that a theology of reconstruction should concentrate on middle axioms, that is, realistic, attainable goals in the present circumstances or the next step on the road to economic justice, human dignity, and political liberation.

Villa-Vicencio made two very fundamental postulations. The first is that the ultimate spiritual and social obligation of all religions is indeed resolute and simple obedience to God.[18] His second postulation is that the church in a post-exilic period is obliged to work with a democratically elected government with the proviso that it does not lead to disobedience to God.[19] The church has the biblical mandate to be the servant of the people in working with a democratically elected government. Taking his secondary postulation as guide, he then continued to unfold its meaning methodologically. Villa-Vicencio took his cue from the idea that God acts in history. Such divine action must be discerned through the hermeneutics of "newness." Thus he conceptualized a metaphorical theology of reconstruction.[20] The post-exilic metaphor in the Judeo-Christian tradition is taken as the guiding star for his "theology of reconstruction." He believed that a post-exilic biblical theology is required in situations of nation-building. The dichotomy suggested by some scholars between doom, judgment, and law in the pre-exilic period over against hope, salvation, and grace in the post-exilic period is an oversimplification of the more complex biblical shift in emphasis at the time of the return from exile. He then took this understanding of a "complex biblical shift" that he found in the post-exilic prophecy and applied it as *the* biblical metaphor for a theology of reconstruction and political stability. He activated this logic within the frame of democratic nation-building as religious obligation in the interest of the common good.

---

16. Villa-Vicencio, *A Theology of Reconstruction*, p. 8.

17. Villa-Vicencio, *A Theology of Reconstruction*, p. 9.

18. Villa-Vicencio, *A Theology of Reconstruction*, p. 272. With this position he concurs with the theological focus of Dietrich Bonhoeffer (p. 273).

19. Villa-Vicencio, *A Theology of Reconstruction*, pp. 168-273.

20. Cf. his reference to Sallie McFague in *A Theology of Reconstruction*, p. 27.

How does he activate his metaphorical theology within this frame? Villa-Vicencio stated that, within the frame of democratic nation-building,[21] *law is key to just reconstruction.* Biblically speaking, he maintained, the notion of law becomes the key that energizes the post-exilic metaphor. The law reveals the presence of God. The notion of law in the Bible is not understood as negative and/or oppressive, but as positive incentive, enabling and drawing a people forward to what they ought to be.[22] Villa-Vicencio accepted that law as we know it today was unknown in ancient Israel. "Culturally, this (ancient Israelite) tradition has nevertheless informed secular legal debate in a way that legitimates metaphorical hermeneutical links being made between biblical reflection of law and the contemporary quest for social and legal renewal."[23] The making of just law is the final quest of *A Theology of Reconstruction.* Villa-Vicencio asserts that South Africa is presently standing on the brink of a new society.

Villa-Vicencio specifically attended to the notions of nation-building and human rights. Until recently liberation theologians had essentially the task of saying "No" to all forms of oppression. "As the struggle for democracy in some parts of the world begins to manifest itself," he said, "the prophetic task of the church must include a thoughtful and creative 'yes' to options for political and social renewal."[24] *A Theology of Reconstruction* is an interdisciplinary attempt to come to terms with the paradoxical relationship between the prophetic "no" and a creative or constructive "yes." He decided to define this relationship in terms of the contextual "demand."[25] The manifestation of democracy requires a new format of liberative theology, a "reconstructive" one. A reconstructive theology articulates the "yes" for democracy, human rights, and nation-building. This is the "demand"[26] of the context in South Africa, Eastern Europe, and the former Soviet Union.

Villa-Vicencio's position is actually an interdisciplinary attempt to give credence to the positive elements of the debate on "middle axioms."[27] While being acutely aware of the opposition of Paul Lehmann to the theo-

---

21. Villa-Vicencio, *A Theology of Reconstruction,* pp. 51-53.
22. Villa-Vicencio, *A Theology of Reconstruction,* p. 52.
23. Villa-Vicencio, *A Theology of Reconstruction,* pp. 113-14.
24. Villa-Vicencio, *A Theology of Reconstruction,* p. 1.
25. Villa-Vicencio, *A Theology of Reconstruction,* p. 2.
26. Villa-Vicencio, *A Theology of Reconstruction,* p. 2.
27. Cf. Dennis McCann, "A Second Look at Middle Axioms," *The Annual of the Society of Christian Ethics* (1981).

logical significance of middle axioms,[28] Villa-Vicencio concluded never-theless that "this concern is what ultimately drives the middle axiom debate in the direction of contextual theology . . . ," and further that "it integrates the contextual and transcendental demands of the gospel."[29] On the basis of this understanding, Villa-Vicencio claimed that "story, tradition and biblical teaching are important . . . however, if the church is to share creatively in the reconstruction process it is obliged to translate this heritage into concrete proposals."[30] It is no longer enough to say that we will not allow the world to propose the agenda. The church should state its agenda: "It is required to say something 'new'. More than this, it is required to be part of a new creation, a new social order and the birth of social, political and economic structures. Goals, principles and guidelines are not enough."[31] Charles Villa-Vicencio claimed that the prevalent social conditions in South Africa are calling for a church that is capable of making sociopolitical proposals. According to Villa-Vicencio, this calls the church to the next practical step or middle axiom.[32]

Critical Interaction with a Theology of Reconstruction

Tinyiko Sam Maluleke, missiologist of the University of South Africa, and I have publicly stated our critical response to Villa-Vicencio's proposal of "a theology of reconstruction." Maluleke does so in claiming a much more committed return to questions raised by African theologies and the reservoir of South African prophetic theologies in an assertive return to cultural and critical prophetic positions. Although I have serious concerns re-

28. In fact he concurs with the viewpoint of Paul Lehmann, who correctly identified the danger of middle axioms being no more than a middle term between abstract ethical principles and action in a specific situation (Villa-Vicencio, *A Theology of Reconstruction*, pp. 280-84).

29. Villa-Vicencio, *A Theology of Reconstruction*, p. 281. He argues that a different position is possible when the argument for "middle axioms" is made not on its basis in universal principles but, instead, on its contextuality (p. 283).

30. Villa-Vicencio, *A Theology of Reconstruction*, p. 283.

31. Villa-Vicencio, *A Theology of Reconstruction*, p. 283.

32. Instead of opting for the paradigm of middle axioms, Lehmann would find a closer affinity to Bonhoeffer's proposal of discipleship as the most proper paradigm in a situation of crisis and opportunity. Paul Lehmann's appreciation of Bonhoeffer's discipleship will be attested to in this research.

garding "a theology of reconstruction," I want to see a biblically developed theology that inspires critical loyalty, brings vision for the future, serves the church, and mobilizes the priesthood of believers without sacrificing the prophetic task of theology.

African Theology from Our Former Prophetic Wells

Strong voices are being raised in South Africa arguing for the need to break the long-standing academic impasse between liberation theologies and African theology. The post-colonial and post-liberation needs of Africa should be brought to the ecumenical agenda. The need for Africanization should receive more attention without reducing the biblical place of the poor in theological construction. This project has already begun. The publication of two important books and one celebrative journal at the end of 1997 are the first fruits:

1. *An African Challenge to the Church in the Twenty-first Century*, edited by Mongezi Guma and Leslie Milton. Cape Town: Salty.
2. *Christianity in South Africa: A Political, Social and Cultural History*, edited by Richard Elphinck and Rodney Davenport. Cape Town: David Philip.
3. "Africanisation and the Future of Theology," *The Journal for Theology for South Africa*, 25th celebration edition, No. 99, November 1997.

Almost every article in these publications argues for a shift to the next phase in contextual theologies, some critical, others more definitive. Such a theology should translate into a theology capable of a pluralistic public discourse with a distinct African voice and culture.

Maluleke questions the theological shift to a debate over law and order in Villa-Vicencio's work. He sees this debate as a retreat from the prophetic task of the church, a retreat that leads to apathy regarding the plight of the victims of apartheid. He accuses Villa-Vicencio of engaging the new world order in highly middle-class terms. A theology of reconstruction is to him an improper strengthening of vague notions such as universal human rights, nation-building, economy, civil society, and democracy. It lowers theology to the level of human rights campaigns, nation-building exercises, and the like. This, he claims, will not help abolish racism, sexism, and poverty. These issues constitute his list of priorities for theological discourse.[33]

Towards a Theology of Transformation

I have proposed "a theology of transformation" over against Villa-Vicencio's choice for "a theology of reconstruction." He has chosen the theological course of the next practical step in nation-building, which to him is lawmaking. I have chosen to search for an option embedded in the ultimate question regarding obedience to God and the biblical design of sociopolitical responsibility. The term "transformation" can best be described according to Bonhoeffer's distinction between the penultimate and the ultimate. Instead of Villa-Vicencio's choice for the penultimate as the praxeological category of theology, I have argued in favor of a specific orientation to the ultimate obedience to God. A theology of reconstruction assumes that changes to structure constitute the new theological core. I find myself in full agreement with Maluleke, that new structures, however important they may well be in legal and political terms, will not rid the country of racism, sexism, and poverty. I believe that the situation in America is a sound warning to South Africans that while participation in the formation of political policy, struggling for a bill of human rights and developing a democratic constitution are of great theological significance, they do not form new humanities (as in human beings). The latter is the essential promise of Christianity.

I have chosen to speak of "a theology of transformation" also because it suggests a paradigm of growth and formation rather than of engineering and mechanization. While it is necessary to think of reconstructing a new South Africa, it is important not to lose sight of the extent to which society is an organism that grows rather than a structure that can be dismantled and reassembled like a motorcar engine. It is a way of thinking about human beings that sets theology apart from any ideology of reconstruction. A theology of transformation calls for a change in the *forms* of acting and the *forms* of being (1 Corinthians 7:29-31). Therefore, it represents the calling of a society, a community, or an individual to reach beyond itself for its new form.

33. Cf. Tinyiko Sam Maluleke, "Truth, National Unity and Reconciliation in South Africa: Aspects of the Emerging Agenda," in *An African Challenge to the Church in the 21st Century*, ed. Mongezi Guma and A. Leslie Milton (Cape Town: Salty, 1997), pp. 109-32.

Although I am also critical with regard to "a theology of reconstruction" I am not prepared to discard the issues of nation-building, economic development, public policy formation, etc. as the narrow concerns of middle-class people. I regard them as social factors that inform and form identity. Every question of identity, South Africa has shown us, has deep theological meaning. A theology of transformation is the quest for identity as being and as practices. Although the nature of the formative power of the nation state has seriously declined, the questions of free and responsible citizenship remain important notions of identity practiced and lived. The same citizens who have adopted the stance of nonresponsibility now stand the chance of falling into lawlessness, lethargy, and apathy. It is possible that the people may shift all sociopolitical responsibility to professional politicians. It is even possible that they may become back-seat drivers or even worse, disgruntled passengers of the vehicle that has to deliver the future.

However, my proposal for a theology of transformation is not informed by the so-called new world order, or by a high regard for legality. It is informed by a Christology that takes the practices of Jesus seriously as a category that is formative to human identity. Conditions in South Africa call for a vocational paradigm that returns to the following of Jesus of Nazareth with the ultimate aim of continuing his liberative practices. Dietrich Bonhoeffer can point us in the right direction in the search for such a liberative Christology.

The anonymous spirituality of the mass-democracy is not enough. To stabilize society juridically with individual human rights is not sufficient. Bonhoeffer warned us against the danger inherent in the belief that legality can save the world. There is a dire need to be a human person and to have a human responsibility for the future of all our children as an expression of communal social responsibility.

My proposal for a theology of transformation is based on the conviction that it is virtually impossible to move from political disobedience to political obedience without coming to terms historically with the very ultimate question, namely, the notion of obedience to God and *its* design of responsible citizenship. A theology that proposes step-by-step to make the next practical move in reconstructing law and order faces the danger of elevating the "new law," the "new and more democratic jurisprudence," to a level where critical consciousness with regard to legality is lost. The loss will be the loss of Christian integrity and the normative question of legitimacy.

A theology of transformation argues for a hermeneutic of transformation instead of the current choice between a hermeneutic of suspicion (as in conflict thinking) over against a hermeneutic of trust (as in functional thinking). The transformational task of theology is defined within the frame of the essential calling of the community of believers (to praise and obey God), and should be portrayed against its present contextual setting, which is its historical manifestation in rapidly changing situations. A theology of transformation calls for the revisitation of discipleship and its practices as epistemological categories of theology. This does not mean discipleship as in *imitatio Christi* or *conformitas Christi*, but as in *transformitas Christi*.

As a contextual theology a theology as transformation is only possible upon the foundation of the form of Jesus Christ which is present in the church as the embodiment of the narratives and practices which go by the name Christian.

This establishes (i) the organizing metaphor of a theology of transformation, i.e., *discipleship;* (ii) the foundation of a theology of transformation, i.e., *the form of Jesus Christ;* (iii) the locality of a theology of transformation, i.e., *the church in its sociopolitical, socio-economic, and personal context;* and (iv) its cosmic-eschatological orientation.

Discipleship reaches its purpose in the twofold love of the church, authentically loving God and the cosmos (John 3:16). In this way, the Reformed principle of *semper reformanda* is reaffirmed and galvanized. The church this principle calls for is a community of transformation: a community being and practicing the vocation of a *transformitas Christi.*

The purport of Christianity is not to follow Descartes, Aristotle, Goethe, Martin Luther King, Jr., Desmond Mpilo Tutu, or any such hero, but simply to follow Jesus Christ, concretely and faithfully. It is Jesus Christ who helps us to see how important the connection between speaking and doing is to the gospel. He was concerned that people not only hear and see, but also practice the gospel. Craig Dykstra's rethinking of the relationship between theology and the practices of the faith community is very instructive to a theology of transformation.[34] He takes Alasdair MacIntyre's posi-

34. Cf. Craig Dykstra, "Reconceiving Practice," in *Shifting Boundaries: Contextual Approaches to the Structure of Theological Education,* ed. Barbara G. Wheeler & Edward Farley (Louisville: Westminster/John Knox Press, 1991).

tion further and wider to claim that practices bear more than moral meaning; they also bear epistemological weight. Engagement in certain practices may give rise to new knowledge. He has correctly seen that MacIntyre's thoughts are applicable to the full house of a theological epistemology. I argue that discipleship is such an epistemological category. The quest for a theology of transformation is based on the acceptance of the fact that theology is always done on shifting ground. It reminds us that every day we enter a very special place in the revelation of God's renewal work in history. It calls for the embrace of the idea that although there is a time for everything — a time to abolish and a time to form, a time to uproot and a time to plant — every now and again God gives us times in which a more complex calling beckons us. At such times abolition and building merge. If you then do only one of these, you selectively obey the call. The usefulness of theology tomorrow depends on its ability to discern the times and the hand of God in history today. A theology of transformation challenges the social constructions of the society and of the church. Its intention is not to obliterate differences. In fact its hermeneutic of transformation welcomes the argument which is a necessary factor for both the enrichment of the community and reconceiving the mission of the church.

A Question to Theologians

President Thomas Gillespie of Princeton Theological Seminary is known for his insistence that theology exists for the church. This paper breathes that same commitment and spirit. The challenges theology faces have become global and call for a renewal of this commitment in all places where theology is done. As I honor President Gillespie with this brief overview, I am also aware that we have come to the end of a millennium. Bonhoeffer, writing his final words in prison, poses an important question which theologians everywhere should face as we prepare for the task of doing theology in the next millennium. This question is also about the future usefulness of theologians. The 1996 International Bonhoeffer Congress, which was held in Cape Town, South Africa, had this question as its theme.[35] "We have been silent witnesses of evil deeds; we have been drenched by many

35. Cf. my article "Afterword: Is Dietrich Bonhoeffer Still of Any Use in South Africa?" in de Gruchy, ed., *Bonhoeffer for a New Day*, pp. 366-72.

storms; we have learnt the arts of equivocation and pretense; experience has made us suspicious of others and kept us from being truthful and open; intolerable conflicts have worn us down and even made us cynical. Are we still of any use? What we shall need is not geniuses, or cynics, or misanthropes or clever tacticians, but plain, honest, straightforward people. Will our inward power of resistance be strong enough, and our honesty with ourselves remorseless enough, for us to find our way back to simplicity and straightforwardness?"[36]

36. Dietrich Bonhoeffer, *Letters and Papers from Prison* (New York: Macmillan, 1971), pp. 16-17.

Christian Equal Regard
and the Male Problematic

DON BROWNING

What validity is there to the popular belief that Christianity teaches male headship and for this reason is a chief carrier of patriarchy and female oppression?

An honest response requires us to say that all of the ancient world was in some sense patriarchal and all of its religions, including primitive Christianity, were implicated in the elevation of males over females. But this confession opens a deeper question: *in what direction was the Jesus movement we now call Christianity actually moving on family and gender issues?* Was early Christianity in tension with, and subtly undermining, what scholars call the patriarchal "honor-shame" codes of the Greco-Roman world that surrounded it?

There are good reasons to believe that the earliest forms of Christianity were in conflict with their surrounding cultures on gender issues. When placed in context, early Christian communities, along with other historical forces, were working to mitigate male power and elevate women. Furthermore, their inner-theological direction was to bring the principle of neighbor love or "equal regard" — a concept I will later define — into the center of family life and the husband-wife relation.

This was the argument of *From Culture Wars to Common Ground: Religion and the American Family Debate*, the summary book of the Religion, Culture, and Family Project.[1] In the early days of this project, biblical scholar David Balch (co-author with Carolyn Osiek of *Families in the New Testament World*) often said at our seminars, "the early Christian family was the Greco-Roman family with a twist."[2] With this formula he reminded us that in urban centers throughout the Middle East the theory of the relation of the family to society (the *polis*) was shaped predominantly by Hellenistic philosophical traditions. Specifically, it was shaped by Aristotle's threefold household theory about the rightful tyrannical rule of master over slave, the aristocratic rule of husband over wife, and the monarchical rule of father over his children. Aristotle preceded the writing of the New Testament by several hundred years, but Alexander the Great, who was his student, spread his influence throughout the Mediterranean world.

Recent pronouncements of the Southern Baptist church on the biblical mandate for wives to submit to their husbands failed to identify this source of the male headship tradition. This knowledge, however, is common among New Testament scholars, even those located in Southern Baptist institutions. Is it possible that Southern Baptist leaders do not want lay Christians to know the origins of this male-centered family theory for fear it would undermine their version of Christian authority on gender issues?

This threefold theory can be found in both Aristotle's *Nicomachean Ethics* and his *Politics*.[3] These treatises provided the chief justification for patriarchy in ancient urban centers surrounding early Christian communities. This Aristotelian influence worked its way into the texts of early Christianity and can be found in Ephesians 5:21-33, Colossians 3:18-25, and 1 Peter 3:1-7. To give an example, note the threefold structure of the

1. Don Browning, Bonnie Miller-McLemore, Pamela Couture, Bernie Lyon, and Robert Franklin, *From Culture Wars to Common Ground: Religion and the American Family Debate* (Louisville: Westminster/John Knox, 1997). This was the summary book of the eleven-volume Religion, Culture, and Family Project, located at the University of Chicago, and funded by the Division of Religion of the Lilly Endowment, Inc.

2. For the development of this point of view, see Carolyn Osiek and David Balch, *Families in the New Testament World: Households and House Churches* (Louisville: Westminster/John Knox, 1997).

3. Aristotle, "Politics," Bk. I, 12 and "Nicomachean Ethics," in *The Basic Works of Aristotle*, ed. Richard McKeon (New York: Random House, 1941).

Colossians passage: "Wives, be subject to your husbands. . . . Children, obey your parents in everything. . . . Slaves, obey your earthly master. . . ."

To catch the parallel with Aristotle, it helps to hear the philosopher's own words. In the *Politics,* he wrote, "Of household management . . . there are three parts — one is the rule of a master over slaves, another of a father, and the third of a husband." In the *Nicomachean Ethics,* he gets more specific. "For the association of a father with his sons bears the form of monarchy, since the father cares for his children. . . . Tyrannical too is the rule of master over slaves; for it is the advantage of the master that is brought about in it. . . . The association of man and wife seems to be aristocratic; for the man rules in accordance with his worth."[4] Notice that the rule of the man is grounded in his superior worth. This was thought to refer specifically to his alleged superior powers of reason and deliberation.

Christianity and the Honor-Shame Culture

To further understand early Christian families as a "twist" on Greco-Roman patterns, Professor Osiek directed us to the anthropological and historical work on the honor-shame codes governing male-female behavior in ancient Mediterranean areas. These codes had much in common with Aristotle's philosophical formulations of worth (or honor) and their implications for family hierarchies. These codes reflect what many scholars call an "agonistic" culture. This is a culture organized around conflicts between men over issues of honor. In such cultures honor was associated with male dominance and agency while shame was associated with male weakness and passivity.[5] A sign of male weakness and shame was permitting the violation of the women of a man's household — wife, sister, or mother — without proper defense or retaliation. To keep such encroachments from happening, males enforced the systematic restriction of women to the domestic sphere.[6] If such an offense did occur, any self-respecting male was to challenge and subdue the violator with physical force. At the same time, free men were entitled to a great deal of public, po-

4. Aristotle, "Nicomachean Ethics," Bk. VIII, 10.

5. Halvor Moxnes, "Honor and Shame," *Biblical Theology Bulletin* 23 (Winter 1993): 167-76.

6. David Cohen, *Law, Sexuality, and Society* (Cambridge: Cambridge University Press, 1991).

litical, and sexual freedom. They also could gain honor if they could get away with shaming other men by seducing or offending the women in their households.

Although primitive Christianity never completely escaped the patriarchal honor-shame codes of Roman Hellenism, it did fracture or partially undermine them.[7] The early church required Christian men to restrict their sexual activity to their wives. The church also rejected the agonistic challenge-riposte pattern of the Greco-Roman male honor code. The ancient custom of infanticide, largely practiced when men rejected for various reasons their unwanted infants, was condemned by early Christian communities. Christian men were exhorted to imitate in their family relations Christ's sacrificial love for the church (Eph. 5:25). Women helped administer the love feast in the early Christian house churches and exercised leadership in evangelism.[8]

The new gender patterns occurring in the *ecclesia* spilled over into the everyday domestic life of early Christians. Husbands and wives related in more egalitarian ways at home, following patterns first established at their house churches. This happened to such an extent that early Christian families were seen by their pagan neighbors as threatening the official relation of family to *polis* in ancient cities, provoking authorities to persecute them for offenses to the established order. This in turn precipitated a retrenchment on gender equality in the post-Pauline church, as we see in 1 Peter.[9]

Ephesians versus Aristotle

Those who believe that early Christianity is a blatant teacher of male headship must confront the following question: What direction was early Christianity going on this issue? Evidence that it was experimenting with new ideas on gender relations is found if we compare Ephesians 5:21-33 to

7. Bruce Malina, *The New Testament World: Insights from Cultural Anthropology* (Louisville: Westminster/John Knox, 1993).

8. Stephen Barton, "Paul's Sense of Place: An Anthropological Approach to Community Formation in Corinth," *New Testament Studies* 32 (1986): 74.

9. For an interpretation of 1 Peter that shows this letter as an apology to pagan authorities for the alleged new freedoms in Christian families, see David Balch, *Let Wives Be Submissive: The Domestic Code in I Peter* (Atlanta: Scholars Press, 1981).

Aristotle's theory of male responsibility in the *Politics* and *Nicomachean Ethics*. First, Ephesians begins with a radical injunction toward mutuality of husband and wife: "Be subject to one another out of reverence to Christ" (5:21). This precedes and frames the soon-to-follow words asking wives to be "subject" to their husbands (5:22). But notice the difference when compared to Aristotle. Aristotle, as we saw, spoke of a proportional equity between husband and wife and a constitutional aristocracy of the husband over the wife based on the man's superior worth. There is nothing approaching the idea of mutual subjection between husband and wife to be found in Aristotle's thought.

Second, Ephesians based this mutual subjection on reverence for Christ. Aristotle, on the other hand, grounded proportional equity in the alleged higher deliberative powers of males. Aristotle writes, "For although there may be exceptions to the order of nature, the male is by nature fitter for command than the female."[10]

Third, Ephesians tells husbands to love their families as Christ loves the church, thereby developing a theory of male servanthood. Aristotle, on the other hand, writes that the higher honor should go to the better, which of course is the husband: "The friendship of man and wife, again, is the same that is found in an aristocracy; for it is in accordance with virtue — the better gets more of what is good."[11] Aristotle is for equity between husband and wife but one based on worth; the man, because of his supposed superior rationality, is worth more.

Finally, Ephesians tells us that husbands should love "their wives as they do their own bodies. For no one ever hates his own body but he nourishes and tenderly cares for it, just as Christ does for the Church, because we are members of his body" (5:28-29). In these words we hear the love commandment — "You shall love your neighbor as yourself" (Matt. 22:39) — brought directly into the inner precincts of marital relations. Nothing similar to this can be found in Aristotle or, for the most part, in other pagan philosophical writings on marriage and family.

10. Aristotle, "Politics," Bk. I, 12.
11. Aristotle, "Nicomachean Ethics," Bk. VIII, 11.

Christian Neighbor Love and the "Male Problematic"

These striking contrasts between Aristotle and Ephesians do not completely deliver early Christianity from patriarchy, but they suggest that its trajectory is away from it. It is generally thought that the principle of neighbor love is the interpretive center of Christian ethics. We learn this in Jesus' response to the lawyer who asked: "Teacher, which commandment in the law is the greatest?" In answering, Jesus lists first the command to love God with all our heart, soul, and mind and, second, the command, "You shall love your neighbor as yourself." It follows from this, I would argue, that the present task of Christian theology is to complete the early church's critique of male headship and the honor-shame code and further implement its direction toward a marriage ethic of equal regard.

But the idea of neighbor love — and the concept of equal regard between husband and wife that it implies — does not give a complete ethic for families. More is needed. In *From Culture Wars to Common Ground*, we took the concept of male servanthood very seriously. The point is that fathers and husbands, in being servants to their families, are not only going against ancient honor-shame patterns, they are also imitating — indeed recapitulating — the nature of God as revealed in the love of Christ. This is a very heady idea, but one worth considering. This thought may reveal something very profound about the nature of humans, the nature of God, and what is unique about Christian family theory.

Insight into how early Christianity redefined male responsibility can be discovered by retrieving some startling formulations of Christian family theory found in the writings of the great medieval theologian, Thomas Aquinas. In his various writings, Aquinas made some remarkable observations, quite consistent with certain modern social-science views, about the natural human needs that lead to the formation of families among humans.[12] These observations do not constitute a Christian theory of marriage and the family as such, but they do give us insights into the natural conditions of family formation that we should keep in mind in building a theologically responsible view. Aquinas's observations deepen our understanding of why human males have become involved in families, generally with considerable ambivalence. They also help us see how Christianity

---

12. See Thomas Aquinas, *Summa Theologiae*, "Supplement" (New York: Benziger Brothers, 1948) and *Summa contra Gentiles* (London: Oates and Washbourne, 1928), pp. 3, ii.

both appealed to these natural tendencies yet added concepts and symbols that transformed them, thereby further stabilizing male commitment to their children and wives.

Aquinas's ideas may seem strange at first. But when we learn that many contemporary psychologists and anthropologists have similar theories, they may not seem so unusual.[13] For instance, he was aware, as are contemporary evolutionary theorists, that human males were unique among animals in learning to care for their progeny and becoming attached to their consorts. Other male primates, for the most part, do not help care for their infants after fathering them. Aquinas advanced several reasons why human males in the course of history became involved in families. He listed (1) the long period of human infant dependency that leads the human female to demand help from her sexual partner in raising her offspring, (2) the recognition by a human male that a particular child is most likely his and therefore a part of his very biological existence, (3) sexual exchange that integrates the male into a more stable relation with his female partner (Aquinas followed Paul in calling it paying the "marital debt"), and (4) useful mutual assistance between male and female that further consolidates their relationship. These are all natural reasons Aquinas gives for how and why human males are pulled into long-term relationships with their offspring and consorts.

It is widely known that Thomas Aquinas believed that marriage was an unbreakable sacrament. But a very important part of that theory is almost always overlooked. The logic of his argument for the permanence of marriage reveals that he wanted to find a ground for the stabilization of fragile human male commitment to families. He was aware that a human female knows that the infant she births is hers; for instance, she experiences the burdens of pregnancy and the trials of delivery. Males have much more tentative, and sometimes difficult-to-discern, relations to the infants they father. Behind Aquinas's theory of sacramental permanence of the marital bond was his insight into human male ambivalence about fatherhood — an ambivalence that I sometimes call the "male problematic."

Aquinas was similar to contemporary evolutionary biologists in his

13. See for instance the work of Don Symons, *The Evolution of Sexuality* (Oxford: Oxford University Press, 1979); Pierre Van den Berghe, *Human Family Systems* (New York: Elsevier, 1979); Martin Daly and Margo Wilson, *Sex, Evolution, and Behavior* (Belmont, Calif.: Wadsworth, 1978).

awareness that human males are almost unique among mammals for their capacity to bond with their children and mates. I agree with John Miller in his *Biblical Faith and Fathering* that stabilizing male responsibility and giving it sacred meaning was one of the great accomplishments of both Judaism and Christianity.[14] This happened in these religions, in part, by depicting God as a caring father that human males were commanded to imitate. We find, however, a particularly helpful model for understanding the transformation of men into fathers in the thought of Aquinas.

As I have suggested, Aquinas's view of how human males became involved in the care of their children and wives shares many observations current in evolutionary biology and psychology. These disciplines recognize variations of the same four factors that Aquinas discussed. They add, however, an important additional theory — the theory of "kin altruism" — that Aquinas took over from Aristotle but did not explicitly state. This is the idea that all creatures, including humans, are more likely to invest in and sacrifice for kin sharing their own genes than they are for non-kin. Aquinas had no theory of genes, but both Aquinas and evolutionary biologists believe that the reality of kin preference is a major, although not the only, factor behind paternal recognition and investment. Certainly Christian love and self-sacrifice add more to the motivation of Christian fathers, but these virtues build on and guide natural kin altruism. Kin altruism is a finite and partial value not to be ignored, suppressed, or disregarded. It is to be encouraged, developed, extended, and transformed. When it becomes idolatrous, it must also be constrained. The highest commitment of Christians should be to the kingdom of God, but within that the energies of kin altruism have their rightful place.

Both Aquinas and evolutionary theory, however, believe that more is required to truly stabilize male investment. Aquinas went so far as to interpret the Ephesians analogy between Christ's sacrificial love for the church and a husband's love for his family as having the clear intent of stabilizing male hesitancy to bond, i.e., the male problematic. Ephesians and Aquinas had different analyses of this problematic, but both see Christian symbols as addressing and overcoming it.

14. John Miller, *Biblical Faith and Fathering* (New York: Paulist Press, 1989).

Don Browning

Christianity and the World Fatherhood Problem

Family changes are occurring throughout the world. We overlook, however, that the central feature of these changes is that more and more children are raised without the guidance of their fathers. One-third of all children in the U.S. are presently living apart from their biological fathers at any one time; nearly one-half live apart from their fathers for a period of three years before age 18. Princeton sociologist Sara McLanahan has demonstrated on the basis of the analysis of large sets of demographic data that children raised apart from their biological parents are two to three times more likely to do poorly in school, have difficulty getting jobs, and more likely to have children out-of-wedlock.[15] The Western religious tradition, evolutionary theory, and empirical evidence all suggest that fathers are important. From a Christian perspective, having an engaged father is not a guarantee of salvation; but it does on average contribute to the health and strength of children and is an important order of society to be preserved.

In *From Culture Wars to Common Ground,* we acknowledge that many conservative religious forces of our society — Protestant Evangelicalism, the African American Church, and the Roman Catholic Church — are more aware of the male problematic than liberal religious movements. To this extent, Southern Baptists and the Promise Keepers, with their emphasis on male responsibility, have their finger on something important. But conservative religious groups are wrong in believing that male responsibility must necessarily be coupled with models of male headship. They seem to suggest that a little soft patriarchy is the price to be paid for male responsibility.

I agree that there is something important in the idea of male servanthood, but not necessarily male servant *leadership.* I recommend following Paul's belief that servanthood should apply to wives as well as to husbands: "For the unbelieving husband is made holy through his wife, and the unbelieving wife is made holy through her husband" (1 Cor. 7:14). Although my colleagues and I argue in *From Culture Wars to Common Ground* that the equal regard implicit in neighbor love is the heart of the Christian theory of marital obligation, we follow Aquinas and his contemporary disciples in locating self-sacrifice (the cross) as a moment of loving

15. Sara McLanahan and Gary Sandefur, *Growing Up with a Single Parent* (Cambridge, Mass.: Harvard University Press, 1994).

60

steadfastness, renewal, and grace within love as mutuality. The self-sacrifice of the cross, in this view, is not an end in itself, but tries to restore love as equal regard when it is in crisis and out of balance.[16] In this respect both husband and wife are called to bear the cross in relation to each other and to their children, albeit in the service of love as equal regard.

16. Some neo-Thomistic statements of the role of self-sacrifice in service of marital love as mutuality and equal regard can be found in the following: Louis Janssens, "Norms and Priorities of a Love Ethics," *Louvain Studies* 2 (1977): 207-37; Barbara Andolsen, "Agape in Feminist Ethics," *Journal of Religious Ethics* 9 (Spring 1981): 69-81; Christine Gudorf, "Parenting, Mutual Love, and Sacrifice," in *Woman's Consciousness, Woman's Conscience: A Reader in Feminist Ethics,* ed. Barbara Andolsen et al. (New York: Harper and Row, 1985).

Theology as Servant of Ecumenism: Some Reflections on the Encyclical Ut unum sint

EDWARD IDRIS CARDINAL CASSIDY

It is my pleasure to contribute to this Festschrift in honor of Dr. Thomas W. Gillespie. I have fond recollections of my visit to Princeton Theological Seminary for an ecumenical symposium in September 1996. The intellectual atmosphere of the symposium which took place at Miller Chapel and the spiritual experience of the vesper service held at the Princeton University Chapel illustrated that two factors, necessary for ecumenism, were given significant attention in that program. These were theology and prayer. As host, Dr. Gillespie guided events in such a way as to keep in view the necessary and pastoral links between theology and prayer required in ecumenism.

Theology is vital for ecumenism. But the ecumenist must keep always in mind that, to be authentic, theological discourse and every other stage of ecumenical engagement must be undertaken in the awareness of prayer, especially in the awareness of Christ's prayer for his disciples ". . . that they may all be one . . . so that the world may believe" (John 17:21). Theology is primarily effective in the prayerful conviction that it is God to whom alone is the glory. While Christians can contribute to Christian unity, it is God who eventually will bring about the unity of the disciples for which the Lord prayed.

One expression of the theme suggested for this Festschrift was "theology as servant of the church." The particular focus I choose to stress in this contribution is "theology as servant of ecumenism." By serving ecu-

62

menism, theology serves the Church. In this essay I wish to illustrate the appreciation for the contribution of theology to ecumenical progress that can be seen in the 1995 encyclical of Pope John Paul II, *Ut unum sint,* on commitment to ecumenism.[1]

The Encyclical *Ut unum sint*

The encyclical *Ut unum sint (Uus)* underscores the significance of theology for ecumenism, especially in relation to ecumenical theological dialogue, but also places the need for theology in the broader context of a more holistic ecumenism. Since the encyclical itself is a theological text, we can only limit ourselves to outlining some broad themes of its appreciation of theology.

We use *Uus* for our reflection not only because as a formal papal document it possesses a particular authority in the Roman Catholic Church, but also for other significant reasons. For example, the encyclical points to the firm ecumenical direction that has been set in the Catholic Church in the most authoritative ways over thirty years. The magna carta of Catholic involvement in ecumenism was the conciliar statement, the Decree on Ecumenism *(Unitatis Redintegratio)* of the Second Vatican Council (1964). The publication after the Council by the Pontifical Council (then, Secretariat) for Promoting Christian Unity of the first Ecumenical Directory (Part I, 1967 and Part II, 1970)[2] and the revised Ecumenical Directory (1993)[3] have underscored the pastoral priority that ecumenism must be given in the Catholic Church. The revised code of Canon Law (1983) said, in theological terms, that the church is bound to promote the restoration of unity among Christians "by the will of Christ" (Canon 755). And now, the encyclical *Ut unum sint* (1995), an expression of the papal magisterium, speaks of commitment to ecumenism "as a duty of the Christian conscience" (#8), insists that the way of ecumenism is "the way of the Church" (#7), and that ecumenism is "an organic part" of the

1. Encyclical Letter *Ut unum sint* of the Holy Father John Paul II on Commitment to Ecumenism (Vatican City: Libreria Editrice Vaticana, 1995).

2. Part 1 is found in Pontifical Council for Promoting Christian Unity, Vatican City, *Information Service* 2 (1967): 5-12; Part 2 in *Information Service* 10 (1970): 3-10.

3. Directory for the Application of Principles and Norms on Ecumenism, Vatican City, March 25, 1993.

church's life and work "and consequently must pervade all that she is and does" (#20).

Individually, each of these texts since Vatican II has been for Catholics a *beacon,* initiating them into the ecumenical movement or guiding and deepening their involvement in it during these last decades of the twentieth century. But together, as we come to a new century and millennium, these texts can be seen as a kind of *platform* to support a firm Catholic commitment to the search for unity in the twenty-first century, into which we are now making our transition. The encyclical is one of the authoritative posts for this "platform."

Theology and the Ecumenical Movement

In an important article entitled "The Place of Theology in the Ecumenical Movement: Its Contribution and Its Limits,"[4] my predecessor Johannes Cardinal Willebrands gave tribute to the contribution of theologians and theology in the quest for Christian unity. His views are worth recalling here.

Referring to the contributions of Catholics to ecumenism, he said that even if the spark has often been struck by lay folk or pastors, "most of the great architects of ecumenism have been theologians."[5] The ecumenical movement, at least in the Catholic tradition, "would die without the theology."[6] Theological research has been "in the help of the Holy Spirit, the instrument of God, for the increase of unity in truth among Christians. Without theology, ecumenism would be a tactic, a 'policy,' not the quest for 'unity in Truth' which Thomas Aquinas acclaimed."[7]

The Second Vatican Council not only did *not* set a limit to the dynamism of theological research, but rather, the Cardinal stated, "in some ways relaunched it."[8] Willebrands recalls some of the key theological insights or developments of the Second Vatican Council significant for Catholic participation in the ecumenical movement, developments which come

4. Johannes Cardinal Willebrands, "The Place of Theology in the Ecumenical Movement: Its Contribution and Its Limits," *Mid-Stream* (April 1991): 101-10.
5. Willebrands, "The Place of Theology in the Ecumenical Movement," p. 101.
6. Willebrands, "The Place of Theology in the Ecumenical Movement," p. 101.
7. Willebrands, "The Place of Theology in the Ecumenical Movement," pp. 104-5.
8. Willebrands, "The Place of Theology in the Ecumenical Movement," p. 103.

from the reception by the Council Fathers of the work of a long list of theologians (exegetes, dogmaticians, liturgists, patrologists) who for decades had explored the content of the Christian tradition. Thus, without paragraph 8 of *Lumen Gentium,* especially the famous phrase *subsistit in,* "the Catholic Church would never have been able to break out of the circle of the old conception of the ecumenism of return. . . ."[9] Without the Council's reflection on *Koinonia* "we should not have been equipped to enter into dialogue with other Christian communities with deep respect and a just appreciation of their diversities, when these are found to be coherent with the apostolic tradition."[10] Without the explanation given in *Dei Verbum* on Scripture and Tradition "we should still be at the stage of implicit polemics with the Reformed churches."[11] Without Vatican II's completion and rereading of the constitution *Pastor Aeternus* of Vatican I, "we should be unable to rethink the Bishop of Rome's ministry of unity and its place in ecclesial communion."[12]

In short, the role of theology in the ecumenical task comes from the fact that faith itself is involved in this task. The specific purpose of ecumenism is "not 'reunion' resulting from human efforts mainly political or sentimental," but rather, very differently, that specific purpose "is *the unity which God wills.*"[13]

And yet, in regard to ecumenism, the Cardinal also made clear the limits of theology. "Ecumenism certainly needs theology," he said, "but because unity can only be given by God, ecumenism above all needs prayer."[14] Even the great "testament" of Jesus on unity has been a prayer, which forms chapter 17 of the Gospel of John. Jesus turns to the Father, praying that the community of disciples remains solid in unity, giving us an example.[15] Theology is critical, but it is not enough, in our quest for visible unity.

9. Willebrands, "The Place of Theology in the Ecumenical Movement," p. 102.
10. Willebrands, "The Place of Theology in the Ecumenical Movement," p. 102.
11. Willebrands, "The Place of Theology in the Ecumenical Movement," p. 102.
12. Willebrands, "The Place of Theology in the Ecumenical Movement," p. 102.
13. Willebrands, "The Place of Theology in the Ecumenical Movement," p. 105.
14. Willebrands, "The Place of Theology in the Ecumenical Movement," p. 109.
15. Cf. Willebrands, "The Place of Theology in the Ecumenical Movement," p. 109.

Importance of Theological Dialogue

Appreciation for what has been achieved with the help of theology, particularly in the context of ecumenical theological dialogue, is also found frequently in the encyclical *Ut unum sint*. In its opening passages, the encyclical speaks of the progress along the path of unity, saying that "Interconfessional dialogues at the theological level have produced positive and tangible results: this encourages us to move forward" (2).[16] Theological dialogue has led to a "growth of communion" among Christians (49).

The encyclical underlines the importance of theological dialogue for the church's commitment to ecumenism, saying that in fact, dialogue "has become an outright necessity, one of the church's priorities" (31). The encyclical underscores the role of theologians by citing the Decree on Ecumenism, that dialogue means "in the first place 'dialogue between competent experts from different Churches and Communities,'" who take part in meetings in which "'each explains the teaching of his [or her] Communion in greater depth and brings out clearly its distinctive features' (UR 4)" (31).

The importance of theological dialogue in ecumenism is rooted in, among other things, the fundamental importance of doctrine through which the faith of the church is expressed. For "the unity willed by God can be attained only by the adherence of all to the content of revealed faith in its entirety" (18). In dialogue each side presents its understanding of revealed faith, as both seek convergence and eventually consensus about the content of revealed faith. The dialogue is "marked by a common quest for truth, particularly concerning the church" (33).

The delicacy of theological dialogue is noted. It must be scientific, but more than that. It includes "difficult and delicate research, which involves questions of faith and respect for one's own conscience as well as for the consciences of others . . ." (70). And therefore it has been and must be accompanied and sustained by prayer. "Precisely because the search for full unity requires believers to question one another in relation to their faith in the one Lord, prayer is the source of enlightenment concerning the truth which has to be accepted in its entirety" (70).

16. Numbers in parentheses, as earlier, refer to the numbered paragraphs of the encyclical *Ut unum sint*.

Spirituality and Dialogue

The encyclical notes the spiritual roots of dialogue in saying, in the spirit of the Decree on Ecumenism, that ecumenical dialogue becomes a "dialogue of conversion" because it cannot take place merely on a horizontal level, restricted just to exchanges of points of view or even the sharing of gifts proper to each community. But rather it has also "a primarily vertical thrust, directed towards the One who, as the Redeemer of the world and the Lord of history, is himself our Reconciliation" (35). This vertical aspect helps us to acknowledge jointly that we have sinned. It is precisely this acknowledgment "which creates in brothers and sisters living in Communities not in full communion with one another that interior space where Christ, the source of the Church's unity, can effectively act, with all the power of his Spirit, the Paraclete" (35).

Dialogue is fostered by spirituality and also fosters it. Thus thanks to ecumenical dialogue we can speak of a greater maturity in our common prayer for one another. This is possible inasmuch as dialogue also serves as an "examination of conscience" (34). Thus, in this context, how can we fail to recall the words of the First Letter of John? "If we say we have no sin, we deceive ourselves, and the truth is not in us. If we confess our sins, God is faithful and just, and will forgive our sins and cleanse us from all unrighteousness" (1:8-9) (34).

According to *Ut unum sint*, the examination of conscience must extend to the sins committed against the Church's unity, to the "many sins which have contributed to our historical divisions" (34). We must be "humbly conscious of having sinned against unity and . . . convinced of our need for conversion" (34). And therefore "such a radical exhortation to acknowledge our condition as sinners ought also to mark the spirit which we bring to ecumenical dialogue" (34). This dialogue must be a "dialogue of consciences" (34).

The spiritual foundation of ecumenical dialogue is a "dialogue of conversion" which takes place before God, and into which the Catholic Church must enter. It is basic to all theological dialogue. In this dialogue, "each individual must recognize his own faults, confess his sins and place himself in the hands of the One who is our Intercessor before the Father, Jesus Christ" (82). The "dialogue of conversion" with the Father on the part of each community holds before us the fact that the purpose of theological dialogue, and ecumenical relations in general, is not simply a cordial understanding or external sociability. Rather "the bonds of fraternal *Koinonia* must be forged before God and in Christ Jesus" (82). Thus, since the ultimate goal of the ecumenical movement — to reestablish "full visible unity" (77), "full communion of all the baptized" (100) — requires "the adherence of all to the content of revealed faith" (18), theological dialogue that serves this goal must itself be rooted deeply in faith.

Achievements of Theological Dialogue

The encyclical gives a strong tribute to the role of theological dialogue in promoting unity. "A valuable result of the contacts between Christians and of the theological dialogue in which they engage is the growth of communion. Both contacts and dialogue have made Christians aware of the elements of faith which they have in common. This has served to consolidate further their commitment to full unity" (49).

Furthermore, a method of dialogue is noted when the encyclical says that the bilateral theological dialogues start from a recognition of a degree of communion already present, and then go on to discussion of specific areas of disagreement. A theological interpretation of the results of dialogue is also given, namely, that "the Lord has made it possible for Christians in our day to reduce the number of matters traditionally in dispute" (49).

The encyclical refers to several areas of progress in ecumenism, achievements that have resulted or benefited from dialogue, as well as from other contacts. Dialogue is one aspect of ecumenism, although a central aspect. Dialogue can build on what has been done previously, and/or it can be a means to promote other aspects of ecumenism. I will briefly mention here some of these achievements, noted by Pope John Paul II.

With the Eastern Orthodox, from the time of the Second Vatican Council, there had been an increasing number of healing events, a "dialogue of love," contacts that put in a whole new light the relationship between the Church of Rome and the Orthodox Church, which have been estranged from each other for nine centuries. It was Pope John Paul II and the Ecumenical Patriarch Dimitrios I who decided in 1979 to begin the theological dialogue. Concerning this dialogue, the Holy Father notes that doctrinal discussion in the Joint International Commission for the Theological Dialogue between the Catholic Church and the Orthodox Church, which began in 1980, benefited from positions previously taken by the

Second Vatican Council, which urged (in *Unitatis Redintegratio, #14*) that due consideration be given to the "special aspects of the origin and growth of the Churches of the East, and to the character of the relations which attained between them and the Roman See before the separation . . ." (50). According to the Pope, both the "dialogue of charity" with the Orthodox and the international theological dialogue have benefited from this approach, which has proved most useful also in relations with the Ancient Churches of the East. In fact "it has led to the gradual rediscovery of brotherhood" (51).

To illustrate the progress made by the joint international dialogue with the Eastern Orthodox, the Pope recalls that in 1987 he and Patriarch Dimitrios, in a common declaration on the occasion of the Patriarch's visit to Rome, were able to state a conclusion of that dialogue, namely "that the Catholic Church and the Orthodox Church can already profess together that common faith in the mystery of the Church and the bond between faith and sacraments" (59). The encyclical also gives other examples of what has been achieved with the aid of the theological dialogue.

Concerning relations between the Catholic Church and the Ancient Churches of the East, which had rejected the dogmatic formulations of the Councils of Ephesus and Chalcedon, the Pope affirms the ecumenical progress that has been made. "Precisely in relation to Christology," he says, "we have been able to join the Patriarchs of some of these Churches in declaring our common faith in Jesus Christ, true God and true man" (62). The Pope cites joint statements made by either Pope Paul VI or himself with Patriarchs of the Coptic Orthodox Church, the Syrian Orthodox Church, and the Assyrian Church of the East. Differences held for 1500 years have been put in an entirely new light in these agreements. And thus, "Once again it must be said that this important achievement is truly a fruit of theological investigation and fraternal dialogue" (63).

Concerning ecumenical progress between the Catholic Church and those churches and ecclesial communities of the West, the encyclical indicates that what is at stake essentially is the question of faith (65). "Doctrinal and historical disagreements at the time of the Reformation emerged with regard to the church, the sacraments and the ordained ministry." The encyclical reports the Vatican Council's call for dialogue on these and other issues (67). Multilateral dialogue such as in Faith and Order is necessary, as is bilateral dialogue between two communities (cf. 69).

According to the encyclical, "this dialogue has been and continues to be fruitful and full of promise" (69). Many disputed questions have been taken up. The theological dialogue is commended for what has been achieved, and also viewed as necessary to continue. It is commended because "as a result, unexpected possibilities for resolving these questions have come to light" (69). It must be continued because of the "realization that certain questions need to be studied more deeply" (69). What has been achieved thus far is only "one stage of a journey, however promising and positive" toward the ultimate goal of reestablishing full visible unity among all the baptized (77).

The Pope's Theological Challenge

In praising theological dialogue, *Ut unum sint* also brings fresh challenges for ecumenical theological reflection. I will mention three. We have already pointed to the first. In *Ut unum sint*, the Pope reminds us of a deeper theology of dialogue itself. He calls to mind in a lively way the profound spiritual basis required for successful ecumenical dialogue. The (horizontal) ecumenical dialogue between representatives of two or more Christian communities must be rooted in a (vertical) "dialogue of conversion," on the part of all, before God. In short, successful dialogue with others requires first conversion and repentance of each before God. This is a strong reminder of the need for a holistic ecumenism.

Secondly, the Pope repeats an often stated ecumenical view that divided Christians already preserve an imperfect but real communion, which is even growing at many levels of ecclesial life. But he adds a further challenging theological insight, indicating an eschatological way in which the present ecumenical struggle for full communion can take hope because it is grounded in the full communion of the Saints:

> I now add that this communion is already perfect in what we all consider the highest point of the life of grace, *martyria* unto death, the truest communion possible with Christ who shed His Blood, and by that sacrifice brings near those who once were far off (cf. Eph. 2:13).
>
> Albeit in an invisible way, the communion between our Communities, even if still incomplete, is truly and solidly grounded in the full communion of the Saints — those who, at the end of a life faithful to grace, are in communion with Christ in glory. These Saints come from

all the Churches and Ecclesial Communities which gave them entrance into the communion of salvation (84).

While the dialogue and other ecumenical efforts must continue, the Pope explicitly acknowledges that the reality of holiness is a common heritage that the various churches and Ecclesial Communities share. This gives hope for the ecumenical achievement of the visible unity sought in ecumenism. For the universal presence of the Saints is a proof of the transcendent power of the Spirit. It is the "sign and proof of God's victory over the forces of evil which divide humanity" (84). For if communities are able truly to "be converted" to the quest for full and visible communion, God will do for them what he did for their saints, namely, "He will overcome the obstacles inherited from the past and will lead Communities along his paths to where he wills: to the visible *koinonia* which is both praise of his glory and service of his plan of salvation" (84).

Thirdly, in the encyclical, the Pope proposes to ecumenical partners a theological challenge in regard to the papacy itself. Aware that the ministry of the Bishop of Rome, which the Catholic Church preserves "in fidelity to the Apostolic tradition and the faith of the Fathers," nonetheless "constitutes a difficulty for most other Christians" (88), the Pope proposes ecumenical theological dialogue on the exercise of that ministry. John Paul II recalls what he had said already in 1987 in an address to Ecumenical Patriarch Dimitrios I, when he expressed the hope that the Holy Spirit might enlighten "all the Pastors and theologians of our Churches, that we may seek — together, of course — the forms in which this ministry may accomplish a service of love recognized by all" (95). In the encyclical, the Pope comes back to this offer concerning papal primacy, but now brings it to a wider audience. "While in no way renouncing what is essential to its mission," the primacy, he says, is "nonetheless open to a new situation" (95). He therefore makes this proposal:

> Could not the real but imperfect communion existing between us persuade Church leaders and their theologians to engage with me in a patient and fraternal dialogue on this subject, a dialogue in which, leaving useless controversies behind, we could listen to one another, keeping before us only the will of Christ for his Church and allowing ourselves to be deeply moved by his plea "that they may all be one . . . so that the world may believe that you have sent me" (John 17:21)? (96).

71

If some were surprised that a papal encyclical on ecumenism would be published, others may have been surprised that the encyclical would include an invitation by the Pope for ecumenical theological dialogue on the way in which his ministry of unity could "accomplish a service of love recognized by all" (95).

Concluding Observations

Theology has been effectively employed in the service of ecumenism, in the search for the visible unity of Christians. This is one particular and important way, among others, in which theology has functioned in the service of the church.

In the Catholic Church, as Cardinal Willebrands reminded us, important theological insights helped the Second Vatican Council to develop, especially with the Decree on Ecumenism *Unitatis Redintegratio,* its mandate for ecumenism, as well as perspectives on some issues which have helped Catholics and other Christians to engage one another in ecumenism.

The encyclical *Ut unum sint* is Pope John Paul II's personal reflection on the Decree on Ecumenism in light of his own ecumenical experience. There is much in the encyclical that praises the contributions of theology, and theological dialogue, by showing ways in which theological dialogue has been a prominent factor contributing to progress toward the goal of the visible unity of Christians. The encyclical thus affirms that ecumenism is one area in which theology has been employed effectively in the service of the church. While explicit praise for theological dialogue in an encyclical about ecumenism should not be surprising, it nonetheless encourages further theological research in support of the goal of seeking the unity of presently divided Christians.

To What End Knowledge?
The Academic Captivity of the Church

ELLEN T. CHARRY

I

There is today a growing concern within the main/old-line Protestant denominations that despite a secularly well-educated laity, the pious faithful are poorly informed about the faith they profess. There are several reasons for this, among them that academic theology and biblical studies are marginal to the churches. The theological disciplines are more oriented to the academy than the church. Some in the churches are suspicious of theology and scripture, and scholarship does not assuage their concerns. Some counsel casting off Bible and theology and starting over. Others gather the wagons round to defend the camp. Scholars who prescind from the political fray keep their heads down in the library. Busy pastors have little time to entertain the problem.

At the same time, the dominant culture is post-Christian, even though many still profess belief in God. The verdict of post-Christianity generally is that Christianity is passé. This puts the faithful in a bind. Theological scholarship is also caught in this dilemma. Having absorbed the methods of modern science, theology is still distrusted by the larger secular academy and by the church as well. Theologians find themselves talking among themselves, with both the wider academy and the churches having turned off their hearing aids.

Although the foregoing pertains to several theological disciplines, this essay will focus on theology proper which interprets Christian doctrine. Several factors contribute to the marginalization of theology from the churches, some having to do with the discipline itself. The argument here will be that one factor contributing to the decline of theology is that academic theology has ceased to be concerned with the cure of souls.

Classical theology, following Paul, developed in response to specific problems that arose in the church. In the ancient church, theology defined and defended the church's teachings in order to help it help people know, love, and enjoy God, that they might live a noble, righteous, and godly life by dwelling in God on earth and beyond.[1] Knowing God was essential to being transformed by and partaking of God's sapience, goodness, and beauty. In short, the cure of souls was central to the theological task.[2]

The burden of this paper is to suggest that although the Reformation did not dispense with the cure of souls, it set in motion structures that could. John Calvin was the last classical theologian whose doctrinal exegesis served the cure of souls and whose pastoral theology required doctrinal and scriptural exegesis. If one were to venture a judgment as to which had priority for him, this writer would say that for Calvin, what truth was to goodness, doctrinal exegesis was to the cure of souls. In the ensuing post-Reformation struggle to establish the authority of Protestantism over against Rome, Protestant theologians turned in a different direction and created biblical scholasticism.

The crisis of authority, precipitated by the Reformation, was also an epistemic crisis. What true knowledge of God is and where such knowledge is found became open questions. Following the Council of Trent, Protestant orthodoxy invented biblical scholasticism, which defines the truth in terms of well-organized doctrines, ostensibly found in scripture, in order to compel rational consent. This already reflects a radically different understanding of truth and knowledge than had guided Calvin's elaboration of articles of religion. Defining truth and knowledge as that which compels assent to logically presented ideas is a clear departure from truth as knowing the sapience of God.

While biblical scholasticism was taking shape, Copernicus's radical scientific ideas were also being picked up, and a new understanding of

1. This is not to deny that even the greatest theologians erred at times.
2. E. T. Charry, *By the Renewing of Your Minds: The Pastoral Function of Christian Doctrine* (New York: Oxford University Press, 1997).

truth and knowledge was being created. The experimentally revealed idea that the earth moves around the sun shook the notion, so central to the cure of souls, that God is the center of our world and of ourselves, as Calvin had assumed. Kepler and Galileo confirmed Copernicus's findings. Francis Bacon invented scientific method to combat the ignorance, alchemy, and superstition associated with medieval science and theology and to make way for the new. The need was to redefine truth and knowledge so that neither ignorance and superstition nor the power of the institutional church could withstand its power. The struggle would continue through the end of the eighteenth century.

The crisis of theological authority could not insulate itself from the larger epistemic crisis caused by the emergence of the beginnings of the scientific revolution. Both the Protestant theologians and the scientists pointed their fingers at received religious knowledge as defined by Rome. Each grasped one side of the crisis of authority and knowledge that reached its height in Descartes and Locke. Scientist and theologian alike had to find a new foundation for knowledge. Yet more, they had to reinvent truth and knowledge.

Neither of the new foundations of knowledge — theological systematizing and experimental method — had room for knowledge of God as transformative. On the theological side, one reason is that the Reformers did away with the structure that could have ordered it: penance, perhaps repackaged. Although the Reformation internalized and privatized the sequence by which people are convicted of their sins, repent, and are regenerated, the curative power of this process is still prominent in both Luther and Calvin. In this light, it is surprising that sapiential theology vanished so quickly thereafter. The argument here will be that the crisis of authority within the church was supported by the crisis of knowledge in the culture at large, making it necessary to reinvent the notions of truth and knowledge that excluded knowledge as divine wisdom.

II

To explore this problem we must begin with Calvin. Calvin's task as a theologian was twofold, in keeping with his place as a Reformer, yet as a second-generation Protestant who followed Luther's lead. As a Reformer, his goal was to root out corruption and introduce reforms in church practice, polity, and doctrine in order to encourage godliness and faithfulness in the church. As a second-generation Protestant, his task was to promote Protestantism by summarizing the faith of the Reformation for his contemporaries, a means to the former end. Note his friendship with Melanchthon, the original summarizer of Protestant doctrine.

The *Institutes* carry off both tasks simultaneously. In the preface to the 1536 edition of the work, he wrote "My purpose was solely to transmit certain rudiments by which those who are touched with any zeal for religion might be shaped to true godliness."[3] In the prefatory note to the 1559 edition he restated that he had "no other purpose than to benefit the church by maintaining the pure doctrine of godliness" through his "zeal to spread [God's] Kingdom and to further the public good."[4] The consolidating task is evident in the comprehensive presentation of the Reformed faith, the sections that distinguish this interpretation of Christianity from others, and those that defend it in the heat of debate. Still, for Calvin, theology is a first-order pastoral undertaking, not a second-order academic discipline.

For the purposes of this argument, it will be well to note two central notions of Calvin's thought that locate him as the last classical theologian: his notions of knowledge and truth. Calvin did not begin with a methodological preface to the 1559 *Institutes*. Nor did he enunciate a single axiomatic principle. The work opens with a theme drawn from the early church: regardless of one's point of entry into the insight, knowing God is the path to a proper self-concept, the path to the cure of the soul. Scripture, for example, helps us do this — for we cannot do it ourselves. But the turn to scripture does not appear until another source fails. It is, in essence, a fallback position, but one that works.

The notion of knowledge here is both cognitive and affective, as it was for Luther, although neither Luther nor Calvin would understand the distinction. Knowing God requires both reason and sentiment. It is existential in that it is attached, emotionally charged knowledge that transforms the self-concept of the knower by linking her to God and the Church. This knowledge is experiential in the sense that being "grabbed" by a new idea or information may set everything in a fresh perspective,

---

3. John Calvin, *Institutes of the Christian Religion* (Philadelphia: Westminster, 1960), p. 9.
4. Calvin, *Institutes,* p. 4.

even to the extent of redefining one's identity. It is an emotional intellectual experience.

Calvin's understanding of knowledge of God begins with intellectual apprehension that provokes desire for God. Understanding God correctly (itself a miracle of the Holy Spirit) would lead to loving God.[5] On the strength of that attachment, one's self-concept and perhaps behavior may change. To put that theologically, one may say that loving God is necessary for conversion. Knowing God will persuade that the only proper way to understand oneself is as a sinner. And the only remedy for that is to throw oneself on the mercy of God disclosed in the death and resurrection of Jesus Christ, and experience relief, trusting that God loves one in spite of the worst. Grasping the truth, beauty, goodness, and wisdom of this love is the beginning of the cure of the soul.

Knowledge, for Calvin, does not begin with a personal experience of some sort that one then interprets theologically or that induces assent to theological propositions, but rather the reverse. It is an intellectual and emotional grasp of God that compels adoration. Calvin assumed that the knowledge of which he spoke was genuine. While revelation assured that intellectual understanding of God was theoretically possible for anyone who was properly instructed, only the elect can benefit from it spiritually. One cannot force oneself to love God. That is a miracle from God, the secret or inner witness of the Holy Spirit. It may be argued that the separation of doctrinal exegesis from experiencing God's spiritual power is warranted by Calvin's assigning the benefits of Christ to the work of the Holy Spirit. The Holy Spirit has been associated with sanctification ever since Origen, after all. But this neat division, that separated the so-called objective role of theology from the so-called subjective side, does not, I think, finally do justice to Calvin's focus on the transformation of the world by knowing God. For it is the Holy Spirit who enables the written word to become the living Word of God and enables the knowledge of God to cure the soul.

Allied with Calvin's notion of theological knowledge, and undergirding his pastoral skill, was his spiritual notion of truth. This too was grounded in the Augustinian tradition in which Calvin stood. To put it syllogistically: God is truth; truth is the good and the beautiful; therefore,

---

5. Q. Breen, "St. Thomas and Calvin as Theologians: A Comparison," *The Heritage of John Calvin*, ed. J. H. Bratt (Grand Rapids: Eerdmans, 1973), p. 39.

God is good, true, and beautiful. To know God spiritually is to love the beauty of holiness that is God. Augustine sometimes summed this all up with the word *sapience*. Putting this together with Calvin's humanistic understanding of the effects of knowing God, we can safely say that by the grace of the Holy Spirit, the believer dwells in and is transformed by the beauty, truth, and love, this wisdom of God made known in Jesus Christ and made available by the Holy Spirit. The cure of the soul is maturation in this sapience, as it applies to oneself as a sinner, as well as in other aspects of one's life. Faith is the ability to cling to this knowledge when fear and despair overtake one.

III

Calvin marks the end of classical sapiential theology. After that, theology was redefined as the logical and systematic presentation of biblical doctrines in order to encourage cognitive assent to them. Assent became the goal of dogmatics; truth became that which may justifiably be assented. The question is, why was sapience deleted from truth?

In looking even briefly at Protestant orthodoxy, while the continuities with the Reformation are strong, the discontinuities are also striking. Calvin had no need of prolegomenon for his theological opus. He needed no rationale; he was free to write about God and the authority of scripture as he saw fit. But those who followed him were under different pressures. The crisis wrought by the Reformation and the beginning of scientific experiment required a new epistemology.

In response to the crises of authority and knowledge, Protestant Scholastics redefined theology as system-building. System is developed following a self-conscious method, organized around a single central principle: in theology's case, the authority, clarity, and the literal meaning of scripture. This principle orders the doctrines deduced from the Creeds and especially the confessions of the Reformation. Systematization aims at a cohesive presentation of Protestantism to enable it to claim certain knowledge for Christian faith. The reintroduction of prolegomena to provide a rationale for this method suggests that the rationale for theology was no longer self-evident; it had to be demonstrated. Logic controlled where wisdom had once flourished.

Richard Muller, an apologist for Reformed orthodoxy, argues that the urge to systematize and categorize is distinctive to the new dogmatics and constitutes a discontinuity with the Reformation.[6] Yet he argues that the model for prolegomena followed medieval theology, even though the Reformation had set its face against the Aristotelians.[7] It is odd that the Protestant Scholastics, so recently freed from medieval scholasticism, would themselves turn to scholasticism. One possibility is that they too faced an epistemic crisis that meant they had lost viable notions of truth and knowledge, and turned to scholasticism as a method to stand in the breach.

For our purposes here it is not necessary to enter into a full conversation with Muller's comprehensive work. Only one question need be posed in pursuit of our larger theme of the distancing of theology from the churches. Again, why did Protestant theologians invent biblical scholasticism, given the Reformers' attack on scholasticism? One reason, certainly, is that they needed a source of authority that could counter the authority of the Church of Rome. But this argument itself does not explain why theological truth was ordered into logical assent to a presentation of ideas, and the wisdom of God ceased to count as truth at all. Early on, reason was reconstrued as a purely rational activity that left the soul behind.

Theologians as well as astronomers had to respond to the epistemic crisis created by the notion of a heliocentric world, for it implied that God was not the center of the cosmos but the sun was. Just as the scientists found a new epistemology from Francis Bacon, the theologians sought a new epistemology in the doctrine of scripture. The effect of this move from immediate knowledge of God to knowledge of God mediated through scripture, was to enable theology to position itself to engage both fronts at once. It was on-the-job training.

Method became recognized as central to creating stable means of truth and knowledge. Bacon's *Novum Organum* followed the purgative thrust of the Reformation.[8] He divided science into two disciplines, a pseudo-science that calls for assent to undemonstrated opinions ("rash or premature anticipations of nature," §xxvi), and a clearly developed science based on experimental method. Bacon created scientific method and the

---

6. R. A. Muller, *Post-Reformation Reformed Dogmatics* (Grand Rapids: Baker Book House, 1993), p. 87.

7. Muller, *Post-Reformation Reformed Dogmatics*, p. 55.

8. Francis Bacon, "Novum Organum," in Bratt, ed., *The Heritage of John Calvin*.

notion of objective research and scholarship. Theology — perhaps referring to the Roman Church — was based on ignorant superstition, not
knowledge. He classifies types of ignorance into four types of idols: idols
of the tribe, idols of the cave (patterned on Plato's cave), idols of the mar-
ketplace, and idols of the theater (§xxxix, ff.). Religion falls under the last
category. It was essential that Protestants distance themselves from this
condemnation.

The mind, Bacon argued, is unstable and weak. It logs on to whatever
is presented to it fairly indiscriminately, and superstition masquerades as
knowledge, untested. The emotions equally lead the mind into dead ends
and errors to which men become stubbornly attached. The very notion of
knowledge must be reconstructed and the mind provided with methods
that yield objective "truth" — factual information that will enable science
to master the earth for the betterment of humankind. Bacon rejected the
humanistic and moral understanding of truth that characterized the philosophy of Plato and Aristotle in favor of the materialism of Democritus.
"Hard" science, based on fundamental axioms and experimental method,
is the only way, he argued, to eliminate the captivity of the mind to the
emotions or habit, and liberate man's ability to gain control over the natural world.

Bacon already criticizes theology for being unscientific. Early on,
dogmatics scientized theology by objectifying it, using scripture as the authority and clear doctrinal organization as the method. Objectifying theology was analogous to Bacon's experimental science. For both theology and
science, combating superstition, astrology, alchemy, and magic, which
were tied up with religion in their day, had to proceed by rejecting definitions of truth and knowledge based on inherited belief and opinion
(dogma), that is, ideas to which people were emotionally attached. The
whole structure of intellectual life, Bacon argued (as Descartes later
would), had to be razed to the ground and reinvented out of whole cloth.
The theologians, interested in separating theology from the taint of magic
and superstition, and outfitting it for the aborning world, breathed the
same air of epistemic crisis as did Bacon. Their response to the crisis depended on some of the principles that Bacon enunciated: central axioms,
systematization, and method that ruled out emotion and tradition. The result was that truth and knowledge became functions of cognition alone;
cognition was separated from attachment.

In short, the formative period of Protestant Scholasticism is intertwined with early modernity. Its decline after 1700 suggests that modern epistemology had, by then, outstripped orthodoxy's capacity to hold its own on the new terms of truth and knowledge. Scriptural authority and literal interpretation organized systematically were insufficient to fit theology for modernity once it was in full swing.

In France and Holland, Descartes, like Bacon, razed the intellectual and "scientific" establishment to the ground. And, like Bacon, he sought a method that would regularize and standardize scientific inquiry. To this he added philosophical inquiry. But unlike Bacon, Descartes was not given to experiment but to the autonomous work of reason. Descartes's plan was to design a method for reason that took a path quite opposite from that of Bacon as well as, of course, from medieval scholasticism. Taking a cue from the Renaissance idea of the *Dignity of Man,* a pivotal statement of modern humanism by Pico della Mirandola, Descartes sought to rid himself of both attachment and empirical evidence, doubt everything he had been taught, and construct knowledge by the power of reason alone. In so doing he strongly reinforced the redefinition of reason in purely rational terms. Knowledge was the result of objective reason detached from the object known.

Descartes held the mind to be strong and stable in its ability to reason its way to certain knowledge, while Bacon held the mind to be weak and unstable. Yet, Descartes too constructed a set of rules, a universal method for analyzing problems that would transcend the weight of tradition and personal idiosyncrasy: doubting rather than assenting to everything proposed to him by the disciplines he studied, and dissecting problems into manageable increments. Descartes's method is the original hermeneutic of suspicion, and it was radical. He sought to reason his way from ignorance to certainty by categorizing the increments into recognizable units and constructing a comprehensive assemblage from them.

Although Bacon and Descartes would have disagreed strenuously on some important matters, they each took method to be the way to truth and knowledge such that wisdom was excluded by definition. Truth and knowledge are no longer located in God and available to believers through prayer, reflection, and self-scrutiny by grace. Truth and knowledge are the result of either experiment or reason alone. Again we see that moral guidance was irrelevant to rationalist notions of reason, truth, and knowledge. The authority of scripture had a hard time holding its own on these terms. Yet the situation was to get more complex.

John Locke is recognized primarily as an empiricist for his insistence on evidence as the foundation of knowledge. Yet Locke also took a good deal from Descartes, integrating Baconian empiricism and Cartesian rationalism into a modern epistemology in his great *Essay Concerning Human Understanding.*[9] He divides certain knowledge from beliefs and judgments of probability. Certain knowledge is ascertained by seeing whether the agreement or disagreement between ideas is immediately evident, or rationally demonstrable. Where neither of these two conditions obtains, there is not knowledge but belief or faith. Thus, there is no such thing as theological knowledge, only belief. Although he admits intuitive knowledge (that sits awkwardly in his presentation, since the first part of the *Essay* disclaims innate knowledge), he does not allow that it pertains to knowledge of God.

Locke, although honoring faith, agreed with Bacon that Christian doctrines cannot count as knowledge but are opinion or belief. He sharpened Bacon's division between anticipations and interpretations of nature by separating reason from dogmatics altogether, because the latter is "assent to any proposition, not thus made out of the deductions of reason, but upon the credit of the proposer, as coming from God" that "we call *revelation.*"[10] Revelation is neither rational, nor based on evidence; therefore, there can be no "knowledge" of God. What we do have, however, is faith in the propositions offered about God from scripture. Now a wall had been constructed between reason and faith. Protestant Scholasticism had depended on being able to claim truth for its doctrinal system and the authority of scripture. Now scripture failed to count as knowledge. Faith shifted from being trust that God will act mercifully toward one, based on knowing who God is, to being a leap of faith that God exists, despite the absence of rational or empirical evidence. By the end of the seventeenth century we have arrived at modernity.

From even a cursory glance at this intellectual history we can see the radical change in the notions of reason, knowledge, and truth that followed upon Calvin. The new notions of reason, knowledge, and truth all eliminated affect. Being spiritually vulnerable to God's goodness and wondrous deeds no longer counted as truth or knowledge; nor was it rational

---

9. John Locke, *An Essay Concerning Human Understanding* (New York: The New American Library, 1964).

10. Locke, *An Essay Concerning Human Understanding*, p. 424.

because it attached the seeker to God. By the end of the seventeenth century the situation looks something like this: theology was no longer about the cure of souls but about rational assent to ideas; yet biblical scholasticism, developed to meet the epistemic crisis, proved inadequate to render theology a credible science. Theology was already moving toward the position it occupies today: emotionally inaccessible to believers and academically unacceptable to the wider academy. It had to try again.

IV

I have suggested that it would be a mistake at this point to think that theologians divided between those who sought to accommodate to modernity and those who sought to resist it. Everyone had to interact with the epistemic crisis that erupted from the Copernican revolution and the Reformation; the conditions that gave rise to modernity affected scientist and theologian alike. Theologians wanted to distance themselves as much from alchemy, superstition, and other ills of the day as did Bacon, Descartes, and Locke. And there was apparently enough of that to require combat over a sustained period of time.

The scientists and the Protestant Scholastics agreed that they needed new definitions of truth and knowledge that would, to put it anachronistically, elevate the left side of the brain over the right. What we would call right-brained thinking was seen as an obstacle to knowledge. In order to create the sciences, everyone sought a trans-personal method, fundamental axioms, and systematization as a way of employing cognition alone to avoid the traps of superstition, ignorance, and magic. This was important for theology, that had for so long been associated with the very evils moderns and Protestants deplored. The Protestant Orthodox sought to be part of the solution, not part of the problem, in order to bolster its authority.

This strategy itself is understandable. But they paid a price. By grounding itself in the budding objective notions of truth and knowledge applied to the doctrine of scripture, Protestant theology let go of a spiritual/theological vision of truth and knowledge that attached the soul to God. The objectification of scripture meant that theologians now had a subject matter with which to oppose ecclesiastical authority and to harness just as natural science did. The Bible could be analyzed and synthesized according to its parts and criteria for further use. And from the dogmatic principle of biblical authority, and standard methods for its examination, the theologians constructed a discipline that they thought could compete on modern terms. Dogmatics could now explain the faith to whoever would lend an ear. But they neglected to see that salvation requires more than assenting to how it works. Attachment to God is essential to salvation whether understood as union with God or remission of sin. The great exception to this is Johann Gerhard (1582-1637), the great Lutheran dogmatician, who deftly held cognition and affect together in his *Loci Theologici*. But generally speaking, dogmatics chose the new reason.

This problem did not sleep long. Decades before Locke resolutely dismissed dogmatics as knowledge, Pietism reacted to the cognitive turn of dogmatics from another angle. Philip Jacob Spener tacitly accepted the dogmatic definition of theology by offering a religion of the heart as its complement. Schleiermacher, himself a Pietist, and Barth, reacting to Schleiermacher, both retain elements of pastoral guidance in their dogmatics, but their work is rarely read in these terms. Scholasticism and Pietism, reason and faith, went their separate ways. Dogmatics provided right doctrine; Pietism offered practical methods that helped believers connect to the Bible and doctrine emotionally. Eventually, by ridding truth and knowledge of attachment, the modern university captured theology for itself and bifurcated the human soul into head and heart. A recent critique of these two types of theology by George Lindbeck indicates how deeply they have influenced theology.[11]

From Paul to Calvin, knowing God attached people to God's beauty and wisdom made known in history, so that they longed for him. After the Reformation, Protestantism eliminated attachment to God from the task of theology. It was given to preaching. Theology was objectified early on. It no longer aimed to cure souls but to inform people of the coherence of the ideas to which believers assented. The cure of the soul that required loving God slipped away. The new reason, knowledge, and truth eliminated vulnerability and awe before the knowledge sought. Knowledge of God came under the control of human reason; the mind stood tall.

Protestant Scholasticism and the sirocco of modernity burned a hole in the notion that only by yearning for God can knowing God cure the soul. The new reason, truth, and knowledge required Prolegomena and

---

11. George A. Lindbeck, *The Nature of Doctrine: Religion and Theology in a Postliberal Age* (Philadelphia: Westminster, 1984).

system. By mid-seventeenth century, it became appropriate to distinguish the reasoning behind the doctrines from the effects of doctrine. Theology, concerned with the former, eventually became divided from the arts of Christian ministry. And so it is until this day.

The terms of modernity seem to offer no way back to the wholeness of the soul. The Princeton theologians of the nineteenth century, especially Charles Hodge, struggled with this division throughout the century, with no satisfying resolution. The theological curriculum, as structured by Friedrich Schleiermacher, sustains the gap. Biblical studies, theology, and church history have become thoroughly academized in the modern sense, further distancing them from the cure of souls. Ironically, despite all the efforts to modernize theology, it is now marginal not only to the church but to the secular academy as well. Both church and academy suspect it, and for opposite reasons. Academic theology produced an ambiguous result.

The argument offered here has suggested but one reason why theology and the church struggle to work together. For their part, liberation theologies and feminism have distanced theology from the church from other angles. But the point of this discussion has been to suggest that the marginalization of theology from the church is quite a complex matter, more complex than can be unraveled here. While many factors come into play, one has to do with a fundamental shift in the notions of truth and knowledge that happened just after the Reformation.

V

What then have the new reason, truth, and knowledge to do with the gap between theology and the churches? If theology is not only to inform about God, but also to serve God's salvific purposes, it must help believers become vulnerable to God, even though the success of such a venture lies with the power of the Holy Spirit. If so, theology must readmit attachment as a central task of its ministry. This argument has suggested that acceptance of the new reason, truth, and knowledge has rendered the spiritual value of theology negligible. It has bred more information about, rather than yearning for, God. Modern doctrinal exegesis has demonstrated the logic that guides the doctrines, but has hesitated to help those who assent to the doctrines and still long to taste the goodness and wisdom of God and be taken up into it.

In Protestantism, the task of helping people yearn for God has been given to preaching. The preacher translates theology for the believer, so that with the power of the Holy Spirit, hearers of the Word become vulnerable to God. But preaching has become yet another discipline *alongside* theology and biblical studies, rather than expressions of them. And it has its own literature, focus, and goals, which may or may not be biblical and theological, even when it is to the cure of souls. With theology and biblical studies so distant from the church, preachers themselves may have difficulty translating from the academy to the church. To wit, the question, "will it preach?" is often raised of theology and biblical studies.

Despite the complexity of this problem, it may yet be that we have arrived at an appropriate moment to assess it. European and North American theology today is located in a post-Christian culture that has advanced steadily since the eighteenth century. Yet now the power of modern thought, which culminated in Nietzsche's proclamation of the death of God, is in turn being brought low. The modern understanding of truth and knowledge in the name of freedom, so hard-won, is now in shambles. Our moment proclaims the death not only of God but also of truth, knowledge, and morals. Yet it is not readily evident that postmodernism, despite its helpful understanding of the power of language to shape reality and of the relationship between power and morality, will suffice to bring us out of our current *aporia*. With the new reason, knowledge, and truth dead and morality and God dead, where is its constructive offering? The other side of emancipation from these traditional sustainers of goodness, wisdom, and order is despair. We may have to reinvent the wheel.

It may sound outrageous, and it may be beyond our reach, but if postmodernity signals a genuine epistemic crisis, it should be theoretically possible for theology to speak in its own voice again. As the moral, social, and intellectual debasement of at least the United States proceeds, there is little reason to reject theology out of hand. Yet such a reconstruction would have to be carefully undertaken. It could not reimpose the older notions of truth and knowledge, nor could it be built on the nihilistic implications of much of postmodernism. To offer an alternative to the present moment it would have to take cognizance of theology's long journey from its classic forms through its own epistemic crises in the Middle Ages, the Reformation, and under modernity and strands of postmodernity. It would have to construct a plausible theological epistemology, one that invites people to whom theology does not speak to become vulnerable to

God again. This would not discard business, science, and technology, but would question them on the grounds that they too stand before God.

Perhaps we, like Francis Bacon, stand at the dawn of a new age. He was able to begin shaping the epistemic void of his age. Whether we are of his caliber remains to be seen.

Our Separated Presbyterian Church in Japan

YASUO CARL FURUYA

When I arrived at Princeton Theological Seminary in 1952 to work toward a doctorate, John A. Mackay was president. He also taught ecumenics, and when I received my degree in 1959, it was his last commencement as the Seminary's president. Under his leadership, Princeton Theological Seminary was not only a Presbyterian seminary in the Reformed tradition, but also an ecumenical seminary. Those ideas have been carried on by his successors, James I. McCord and Thomas W. Gillespie. Although I was ordained by the New Brunswick Presbytery before returning to Japan, I was transferred a few years later back to the United Church of Christ in Japan, which was my original church.

Princeton Theological Seminary, my alma mater, has always been a Presbyterian but also an ecumenical seminary for me. And for me the Presbyterian church has always been an ecumenically minded church. Besides Mackay, people like Henry P. Van Dusen, Eugene C. Blake, and John C. Smith were all good Presbyterians and leading ecumenical statesmen.

I remember especially in this regard John Coventry Smith, who spoke at our commencement and encouraged me to attend the International Christian University. Having spent twelve years as a Presbyterian missionary in Japan before World War II, he served as secretary of the Foreign Mission Board and the general secretary of the Commission on Ecumenical Mission and Relations of the United Presbyterian Church in the U.S.A. He was elected moderator of the United Presbyterian General Assembly and also a president of the World Council of Churches.

I urged my then colleague Toshio Yamaguchi[1] to translate John C. Smith's memoirs, *From Colonialism to World Community: The Church's Pilgrimage,*[2] into Japanese in order to let his own church, the Presbyterian church in Japan, know how the American Presbyterian church was an ecumenically minded church.

Professor Yamaguchi is an elder of his church, *Nihon Kirisuto Kyokai* (Church of Christ in Japan), frequently abbreviated as Nikki. The Nikki is, however, a Presbyterian church. According to the *Christian Yearbook 1998,* this denomination is composed of 138 churches, 140 ministers, and 13,478 members.[3]

Although the Protestant churches in Japan are as a whole not large, the Nikki is small by comparison. The total number of Protestant ministers is 9,393 and the number of lay members is 587,980. Lay members of the Roman Catholic Church number about 450,000 and the Greek Orthodox Church about 25,000. Thus the total Christian population represents only 0.8 percent of the national population.

But the Nikki was the largest Protestant church before World War II, and this was the church to which Smith was sent as a young missionary in 1929. In his memoirs, he writes: "Our Presbyterian U.S.A. Mission had 65 missionaries. The Nihon Kirisuto Kyokai (The Church of Christ in Japan) had about 65,000 members and was the largest Protestant church in Japan."[4]

The Nikki was also the most theological Protestant church. As Smith also said in his memoirs, he learned a theology he had never heard before at Sapporo in Hokkaido, a northern island of Japan.

There were four churches in this city of 150,000, and the Nikki was the strongest. Its prominent pastor was Rev. Rinzo Onomura, now middle-aged and the leader of Hokkaido Presbytery. Although he never lived outside Japan he was an ardent reader in Japanese, English, and German, and an able preacher and theologian. We became good friends and he took me under his wing. He was already studying Dr. P. T. Forsyth of England, who was a forerunner of Karl Barth. Onomura was surprised that

1. Professor of Biology at the International Christian University.
2. John Coventry Smith, *From Colonialism to World Community: The Church's Pilgrimage* (Philadelphia: The General Press, 1982).
3. *Kirisutokyo Nenkan 1998 (Christian Yearbook 1998)* (Tokyo: Kirisuto Shinbunsha, 1997).
4. *Kirisutokyo Nenkan 1998,* pp. 18f.

I did not know about Forsyth. Most of all he taught me about the church in Japan. I shared with him my dream that we evangelistic missionaries should work under the direction of the presbytery. He was in favor of it and taught me a great deal about the presbytery itself.[5]

Thus while the Nikki was actually a Presbyterian church, its name indicates it never intended to be a denominational church in Japan, but rather an ecumenical one. The first Protestant church in Japan was organized at Yokohama in 1872. Both missionaries (Presbyterian and Reformed) and Japanese converts were to establish a Japanese national church not specifically identified with any denomination. That was why its name was *Nihon Kirisuto Kokai. Kokai* means catholic or universal. But as more missionaries arrived, more denominational churches were organized. However, as Japanese Presbyterians wanted to be interdenominational they organized *Nihon Kirisuto Itchi Kyokai* (Unified Church of Christ in Japan) in 1877. From 1836 to 1890, they worked hard to form an organic union with the Nihon Kumiai Kyokai (Congregational Church in Japan), which was already the second largest church although it had been constituted in 1886. After painstaking negotiations between the two churches, the General Assembly of the Nikki unanimously adopted the constitution of the union; however, its counterpart did not adopt it. The real cause of this failure was not the difference between Presbyterianism and Congregationalism as to church polity, but the lack of an ecumenical spirit among the Congregational missionaries and some Japanese, especially those educated in the United States at that time.

But the ecumenical intent of the Presbyterians was by no means crushed by this failure. On the contrary, ecumenical consciousness was increased even more. After this event, the name of the church was changed in 1891, from *Nihon Kirisuto Itchi Kyokai* to *Nihon Kirisuto Kyokai* (the Church of Christ in Japan). That is why the "Presbyterian" church in Japan never called itself by its denominational name, but simply the Church of Christ in Japan.

The Nikki was the first Japanese church that tried to become independent from the missions of America. The foremost leader in the independence movement was Masahisa Uemura (1868-1925), who was one of the first Japanese Protestants and who eventually became the leader of the

5. *Kirisutokyo Nenkan 1998*, pp. 19f.

Nikki. In the Ninth General Assembly of the Nikki, held in 1894, Uemura introduced a proposal to reorganize a board of evangelism, in order to shift the leadership in financial and personnel matters from the missionaries to the Japanese. He was convinced that Christian evangelism in Japan could be properly carried on only if Japanese Christians were primarily responsible. He was particularly concerned with financial independence from foreign mission boards.

In other words, Uemura and others raised the question of the propriety of an indigenous church that is affiliated with a foreign mission board performing the function of a presbytery or synod in directing local churches. As Charles Iglehart has pointed out, this was probably the first instance in the history of Protestant foreign missions that the issue was clearly raised by younger churches.[6]

In the same way, Uemura founded a theological school run by Japanese. While he was teaching at the Divinity School of Meiji Gakuin, which was administered by missionaries, he was criticized by one of the Southern Presbyterian missionaries for using a textbook of liberal theology. Convinced that theological education also should be independent from missionary control, he resigned from Meiji Gakuin and founded the Tokyo Theological School in 1903, the first theological seminary supported financially by the Japanese.

This is not to say, however, that the Nikki (represented by Uemura) was anti-missionary. As Richard Drummond remarked: "He had a genuine humility in the presence of truth, and his concern for the independence of the Japanese church was rooted in his respect for all people."[7] That was the reason why there were several outstanding women educators among his church members. Uemura was also the first to propose the ordination of women as elders of the Nikki, and in 1933, the Nikki ordained a woman as minister quite naturally and without controversy. In the following year, a daughter of Uemura was also ordained; these were possibly the first instances of women's ordination in the history of the Presbyterian church in the world, if not in the history of the world church. It was not

6. Charles W. Iglehart, *A Century of Protestant Christianity in Japan* (Tokyo: Charles E. Tuttle Company, 1959), p. 122.

7. Richard Henry Drummond, *A History of Christianity in Japan* (Grand Rapids: Eerdmans, 1971), pp. 219f.

until 1956 that the United Presbyterian Church in the United States ordained its first woman as minister.

To use the title of Smith's memoirs, Nikki was a leading church in the pilgrimage away from colonialism and into the world community. At least, it was a leading church in Japan. When Japan entered the so-called "fifteen years war," which began with the Manchurian Incident of 1931 and ended with the atomic bombs dropped in 1945, the Nikki was the largest Protestant church in Japan. According to the statistics of 1932, the numbers of independent churches and membership were as follows: the Nikki had 143 churches and 45,322 members while the Congregational Church had 82 churches and 31,570 members; the Methodist, 91 churches and 20,734 members; and the Episcopal, 34 churches and 15,825 members.[8]

At the same time, the Nikki was the most theologically minded church. Even before the "fifteen years war," as Drummond described it: "Translations of contemporary Europeans and American theologians were read by large numbers. Kierkegaard and Troeltsch continued to be studied: Barth, Brunner, and Heidegger were in some cases better known and at an earlier period than in English-speaking lands. This kind of theological activity was particularly strong in the Presbyterian-Reformed tradition under the leadership of Tokutaro Takakura."[9]

Takakura was the theological successor of Uemura. Though Takakura himself was not a Barthian, many of his disciples became Barthians. Among the younger churches in Asia, the Japanese church was probably the only church in which Barthian theology was read to such a degree before World War II. It is ironic, however, that these Japanese theologians did not resist Japanese militaristic nationalism while Barth himself fought against Nazism.

It is also ironic that Toyohiko Kagawa, a minister of the Nikki who studied at Princeton Theological Seminary (1914-1916) and became the best-known Japanese Christian evangelist and social reformer in the world, was treated with an air of indifference, if not contempt, in his own denomination. The basic reason was Kagawa's criticism of Nikki's "theologism," which was not concerned with social affairs.[10]

8. Arimichi Ebisawa and Saburo Ouchi, *Nihon Kirisutokyoshi, A History of Japanese Christianity* (Tokyo: Nihon Kirisuto Kyodan Shuppankyoku, 1970), p. 545.
9. Drummond, *A History of Christianity in Japan*, p. 252.
10. Yasuo Carl Furuya, "Toyohiko Kagawa (1888-1960): Blessed Are the Poor," in *Sons of the Prophets: Leaders in Protestantism from Princeton Seminary*, ed. Hugh T. Kerr (Princeton: Princeton University Press, 1963), pp. 192ff.

In June 1941, a half year before the beginning of the war, the United Church of Christ in Japan (the *Kyodan*) was organized. The direct cause for the formation of the Kyodan was the pressure by the Japanese government, which was controlled by ultra-nationalistic militarism. In order to mobilize the whole nation for war, the government demanded all religious denominations to be united into several bodies. Thirty-four Protestant denominations were ordered to unite. If they did not follow the order, they were no longer legally recognized as religious bodies.

When it became apparent to the denominations that church union was necessary and indispensable for their survival, even the Nikki, which had the strongest opposition to a union in which the question of creed was not seriously considered, finally decided to move toward union.

This organic union was justified by asserting that this had been the great desire of most Japanese Protestants from the beginning. When we could not fulfill the dream ourselves, pressure from the government provided the opportunity to realize the union, which had been an ideal of the ecumenical movement since the Edinburgh conference in 1910.

Mitsuru Tomita, a minister of the Nikki who had studied at Princeton Theological Seminary (1918-1920), was selected as moderator of the Kyodan. Smith remembered Tomita: "We knew Tomita as the chairman of the board at Meiji Gauin. He was a 'rock.' He reminded me of Darley Down's comment on a previous occasion. Darley was a Congregationalist, but he said, 'if it comes to resistance unto blood, the Presbyterians will be there.'"[11]

I am not going to describe here in detail how the Kyodan did not resist but rather cooperated with the war policy of the military government during the war. One thing I must write about, however, is the original founding of the Kyodan and its behavior during the war — which resulted in the separation and withdrawal of several churches from the Kyodan and strife within the Kyodan itself.

After the defeat in the war in 1945, many missionaries came back to Japan from America. The major American denominations — Presbyterians, Congregationalists, Methodists, and others — organized the Interboard Committee for Christian Work in Japan (IBC) and decided to work together with the Kyodan. But some denominations — Anglican, Baptist, Lutheran, for example, and minor denominations like the Holi-

11. Smith, *From Colonialism to World Community,* p. 19.

ness, Friends, Nazarene, and Free Methodist — were separated and withdrawn from the Kyodan within a few years after the war. The reasons
were various: some were doctrinal and some financial; some were even
political.

The majority of the Kyodan, however, consisting of the former Nikki
(Presbyterian), Congregational, and Methodist churches, decided to stay
as the united church. Why did they stay in the Kyodan even though it was
obviously organized by the pressure of the government, subservient to the
government, and no longer assumed the prophetic responsibility of the
church?

The basic reason was that they believed the union of the churches
was the divine will and good for the advancement of the mission in Japan.
It had long been a dream of Japanese Christians. If the Kyodan disinte-
grated and old denominational churches revived, it would not be easy to
reunite the many denominations as one church. Therefore, it was better to
stay as the United Church. Although there were many questions about its
origin and its behavior during the war, there was no reason to disband the
united church and return to the divided denominations. This was the
main reason that the majority of both ministers and lay members decided
to stay together in the Kyodan. The mainline churches in America, including the Presbyterians, supported their decision and worked together
through the Interboard Committee for Christian Work in Japan.

The separation and withdrawal of thirty-nine churches of the Nikki
and the formation of a new Nikki (calling their new church the same
name, the Church of Christ in Japan) in 1951 was thus a great shock to the
Kyodan. The Nikki was the largest and core church within the Kyodan, and
the reasons for separation and withdrawal were related to theological
questions. John C. Smith's old friend, Rinzo Onomura, was one of the
leaders of the new Nikki.

The reasons concerned not only financial matters of the mission but
also matters of faith. Just as the old Nikki had been critical of the formation of the Kyodan over the question of confession of faith, the new Nikki
churches still thought the Kyodan confession of faith was ambiguous. The
"Greetings" to the other churches, which were adopted at the Founding
Assembly, said: "We have separated and withdrawn from the Kyodan, because we were urged by the consciousness of faith to be loyal to what we
believe as our own mission. Of course, we are not going to be different for
our own pleasure. Accordingly, we respect the traditions and the stands of

faith of other churches, and we hope that we will be friendly as much as possible."[12]

In 1953, at the third General Assembly, they approved the "1953 Confession of Faith," a confession often compared with the "1890 Confession of Faith" and referred to as its "critical successor." Basically they are the same. Just as the name of the church is exactly the same — Nikki — so the confessions of faith of both old and new Nikki are basically the same.

Having been stimulated by the Nikki's Confession, the Kyodan also approved its Confession the following year. Of this Confession, a church historian has said: "To one's surprise, though there was some progress, it is not much different in its form and content from the 'Creed' of the old Nikki, approved in 1890. Not only that, it is almost the same as the 'Rules of Faith' adopted by the Nihon Kirisuto Kokai, the first church at Yokohama in 1872. It is a simple creed; while it speaks clearly at minimum about the evangelical and fundamental matters, its stand is very tolerant about other matters."[13]

The confessions of the new Nikki and the Kyodan are thus basically the same. Almost half a century has passed since the new Nikki separated from the Kyodan. But one cannot say, except in its first decade, that the Nikki was a growing church among churches in Japan. According to the statistics, the active members numbered 3,865 in 1951, 5,071 in 1961, 5,399 in 1971, 5,809 in 1981, 6,336 in 1991, and 6,242 in 1996. The total Protestant population increased from two hundred thousand in 1951 to six hundred thousand in 1996.[14]

The old Nikki was the leading church in theology. This cannot be said about the new Nikki. Sad to say, it has been struggling to have a theological seminary. There is no full-time professor and very few students. The old Nikki used to have several leading theologians and biblical scholars, but now there are very few if any.

The old Nikki was also the leading church in ecumenism, interested in the union of churches and missions in old colonies like Taiwan and Korea. One cannot say the same about the new Nikki. It is not yet a member of the National Council of Churches. Though it is a member of the World

12. *Nihon Kirisuto Kyokai no 35 nen (35 years of the Church of Christ in Japan)*, ed. The Historical Committee of the Nihon Kirisuto Kyokai (Hakodate, 1986), p. 1.

13. Ebisawa and Ouchi, *Nihon Kirisutokyoshi*, p. 622.

14. *Nihon Kirisuto Kyokai Binran (Concise Yearbook of the NKK)* (Sapporo: Nihon Kirisuto Kyokai Shuppankyoku, 1997), pp. 324f.

Alliance of the Reformed Churches, it is not a part of the Christian Conference of Asia nor of the World Council of Churches. It receives no missionaries from abroad and it sends no missionaries elsewhere. Though recently the new Nikki began to have some relations with the Korean churches in Japan, it is in no way an ecumenically minded church.

The polity of the new Nikki is, as the old Nikki, presbyterian. But the presbytery of the Nikki is as large as the synod. For instance, the Tokyo Presbytery covers an area from the north to the middle of the Main Island. The new Nikki is actually run not by the presbytery, but by either individual churches or the general assembly.[15] Thus, one cannot help having an impression of the new Nikki as small and closed, not an ecumenical church. Even one of its ministers openly said:

> The old Nikki lost its subjectivity and identity during the wartime, when it joined in the formation of the Kyodan. After the war, it reflected on its own conduct and founded a new church, being separated from the Kyodan. It was at the same time on a course of independence that cut the financial aid from foreign countries, and especially the relation with missionaries. But it turned out to be a loss of ecumenical fellowship, ecumenical points of view and concerns. It became the cause of spiritual poverty, and the drying up of the spiritual power of the fellowship. Its viewpoints and concerns became domestic. It became a poor church, which can only have thinking from the inside. It seems to have returned to being a nationalistic church, which it once criticized.[16]

On the other hand, even after the new Nikki had separated and withdrawn, the Kyodan remained the largest and leading Protestant church, consisting of the old Congregational church, the old Methodist church, and the majority of the old Presbyterian church. To be sure, the Kyodan has had many problems. It took the initiative among Japanese churches in issuing the "Declaration of Wartime Responsibility" in 1967. The declaration was not, however, the beginning of a new and bright era of the Kyodan. On the contrary, it was the foretaste of even greater division and

15. *Nihon Kirisuto Kyokai no 35 nen,* pp. 104-9.

16. Sozo Koike, "The Seminary Which Opens for the Future," *Shingakko Dayori (Seminary Bulletin)* 27, by the Theological Seminary Committee of the Nihon Kirisuto Kyokai, Kawagoe (November 1997), p. 1.

turmoil, which still continues. Controversy over the declaration was followed by dispute over the Christian Pavilion at the Osaka World Exposition in 1970, and the students' strike and riot police at Tokyo Union Theological Seminary, the Kyodan seminary, in 1970. For the next twenty years the Kyodan was unable to have a General Assembly, being wracked by controversies between the "social action" groups and the "evangelistic" groups. Many meetings were controlled by radical students and ministers calling themselves "problem posers," who used violent and undemocratic actions.[17]

Whenever one looks at Kyodan's chaotic confusion and conflicts, one cannot help but raise the question as to what would have happened if the new Nikki had not separated and withdrawn from the Kyodan. In my opinion, the separation and withdrawal of the new Nikki resulted not only in damage to the Kyodan, which has long been in confusion, but to the new Nikki, which has long been in isolation. Unfortunately both churches have been hindered from carrying out their proper missions in Japan, Asia, and the world for too many years.

Why are they separated from each other? I have some classmates at Tokyo Union Theological Seminary who joined the new Nikki. Some new Nikki ministers have also studied at Princeton Theological Seminary. There are brothers who are separated; the elder is a minister in the Kyodan and the younger a minister in the new Nikki. There is even one couple where the husband is a minister in the Kyodan and the wife a minister in the new Nikki.

It is my sincere hope, therefore, that someday soon the new Nikki and the Kyodan may be united, just as the Presbyterian Church in the U.S.A. and the Presbyterian Church in the U.S. were united after more than a hundred years of separation. And I am quite sure that such a united church will have a more creative and faithful theology as servant of Christ and God in Japan.[18]

17. Yoshinobu Kumazawa and David L. Swain, eds., *Christianity in Japan, 1971-90* (Tokyo: Kyobunkan, 1991), pp. 89-113. Cf. James M. Phillips, *From the Rising of the Sun: Christians and Society in Contemporary Japan* (Maryknoll, N.Y.: Orbis, 1981).

18. Cf. Yasuo Furuya, ed., *History of Japanese Theology* (Grand Rapids: Eerdmans, 1997).

Preaching as a Matter of Trust: Recovering the Nerve of the Pulpit

PETER J. GOMES

The Lord God has given me the tongue of those who are taught,
that I may know how to sustain with a word him that is weary.
Morning by morning he wakens, he wakens my ear to hear as those
who are taught.

ISAIAH 50:4

In 1922, Willard Learoyd Sperry became the fifth dean of Harvard Divinity School. He reports that he was waited upon in his study in The Central Congregational Church of Boston by none other than the president of Harvard himself, the redoubtable Abbott Lawrence Lowell, who came directly to the point and offered the post to Sperry. Sperry replied that he was no scholar. "I know that," Lowell is reported to have said; "all you have to do is to know one when you see one."

Neither man in this account was fully forthcoming. Sperry was in the first class of American Rhodes Scholars, and had good degrees from both Oxford and Yale. He would preside over a great era in the history of the Divinity School, embodying in his own considerable scholarship and pastoral experience the seventeenth-century ideal of the "learned ministry." Shortly after his appointment, Sperry articulated his vision for the ministry in his 1922 Dudleian Lecture entitled "The Call to the Ministry," which enjoyed a wide circulation. Writing in painful proximity to the American

98

experience in the First World War, Sperry defined preaching in the confused climate of the early 1920s as "primarily a process of thinking aloud about life." "We have been told recently that the war discovered a vast fund of 'inarticulate religion' in the rank and file of human life. Inarticulate religion is religion which has never really become conscious of itself, found itself, and got itself stated out in the open. The case for preaching at the present time rests on the inarticulate religion of the average man."[1] The first task, then, of the modern preacher, according to Sperry, is "to help dumb and perplexed men say out what is in them."

Despite the plethora of words in this most wordy of centuries, where no condition goes unlabeled and every constituency is catered to, even after the passage of seventy-five years I think that that vast fund of "'inarticulate religion' in the rank and file of human life" is as vast as it ever was. The persistence of this condition may help to explain the increasing cultural preference for what is called "spirituality" over "theology" or even "religion." When I entered the ministry thirty years ago, and when I began to teach in Harvard Divinity School twenty-five years ago, spirituality was not a subject we Protestants knew or heard much about. Spirituality had a vaguely Roman sound to it and suggested a certain esoteric quietism quite out of sync with our reformed inheritance and neo-orthodox tendencies. For our fathers and mothers, knowledge of the Bible was thought to be sufficient, and the battles of the nineteenth and early twentieth centuries within the Protestant churches were mainly "battles for the Bible." In our day, for a brief and shining moment we believed that if people got their theology right all would be well, and we were all in the business of "doing" theology. Today, in the closing moments of the second millennium, we find with some notable exceptions that neither the Bible nor theology commands the field as they once did. People are woefully ignorant of the Bible, and they know less and care even less about theology. If you want a book on a religious topic to get the attention of readers in the bookstores of America, pray that your book is not shelved under "Theology" or even under "Religion," for there it will languish with the multi-volume biblical commentaries and the systematic theologies of required reading lists. Pray to the bookstore gods that you are shelved in the "Spirituality" section, where you can attain ascribed status by proximity to the mega-selling *Chicken Soup* series, and esoteric inner-help books. Perhaps spirituality,

1. Willard L. Sperry, "The Call to the Ministry," Dudleian Lectures (1922), p. 10.

whatever that may mean or be, is the end-of-century response to that "vast fund of 'inarticulate religion' in the rank and file of human life," discovered by Dean Sperry in the cultural anxiety of the years immediately following World War I.

For those of us in the business of trying to make words make sense, this may well seem a threatening situation. Who cares to hear what we may have to say when people are much more interested in trying to articulate that which is within themselves, permitting that inner self and inner voice an authentic and liberating communication?

In the "old" days, preaching in seminary often suffered at the hands of the hard disciplines, particularly of biblical studies and theology. These cardinal studies regarded themselves as the heart and mind of the church's work, the grammar and syntax of the theological enterprise, and preaching is what you did after you had dealt with these "real" disciplines. The Harvard of Sperry's day, for example, was famous for its neglect of what was then called "Practical Theology," with one's first years in church considered a sufficient laboratory in which to learn it. Sperry, himself a superb pastoral theologian although Dean, tacitly acquiesced in this hegemony.

Today, if we take seriously the experience of many in seminaries and even in churches, preaching suffers no longer at the hands of the hard disciplines which themselves have long been under siege. Preaching, rather, must now commend itself on its merits to those who do not wish to be spoken to, at, or for, who may well prefer the authority not of the word or of the preacher but of their own individual and group experience, and who are, in most cases, as well or better educated and possessed of more experience, spiritual or otherwise, than their pastors. As one of my seminarians reported to me not too long ago, "Preaching is too authoritarian, too top down: nobody does that sort of thing anymore." Nobody does that sort of thing anymore, that is, except for those of us who still do that sort of thing. Preaching, once too soft for the seminary and now too hard for the church, nevertheless maintains a claim upon both seminary and church, a paradox both amusing and frustrating. Preaching courses are more popular now in seminaries than at any point in recent years, perhaps because congregations complain consistently about the poor quality of the preaching under which they sit. The single most requested short courses in continuing education among the clergy, both in school and at professional conferences, are courses in preaching. When congregations conduct the now nearly universal self-study procedures before searching for a new minister, routinely they list skills in leadership, management, and counseling as chiefly desirable in their pastor, but most candidacies rise and fall on the ability to articulate the "inarticulate religion" in the rank and file of human life. Even a spiritual enabler has to be able to articulate in some convincing fashion the gifts within.

In discussing with an old friend my mild theory that spirituality as popularly understood is subversive of preaching, compromising its authority and intimidating its practitioners, I was asked if I didn't think that architecture had as much to do with it as anything else. I asked what he meant, and we launched upon a lively discussion of the demise of the center pulpit in mainline Protestantism. Those of us of a certain age not only remember the defining characteristics of Protestant interiors as the center pulpit but also the wholesale renovation of those spaces, and the installation from the 1920s onward of the divided chancel. Nearly all of the great pre–World War II "Protestant Gothic Cathedrals" in the United States adapted their new interiors to the liturgical ideals most frequently expressed in Anglican interiors. Aping the Anglicans became the fashion, and even as Protestant and word-centered a place as The Riverside Church in New York City, built by Mr. Rockefeller to afford hospitality to the preaching of Harry Emerson Fosdick, offered it with a divided chancel. The college chapels at Princeton, Duke, Chicago, and Harvard all did the same thing within five years of one another. Protestants of what was once called the "Free Church Tradition" are still trying to figure what to do with their chancels and how properly to relate the word to what else goes on there. Ecclesiastical architecture is not necessarily theological destiny, although the question of liturgical space and the function of preaching as a liturgical act is one worth exploring with more than perfunctory care.

The question that continues to concern us is the relationship between preaching which assumes a high degree of articulation, and that vast fund of "inarticulate religion" in the rank and file of human life. Indeed, we might ask if preaching itself gets in the way of articulating the inarticulate. "In this fallen world the preacher cannot always be the clear voice of God twice every week. But he can always be the voice of the people, trying to find and express themselves."[2]

Perhaps the Dean is conceding too much here, and nowadays most preachers do not get an opportunity to express anything twice a week, but

2. Sperry, "The Call to the Ministry," p. 11.

perhaps in sacrificing what some might regard as a "high" view of preaching, the Dean provides a means for the ordinary preacher to enter into the conversation between God and the people of God. Contemporary preachers may not be able to utter with conviction or persuasion, "Thus says the Lord," at least not always, but the listening preacher, the one who hears the people committed to his or her charge, who has and accepts in the old language the "cure of souls," just may be able to utter, "Thus cry the faithful." In doing so preaching begins, as Isaiah puts it, in the voice of "the one who is weary," and as one who is taught, and only then proceeds to teach as God gives utterance. To teach as one who has been taught is to stand not under authority but under instruction. Preaching then begins with the underrated homiletical art of listening both to God and to the people of God. Listening is as important to teaching as discourse is to speech, and to preach the sustaining word to those who are weary is to give expression to those deep and inarticulate matters of heart, mind, and soul which so easily encumber the faithful and make them weary and anxious. I once asked a colleague, a member of our daily congregation for over fifty years, what he expected to get out of a lifetime of so much sermon listening. Rather than novelty or profundity, the Scylla and Charybdis of so much college and other preaching, he said that he hoped to hear what he himself felt but could not begin to articulate. In other words, he looked to be heard in the words and experience of another, and by that transaction to be connected to the sustaining word of God.

Not long ago, I had a chance encounter with one of our graduates now working as chaplain in a nursing home where she is obliged to preach weekly. Hers was a congregation of diminishing expectations. Worlds were shrinking for her people, and at first she said she simply did not know what to do. Her best parish efforts seemed of no account here. Sensing herself floundering, she asked one of the patients what would be most helpful, and she was surprised by the articulate response. What the patients wanted in their sermons, she was told, was humor, personal experience, and a word of hope. Humor reassured them that they were still alive; personal experience likened her life to theirs; and the word of hope suggested that while they may be lonely they were not alone. These basic human elements provided an accessible framework for the gospel to be articulated, and enabled this listenable preacher to find the sustaining word for those who were weary.

To teach as one who has been taught may indeed be an argument for inspiration, and it ought to be our daily prayer that we are inspired by more than our own imagination and agenda. Here, however, I would make the less lofty case that we preach and teach out of the full wealth of conviction provided by the privilege of a rigorous theological education. If theology is to be understood as an effort — systematic or otherwise — to make some sense of the relationship between the human and the divine, then theology is not simply an abstract technical discipline existing in splendid and increasingly neglected isolation in the higher reaches of the curriculum, available only to the long-trained *cognoscenti,* but the means by which the faithful inarticulate are given a voice in the formation of both their questions and the answers to them. That work, I wish to argue, is most perfectly expressed, albeit imperfectly, in preaching. Thus, theology in its most comprehensive sense is indeed the servant of the church, and preachers are the church's servant theologians. The arbitrary distinction between those who "do theology," and those who merely preach, is as unfortunate as it is false, and it has wrought great havoc in contemporary theological education. By this false distinction persons preparing for parish ministry and who accept the responsibility of preaching, are led to believe that theology is "what doctoral students do," and is therefore not for them. Doctoral students, most of whom have neither the desire nor intention to preach, regard theology as that special, esoteric branch of instruction to which they have committed their lives and dissertations. Those who have embraced this specialized notion of theology remain in undisturbed possession of a subject which, to paraphrase the irascible Stanley Hauerwas, has become terminally dull.

To recover the nerve of preaching and to reaffirm that theology is indeed the servant of the church is to recognize, particularly on the part of preachers, that theology is not simply what "they" do in that department, but rather is the whole business of the relationship between the human and the divine, both then and now. "Religion," as John Habgood, former Archbishop of York puts it, "is about making sense of life, of this life first of all, and particularly of those aspects of it which challenge and disturb us." A theological education properly construed considers that enterprise both historically and existentially. It is concerned with the language and experience of the church in its continuing work of making sense, and preaching is both the articulation and experience of that work. Out of this collective experience we are taught, and it is to this collective experience that we both preach and teach. Because we have the benefit of this concentrated experience, because we have now some sense of the formulation of those questions that continue to be asked and have eluded tidy answers, because we are instructed by the living traditions of scripture and sacrament, human history and human hope, we may speak as those who are taught. Those of us who teach in the theological enterprise have the opportunity and the obligation to allow our students, especially those who intend to preach, the full benefit of this experience.

When the ancients famously referred to theology as the "Queen of the Sciences," they did not mean that this formal discipline exceeded all others and held them either in thrall or in contempt, but that in theology all learning was combined to demonstrate nothing less than the knowledge of God. Theology was the comprehension of all disciplines, all knowledge, all wisdom, and all skills, in a whole significantly greater than the sum of its parts or any one of its parts. In a fragmented and anxious world where disunity rather than unity is the order of the day, and fragmentation and specialization drive us further and further apart from each other and our endeavors, preaching understood as the most comprehensive of theological enterprises may well be one of the means whereby some sense of order, grandeur, and purpose may be restored. Such an ambition is indeed a recovery of nerve, and it may be just the radical cure required for the renovation of both church and seminary.

In the final analysis it comes down to a matter of trust. In the way of the world of Harvard Divinity School, I usually have a high number of graduating seniors in my preaching seminar. For some it is their last preaching course, for others it is their only preaching course, for all it is the last chance we have at one another within the consoling embrace of the academy. The anxiety level is high. Those who are about to be ordained and accept a call to their first parish as assistant, associate, or pastor wonder if the Spirit will have anything left for them to say when the moment comes. I remember well the feeling. Our old professor of public speaking, Frederick Clyfton Packard, a Dickensian-looking character and rhetorician of the old school, told us candidates in the Class of 1968, "Remember, do not to try to preach everything you know in your first sermon: you just might succeed." He knew whereof he spoke, having listened to many a first sermon over the course of fifty years of instruction. I ask my students at the beginning and end of the course to remember that preaching is a matter of trust.

First, trust yourself. Trust that you have something to say, and that it is worthwhile. For reasons best known to God, you have been called to this particular and peculiar vocation. If God has enough confidence in you to place the office of preaching in your care, you should share something of the confidence in yourself. You may well have much about which to be modest, and you may need a lot of help, but you are the vehicle, however imperfect, that God has chosen to use: take some comfort from that.

Second, trust the text. Many young preachers ask themselves when confronted with textual preaching, "What can I do to make this interesting? How can I make this text talk?" Or, in other words, "How can I make this text say what I want to say?" These, I suggest, are the wrong questions, as any good exegesis and interpretation course will demonstrate. The question really is, first, "What is this text saying?" then, "What does it give me permission to say? How have others dealt with this? What did they know that I do not? What do I know that they did not? If we believe in the concept of the 'true and lively word,' where are the life and truth to be found? What may I or ought I to do with them?" Trust that the text not only spake, but speaks.

Third, trust the people. Most congregations will their preachers to succeed, for there are better forms of amusement than to watch a preacher die in the pulpit. Most people will listen to you if you listen to them. As Milton might have said, "The hungry sheep [still] look up, yearning to be fed." As my old parishioner at our daily service of Morning Prayers put it, the people hope that you will articulate what is inarticulate within them, not necessarily what they want but what they need; and for the moment of preaching you are the only one with the possibility of doing that for them.

Finally, and this is perhaps piously obvious, trust God. The most sincere prayer of the preacher that I know is the one uttered in the silence just before the sermon begins. We might like to think that we invoke God to speak to us and through us, but our real prayer is the first article in the creed of our colleagues in medicine: do no harm. Trust that God has a word for you, and that out of your prayer and your study, and out of all your choice of words, that word which is God's word for you and for your people will be heard even if it is not the word you had in mind when you began. The preacher who listens both to the people and to God may on occasion get the right Word amidst all of the words. It is in this context that we understand the sacramental nature of preaching, perhaps a Protestant conceit but a necessary conceit nonetheless, that preaching is indeed an outward and visible sign of an inward and spiritual experience. For the preacher, preaching must not stand in the way of the sacrament but must become in itself a sacramental transaction.

When I consider the faithful ministry of my colleague and friend, President Thomas Gillespie, his witness for Christ, and his prudent stewardship of the rich resources of Princeton Seminary, I think indeed of that workman in 2 Timothy 2:15 who "needeth not to be ashamed" of the good work that he has done and which remains to be done. I would not want to ascribe to him in their entirety the views expressed above, but I do know that we share a love for the mind and the heart of the church, and that we do understand theology in its most comprehensive form to be the means for the edification of the whole church. Through the peculiar lenses of an admiring though distant friend I view with appreciation the example he has set for ministry, and the encouragement he has given to those Princeton men and women who adorn the churches of America and beyond. He has been well used of God, for which both church and school must now say Amen and Amen: Thanks be to God.

A Message from Medellín

GUSTAVO GUTIÉRREZ

Thanks to a generous invitation from Dr. Thomas Gillespie, I had the opportunity to spend a semester at Princeton Theological Seminary. The experience was very fraternal and enriching, and one that I will treasure always in my memory. It is a delight and an honor to participate in this book in homage to Dr. Gillespie and to present a few of the topics developed during my stay at Princeton.

Thirty years ago, the second General Conference of Latin American Bishops took place in Medellín, Colombia. The issues defined by the Second Vatican Council gave life to the idea of having a gathering that would address the reality of the continent, evaluate the challenges that it presents and signal the direction to follow in the proclamation of the Gospel. Medellín, similar to Vatican II, had a strong ecumenical emphasis which, unfortunately, weakened in the succeeding Latin American episcopal conferences. This emphasis was expressed through the presence of representatives from diverse Christian churches in a memorable liturgical celebration and in various of the written documents.

Much has happened in the world since this time. There have been important changes in the ecclesiastic field and, without a doubt, today's times are no longer those of Medellín. Does this mean that this conference belongs to a past since overcome? Was it relevant in its moment, but has ceased to be so today? It is said that we confront in this day and age a very different situation, new challenges and other demands; that Medellín has become estranged from all this, and new responses from the Church are now required.

Practically the day after it took place, many people tried to speak of

107

Medellín as if it belonged to the past, for reasons we know well. This perspective still permeates certain circles. However, this should not hide the fact that today, thirty years later, we are facing important developments both in Latin America and globally. Without question, we have entered a different time and are therefore led to ask the question: To what extent and in what manner do historical changes affect the depth of doctrine and the pastoral models stimulated by this historically determined situation?

In the following pages we will attempt to address the relevance of Medellín today. Since there are many factors involved, we will limit our focus to three of them: (1) the identification of Medellín in the conciliar cycle; (2) discerning the signs of the times; and (3) the persistent outcry emerging from those trapped in widespread poverty.

The Context of Vatican II

Historians and theologians agree that the reception of the councils in the Church is a process that takes place with a certain slowness and over the course of extensive periods of time.[1] This has been especially true for Vatican II, which, in view of the opposition faced by the Catholic Church in previous centuries, assumes a historical perspective. At the same time, it presents a broad vision of the world today and solid theological reflection, thereby spreading the word of the Gospel through novel routes. As has been said many times, the Church and its mission was the central theme of the Council.[2]

1. See the classic article of Y. Conger, see "La réception comme réalité ecclésiologique" in *Revue des Sciences Philosophiques et Théologiques* 56 (1872): 369-403. The author defines the notion of reception as follows: "the process through which an ecclesiastical body makes its own, in truth, a decision that it has not yet granted itself, recognizing that the proclaimed measure is a rule that corresponds to its life." The reception, states Conger, is more than obedience, it is "a contribution of one's own consent, eventually of judgement, in which the life of a body that exercises its spiritual capacities is expressed" (p. 370). Cf. the most recent articles of E. Lanne, "La notion ecclésiologique" in *Revue Théologique de Louvain* 25, no. 1 (1994): 30-45, and A. Anton, "La 'recepción' en la Iglesia y eclesiología" in *Gregorianum* 77, no. 1 (1996): 57-96, and idem, 77, no. 3 (1996): 437-69.

2. Paul VI had reinforced this conciliar interest by affirming in his address *Ecclesiam Suam* (1964), "We think that it is the responsibility of the Church today to deepen in the consciousness that it should have of itself, in the treasure of truth of which it is heir and guardian and in the mission that it should exercise in the world" (n. 19). The Council was a great step towards the raising of this consciousness.

However, without question the *"aggiornamento"* of the Church, which accord-ing to Pope John XXIII the Council should bring forth, has yet to be developed to its full potential.

Medellín was a prompt and creative reception by the conciliar as-sembly. The episcopal conference was brought together to study "the Church in the present-day transformation of Latin America in the light of the Council," echoing the Council's concern for the Church's presence in today's world. The conciliar perspective was projected in Medellín specifi-cally with its intention of proclaiming the Kingdom of God in a changing world. This conference took place in the specific environment of a poor continent, whose serious implications and possibilities were not, for easily explainable reasons, fully considered in the Council. However, the Council signaled the primary need to address the continent and its reality. Between the time of Vatican II and Medellín, Paul VI published his encyclical *Populorum Progressio* (1967). Its clear reference to the situation of poor countries and corresponding Christian demands had enormous repercus-sions in Latin America,[3] and has been considered by some to be the *Gaudium et Spes* for the Third World.

Medellín is clearly situated in the span of the conciliar era in which we still find ourselves today. John Paul II explicitly referred to this in his letter, *Tertio Millennio Adveniente,* in which he calls for the celebration of the Jubi-lee in the year 2000 as an occasion to readdress the conciliar demands related to the presence of the Church in the world today and to ecumenical dia-logue.[4] The Pope links the Council with his proposal for celebration of a Ju-bilee that looks toward the future. "It can be affirmed," he says, "that the Vat-ican II Council constitutes a providential event, thanks to which the Church has initiated the preparation for the upcoming Jubilee." He continues, pro-

3. As is known, the texts most commonly cited in Medellín are *Gaudium et Spes* and *Populorum Progressio.*

4. With respect to the Jubilee, John Paul II says in his letter: "Among the most fervent pleas of this exceptional moment in the nearing of the new millennium, the Church im-plores the Lord that the union among all Christians of diverse Confessions prospers until full communion is reached. I wish for the Jubilee to be an occasion on which all that unites us and all that is held in common, which certainly are more than the things that separate us, allow for a fruitful collaboration. For this purpose, it would be very helpful if, in respecting the programs of each Church and Community, ecumenical accords might be met for the preparation and celebration of the Jubilee: this will have more force if the decided will of the disciples of Christ is put as testimony in order to obtain full unity as soon as possible in the certainty that 'nothing is impossible for God'" (n. 16).

viding the foundation for its current relevance, "it will be a Council similar to previous ones, although at the same time very different: a Council focusing on the mystery of Christ and of his Church, and at the same time open to the world" (n. 18). It follows that "the previously unknown wealth and new tone of the conciliar presentation of these contents constitute the announcement of new times." All of this demands a "renewed commitment to apply the teachings of Vatican II, as faithfully as possible, to the life of each individual person and to the Church as a whole" (n. 20). These words clearly reaffirm the relevance of the Council today.

Although we find ourselves living in a time very different from that of the Council, it indeed is not possible to say that it is obsolete. On the contrary, the message found in the texts cited above is explicit: it is necessary to face the present challenges and those of the coming century, starting from the evangelizing ideas provided by Vatican II. It does not mean that we should ignore the changes that have happened in our world since that time, nor the concern about how to confront them. It simply means that analysis about its validity should be more defined. In ecclesial assemblies, as in the Council (as well as in Medellín), attention to the immediate historical context is necessary in order to develop adequate responses and appropriate paths for the proclamation of the Gospel. However, given the character of the proclamation, this cannot be done without a deeper analysis of the ever present mystery of God's love revealed to us in the Bible, and that we never completely come to know.

For this reason, in speeches given in the introduction of the Council, John XXIII simultaneously calls for the sensibility to current questions, as well as for a deeper reflection on the treasure of the biblical revelation. Both tasks are important and cannot be considered apart from one another. Indeed, alerted by the historical appeals, we accept the demands of faith precisely in order to position ourselves as Christians in the world in which we live. It consists of a fertile relationship, a truly hermeneutic circle, one that we do not view in a mechanical and rigid form, outside the dynamism of history. The new vistas of faith stimulated by the historical context are therefore largely independent of the context that set them in motion. At the same time, these vistas enrich the doctrinal patrimony of the Church. Evidently, various things become invalid in light of these vistas in the passing of time; however, insofar as they approach the substantial foundation of the Gospel, they have an enduring significance.

The character of Vatican II emphasized by John Paul II reverberates in that of Medellín and provides an important pull in the direction followed by the Church in the conciliar time, considering the fact that it opened the path for the gatherings in Puebla and Santo Domingo which stressed their continuity with Medellín. This pull is made evident when reception of the Council is prolonged over so many years.

Discerning the Signs of the Times

If we consider the interventions of John XXIII during the preparation of the Vatican, we are able to see that they expressed a greater concern for preaching the Gospel in today's world. The question is serious and has many consequences. "Immensely grave and ample tasks await the Church," says the Pope, "as was true in the most tragic of times in history."[5] The issue is: "How to ensure that the Church is the present, visible sign of the Kingdom of God?"[6]

The evangelizing thrust leads us to the question of what the Lord wants to say to us through the historical process of humanity. Pope John audaciously recalls an evangelical idea with great potential: the need to discern the signs of the times. He affirms that we should heed Jesus' admonition to discern "the signs of the times" (Matthew 16:4). In this way we will be able to see "amid the thick darkness more than a few indications that will appear to announce better times for the Church and humanity."[7] An authentic evangelizing purpose demands an attitude that listens and discerns the conditions in which people are living. To scrutinize the signs of the times is a path, a method of coming closer to an understanding of these realities.

As is known, the Council openly welcomed the perspective suggested by John XXIII. Diverse and rather explicit texts exist on how the Council affirmed this perspective. We face a global reality that, in one way or an-

5. "Humanae Salutis" (Apostolic constitution summoning the Council) in A. and G. Alberigo, *Profezia nella fedelta* (Brescia: Queriniana, 1978), p. 345.

6. Cardinal Landzuri, Archbishop of Lima and one of the presidents of Medellín, put forth this concern at the beginning of the Conference and alluded to the topic of the signs of the times. "The People of God who live and suffer in these lands want to say for themselves, for their loyalty to God, that they desire to serve humanity and therefore search the signs of the times, which is what the Spirit wishes of the Church. Only in this manner will the People of God be in these journeys of history, a raised standard among nations" (Inaugural Speech).

7. "Humanae Salutis," p. 346.

other, can be found in all the conciliar pronouncements.[8] It is an approximation to reality which always maintains an openness to the changes that situations may present. On principle, it does not cling to a determined moment or to the judgments that it may have deserved.

Medellín continued in this path with determination and imagination,[9] as it affirmed in its *Message:* "by the light of the faith that we profess as believers, we have tried to discover God's plan in the 'signs of the times.'" The theological reason is immediately indicated: "We interpret the aspirations and clamors of Latin America as signs that reveal the orientation of the divinely operating plan in Christ's redeeming love that founds these aspirations in the consciousness of a fraternal solidarity" (n. 3). The Conference did indeed constitute an immense attempt to read into the lives of the peoples of the continent, in light of their faith and the Council, that which God wishes to tell us in the opportune and effective announcement of the Gospel.

For this reason, Medellín brings us to renewed reflection about the great Christian themes. The evangelistic concern is always a source of a theology that is fed by the same sources of the biblical revelation. We may recall the role that the conciliar texts and the *Populorum Progressio* have in the spirit and documents of Medellín. However, the confrontation with the harsh reality of the continent means that new paths must be taken, as in the case of poverty and the poor that we will address in the following section.

Developing a specific position and identifying elements favorable to a human life which is both dignified and in the presence of the Gospel was not an easy task in those years. Contrary to what has been said and written at times without concern for seeking precise information, an easy sort of optimism did not exist during the second half of the decade of the 1960s in Latin America.[10] Medellín, without forgetting the reality that it firmly de-

8. It is important to mention that there were difficulties and reservations in the conciliar works in order to accept this perspective; cf. M. D. Chenu, "Les signes des temps" in *Gaudium et Spes*, L'Eglise dans le monde de ce temps (Paris: Mame, 1967), pp. 95-116.

9. The two initial speeches presented in Medellín were dedicated to this theme: M. McGrath, "The signs of the times in Latin America," and E. Pironio, "Christian interpretation of the signs of the times today in Latin America."

10. Long-time dictatorships in Haiti, Paraguay, and Nicaragua, military government in Argentina, an increasingly oppressive regime in Brazil. Guerrilla violence in Colombia, Venezuela, Peru, and Bolivia. In Mexico the massacre in Tlateloco Square in 1968. Instability and serious social problems in various other countries.

nounced, had the perspicacity to go further and value the seeds of life and liberation that were stirring in Latin America.

Puebla and Santo Domingo continue reading of the signs of the times. The references are numerous in their conclusions; however, as in the case of the Council and Medellín, they consisted mainly of addressing the historical context included in the collection of their texts. As has been outlined, this is a method ever open to the present, and which Puebla and Santo Domingo assumed with great creativity.

If being within the temporal span of the Council gives relevance to Medellín, it also comes from initiating a way of viewing the reality and the presence of God in Latin America: being attentive to the sign of the times.[11] We have previously outlined the sources of these positions; it should be mentioned, however, that without Medellín, the message of Vatican II and the discernment of the signs of the times would not have entered into the daily ecclesiastical life in Latin America. Numerous documents of the national episcopates and ecclesiastical meetings, the commitment of so many Christians in these years, and new opportunities for an ecumenical dialogue prove the relevance of this perspective in the continuous reorientation of evangelizing action.

Evangelizing in a World Marked by Poverty

The two aforementioned factors regarding the relevance of Medellín were closely related to Vatican II, at least insofar as this was identified as their point of departure. We would now like to add a third factor, rooted in the conciliar preparation period, although not as prominent in the conciliar texts. This third factor refers to the challenge that poverty presents, not only on the social level, but also as a challenge that lies at the heart of the Church's evangelizing task, as well as its identity.

Discerning the signs of the times led the Medellín conference to face the reality of a continent that lives "under the tragic sign of underdevelopment that not only excludes our brothers from the enjoyment of material goods, but from their own human development," as already said in the

---

11. Puebla takes note of this and indicates that "above all, from the time of Medellín, with clear consciousness of being a loyally open mission to dialogue, the Church scrutinizes the signs of the times" (n. 15).

Message. Underdevelopment "is an unjust situation which promotes tensions that challenge peace" (*Paz* 1). This situation has also been called "painful poverty, in many cases close to inhumane misery" (Poverty of the Church 1). "Misery, in its entirety, is an injustice that clamors to Heaven" (*Justice* 1). Injustice, in turn, expresses "a situation of sin" (*Peace* 1). The texts cited in these quotes can be found at the beginning of these documents and set the tone for the development that will be found in them later.

Medellín considers poverty the most significant challenge confronting the proclamation of the Gospel in these lands, the proclamation of a Kingdom of love and peace, which is incompatible with the "institutionalized violence" in which the poor of Latin America live (*Peace* 16).[12] Therefore, it is impossible to be "indifferent to the tremendous social injustices which exist in Latin America" (*Poverty* 1). The Conference calls Christians to commit themselves to constructing a just society without the existence of impoverishment or oppression. From this call emerges a "clear clamor" for "a liberation that never appears to come" (*Poverty* 2). Medellín (and later Puebla) sought to respond to this call.

Following the Latin American theological reflection of those days, Medellín understands liberation as "a complete liberation" which offers "the wealth of an integral salvation in Christ our Lord" (*Catechizes* 6).[13] Therefore, a "true liberation" demands from all people "a profound conversion so that the Kingdom of justice, love and peace arrives" (*Justice* 3).[14] In the view of this complete liberation, Medellín proposed "the ever more

12. The expression "institutionalized violence" surprised many, and there were those who considered that it was outside the scientific categories of analysis of the society. However, in the following year of 1969, J. Galtung, one of the principal current experts in the area of peace and violence, coined the phrase "institutionalized violence." It is enough to read his texts in order to prove the closeness of his ideas with those presented in Medellín (cf. J. Galtung, "Violence, Peace and Peace Research" in *Journal of Peace Research* 6, no. 3 (1969).

13. The Conference of Puebla was right when it affirmed: "In Medellín a dynamic process of integral liberation was unfolded and its positive echoes can be heard in the *Evangilii Nuntiandi,* as well as in Pope John Paul II in his Message to this Conference" (n. 480).

14. This last text comes immediately after one of the simplest passages about the integral character of liberation: "It is the same God who, in the fulness of the time, sent his Son so that as a man, he would come to liberate all men from misery and oppression, in a word, the injustice and the hate that comes from human egoism" (n. 480).

presence of the face of an authentically *poor, missionary, and pastoral* Church in Latin America, disconnected from all earthly powers and audaciously committed to the liberation of the whole man and all mankind" (*Youth* 15, italics mine).[15] This text suggests a rich ecclesiastical perspective, in tune with the situation of Latin America.

The document *Poverty of the Church* provides important details regarding the testimony of poverty. Following the path defined in these days in Latin America, it provokes an interesting reflection about the biblical sense of poverty. The distinctions it establishes help give order and clarity to this complex and, at times, confusing theme. Moreover, this path constitutes a point of departure for subsequent reflections.

It is important to recognize the convergence of the different notions presented. The first notion refers to material poverty as a lack of worldly goods, far from any idealization, which is considered an evil in and of itself. Secondly, spiritual poverty implies an attitude of spiritual infancy and of disposition to God's will; a consequence of this will be the interior distancing in the face of worldly goods.[16] This interpretation brings us to the question of why one should choose to live in poverty. Medellín's response is that poverty, as a voluntary Christian commitment, should be expressed simultaneously as solidarity with the poor and rejection of a material poverty, as something not desired by God. The christological foundation of this perspective is explicitly highlighted (cf. *Poverty* 4).[17]

Based on these premises, the testimony of a poor Church is seen as a denouncement of poverty and its causes, as well as a commitment to follow, as the Council mentions, "the path of poverty" (*Ad Gentes* 5). In this manner, the Church will be able to "preach and live the spiritual poverty, as an attitude of spiritual infancy and openness to God" (*Poverty* 5). Spiritual infancy means recognizing God as love, the true meaning of Father, and consequently, recognizing all others as brothers and sisters. We are, therefore, at the essence of the message of the Gospel.

15. This is a text that Cardinal E. Pironio held in great appreciation and frequently cited.

16. A constant error (surely a typo) in the edition of the document *Poverty* places the fourth footnote at the end of the paragraph referring to spiritual poverty when, in reality, it corresponds, as originally written, to the end of the paragraph about poverty as evil.

17. From this foundation, "the effective preference for the poorest and most needy sectors and those segregated for whatever cause" (*Poverty* 9) is framed in the universal love of God from which no one is excluded. (Cf. id. 8 and 18.)

It is appropriate to emphasize that for Medellín, although poverty is fundamentally socially and economically rooted, the issues do not stop there. Rather, it is also considered a human and a global situation. The poor are the "insignificant," those who for economic, racial, cultural, and gender reasons have little or no weight in the society and have their rights violated and human development and opportunities impeded. The condition of the poor constitutes, therefore, an authentic interpolation for the mission of the Church and should be welcome as a call to redefine the task presented before the magnitude of a situation so contrary to the will of God.

This is what John XXIII proposed to the Council when he suggested the topic of "the Church of everyone and particularly the Church of the poor" (Speech on September 11, 1962). For various reasons, and in spite of the efforts of Cardinal Lercaro and other Council priests, the issue did not have the presence that the Pope would have liked in Vatican II.[18] It was Medellín that took on the initiative and began to give shape to the Church's task in response to the challenges poverty presents, not only, I repeat, in its social concern, but also in the pronouncement of the Gospel as a whole.

Puebla and Santo Domingo advance Medellín's priorities and creatively deepen the perspective initiated in this conference.[19] Puebla takes from Medellín, as well as from the experience and reflection of the years following this assembly, the expression "preferential option for the poor," and understands this in reference to the distinction of the notion of poverty as defined above. The three words in this phrase (poor, preference, option) refer precisely to the three concepts distinguished in Medellín (material poverty, spiritual poverty, poverty as a commitment).[20] Today, as is well known, the perspective (and the discourse) of preferential option for the poor belongs to the universal magistrate of the Church. John Paul has repeated it on numerous occasions.[21]

18. Regardless, *Lumen Gentium* 8 and *Ad Gentes* 5 are interesting texts in this respect.

19. For example, with the invitation to see the characteristics of Christ in the varied faces of the poor (nn. 31-39). This text was written by two great bishops, Leonidas Proaño of Riobamba and Germán Schmitz, auxiliary from Lima. (Cf. also Santo Domingo 179.)

20. Cf. G. Gutiérrez, "La opción preferencial por los pobres" in *La religión en los albores del siglo* 21 (Bilbao: Universidad de Deusto, 1994), pp. 107-21.

21. This can be found as well in North American, Asian, and other national episcopates.

A paramount focal point around the issue of poverty in Medellín was not limiting the discussion solely to describing it, but rather the concern to identify its causes. This was one of the great novelties and contributions of this conference.[22] The Synod that was summoned to celebrate the twentieth anniversary of the commencement of the Council (1985) frankly recognizes this: "*After* Vatican II, the Church has become more conscious of its mission to serve the poor, oppressed and marginalized" (D. 6, italics mine). The determination of "after the Council" is accurate, for it recognizes the novelty mentioned and remits with certainty the experiences and reflections of the Latin American and Caribbean Church expressed in large part in Medellín and Puebla. The interest in understanding and denouncing the roots of poverty is not an intellectual exercise; it is a manifestation of loyalty to the poor. If we do not address the roots of the problem, it will be impossible to confront adequately the conditions under which the poor suffer. Puebla and Santo Domingo have adopted the same perspective. This attitude is strengthened by John Paul II's many texts clearly denouncing the social and economic mechanisms that generate and perpetuate poverty.[23]

As a consequence, we take a vigorous position with respect to poverty, which reminds the whole Church of the role the most recent "least ones" of history play in God's plan for salvation. Unfortunately, the condition of the poor has far from improved; rather it has become even more serious, and the breach between the poor and the rich (both nations and individuals) is greater than in the time of Medellín. All international reports affirm this to be so. The challenge of poverty and marginalization continues in the present, and therefore it is no surprise that the conferences of Puebla and Santo Domingo frankly assume the priority and perspective

22. Within the World Council of Churches, concern for the situation of the so-called Third World countries (cf. the excellent study by A. Neely, *Protestant Antecedents of the Latin American Theology of Liberation* (Ann Arbor, University of Michigan, Dissertation Information Service, 1992).

23. The last text in this regard can be found in one of the speeches during his visit to Cuba. After denouncing "a form of capitalist neoliberalism that subordinates the human person and conditions that development of the people to the blind forces of the market," the Pope affirms, "In the concert of the nations one can see the exaggerated wealth of a few at the cost of the impoverishment of the growing many, so that the rich get richer and the poor get poorer" (Homily, January 25, 1998).

provided by Medellín. They also recall other goals for the Church's evange-lizing duties,[24] and, while overcoming much opposition, reaffirm the core characteristic of the option for the poor. These conferences contemplate the complicated situation, with its economic, cultural, racial, and gender dynamics, and present an important contribution to the reflection regard-ing this preferential option on behalf of the poor, as well as to the pastoral priorities.

For these reasons among others, thirty years later, the Episcopal Con-ference of Medellín continues to be an essential point of reference. At the same time, we do not deny that certain aspects of its texts reflect different times. The substantial part of its message, however, continues to be rele-vant. As we have mentioned, the fact that it falls within the conciliar span, the initiative from Vatican II, the flexibility and fidelity to the new chal-lenges presented by the interpretation of the signs of the times, and the in-terpolation that comes from an increasing poverty, make its relevance in our current times clear.[25]

One of the most important and lasting meanings of Medellín is the maturity expressed by the Latin American Church. To be an adult Church that openly confronts its historical reality is the condition of authentic communion with the universal Church. In his closing speech at the Con-ference, Cardinal Landzuri (following the example of Paul VI in the text cited above, *Ecclesiam Suam*, which seeks to respond to the question: Who are we?), took up this clear and exciting perception: "we are members of a people that has begun to discover the crossroads of nations, its own con-sciousness, its own duty." I add to this: "we are pastors among these people of God who, as witnesses to the Teacher in all the world, will discover new directions of the Father."[26]

24. Secularization, for example, present in some areas of Latin America and the Ca-ribbean, also mentioned in Medellín: *Youth* 4, *Catequesis* 2.

25. Without doubt, the fertile proposals of the Jubilee made by John Paul II will pro-vide a new current to the issues of Medellín and are precisely those that present the biblical roots of the Jubilee.

26. In another passage, it is declared, "There is something very characteristic in the proposals that we have made during these days and that I would like to emphasize, that is: we confront our problems. There is a servitude that is not communion. There is a psycho-logical and sociological dependence that does not respond to the intimate interdependence of the Body of the Lord. Facing our problems demands maturity. This is a privileged form of expressing the episcopal collegiality and the communion with all the Church." For this rea-son, the following was added: "We try to find solutions from within our own realities and

The search for these "new directions" has not been an easy one. However, its evangelical fecundity leaves us in no doubt, for, among other reasons, many along this path have violently lost their lives. Monsignor Juan Gerardi of Guatemala is the most recent name in this long and painful list. People and close friends such as he feed our faith and our hope, and help us finally to understand the relevance of Medellín today.

possibilities: this permits the universal Church, as in other historical stages, to enrich itself with new ecclesial and pastoral forms."

Once More into the Breach:
The True Historical Jesus

ROBERT W. JENSON

M y revered *"Doktorvater,"* Peter Brunner, was generally a misfit in modernity, not least by his preternaturally early understanding of National Socialism's true character. Perhaps this may suggest respect for some of his other sins against the times, among which was the assertion that faith has its own access to history, and to history precisely in the common notion, to what *"eigentlich gewesen ist."*[1]

There are, according to Brunner, events that have occurred in the time and space we inhabit and are within the view and task of the historian, which nevertheless the historian as such cannot now get hold of. Yet the fact of their occurrence can be known, by faith hearing the gospel's account. Faith's knowledge transcends what research according to empiricist canons can know, *without* transcending "what happened." Thus only the believer can fully know what historians, at least in their modern secular identity, seek to know.[2]

It will perhaps be granted that if Brunner's claim could be sustained, some recent and contemporary theological anguish would be alleviated. I find Brunner's own argument for his position convincing, and will return

1. Von Ranke's famous motto has, I confess, continued to seem right to me, through all fits of skepticism.

2. For this and subsequent references to Brunner, see Robert W. Jenson, "The Doxological Concept of History in the Theology of Peter Brunner," *Zur Auferbauung des Leibes Christi,* ed. Edmund Schlink and Albrecht Peters (Kassel: Johannes Stauda Verlag, 1965).

to one part of it. But in most of this essay I will move from somewhat different concerns than his. And I will narrow the problem to that about "the historical Jesus."

From the mid-eighteenth century on, three doctrines have determined our reading of Scripture about Jesus. The one is that what Scripture tells us about Jesus is to be treated as evidence for the historical truth about him rather than as itself that truth; that whatever may otherwise be the power of Scripture or the reality of the Lord Jesus, if it is the historical Jesus we want to know, we must cleave to the evidence-weighing mode of cognition. The second — not so often noticed, perhaps because it is taken as obvious — is that the scriptural evidence consists of the Gospels and a few clues wrested from other New Testament documents. The third is that, although this material has been preserved by faith for faith's unique purposes, when we turn to use it as evidence we must abstract from faith. The last is the one Brunner directly denies.

Brunner's claim will not immediately be plausible to anyone with a standard education, including the present writer. Yet it is less and less obvious that faithful scholarship can get along without something like it. The homiletical, catechetical, and devotional deficiencies of modernity's traditional exegetical procedures, and of seminary education controlled by them, and of pastors and other teachers educated in such seminaries, are increasingly noticed and lamented. It has turned out again and again: the latest "historical Jesus" delivered by some scholar or group of scholars is not the Jesus in whom believers believe, or indeed in whom anybody could exactly "believe." And those who with increasing desperation persist in the "quests" are in these latter days driven to proposals that are bizarre intellectually and useless or destructive ecclesially. Yet what else are we to do?

Much late-modern theology has made a virtue of the difficulty, and has sought the object of faith elsewhere than in the risen Jesus of Nazareth *wie er eigentlich gewesen ist.* Indeed, readers may have taken my reference to "the *Jesus* in whom believers *believe*" as a category mistake. The proposed object of faith has then been "the biblical image of the Christ," or the momentary word-event whose saving accidentality is guaranteed by mention of an otherwise theologically irrelevant historical Jesus, or one or another "Christ-principle" — often of conveniently flexible gender, ethnicity, or personality — or a thoroughly unfleshed *Logos asarkos,* or the Christ of dogma taken as truth without necessary historical reference, or for that matter just "what Jesus means to me."

121

Perhaps only those most tenuously related to the faith now find these decidedly pre-postmodern *theologoumena* satisfying, even though many of the faithful can see no option but to cling to one of them. It is otherwise generally recognized that Christianity, of all religions, cannot find shelter in a "storm-free region"[3] immune to historical study. Unless of course we plunge on into the region of sheer "deferring" textuality in which all histories are equally false. But — again — what else are we to do?

Sometimes in this situation it is said we must quit the entire enterprise of treating the New Testament testimony to Jesus as "evidence" for what the historical Jesus did, said, and suffered, and just plow ahead with the texts as they are: this is what Matthew, Mark, Luke, and John said Jesus was like, and we can take it or leave it. We must drop the first of those three exegetical doctrines. This has a nice ring of faithfulness to Scripture, but for myself I confess that my epistemological conscience is not quite that hardened against the Enlightenment. Moreover, there is a strictly theological mandate.

In the hermeneutical event of the gospel being spoken, one pole is always the claim "Jesus is risen." The import of such a proposition depends, of course, on who is risen; "Stalin is risen" would lift few hearts. It is therefore a regular task of those who would speak the gospel: we must identify this "Jesus" to those for whom, unlike most of the crowd at Pentecost, the sheer proper name does not suffice. And in all such situations we do this by telling some of the person's story. So in the case of Jesus such things are said as, "He was a prophet who proclaimed the Kingdom with strange personal authority, a rabbi who taught Scripture as if he were the author, a friend of publicans and sinners," etc. The outcome of this necessity in the primal church is the genre of the Gospels, each of which is a long proposition of the form, "The one who . . . and who . . . and who . . . is risen."

Where we go from here depends on how — or rather, I think, if — we understand the Resurrection. If the risen Jesus Christ is a spook or a meaning or an occasion of richly varied experience or whatever such, we can as well identify him by fiction as any other way (I am of course assuming that "fiction" is an opposite to something, and I note also that those who make this assumption have conceptually undercut their right to it).

---

3. The phrase is from the debate about Martin Kaehler's tract, "Der sogenannte historische Jesus und der geschichtliche, *biblische Christus*" (Leipzig: Deichert'sche Verlagsbuchhandlung, 1896), to which recurrent reference will be made.

But if the risen Jesus is to be the actual human being Jesus, with a mother, an executioner, and all other accouterments of individual embodied humanity, then we need to identify him in the same way as we identify other actual human persons, by the knowable facts about him, by such biography as we can muster. Trying to our best ability to tell of Jesus as he "actually was" is in my judgment a theological requirement of the first order. We cannot help doing what Luke did: look at the existing accounts and try to get closer to the facts.

The classical liberalism that carried so much of the older Jesus-research encountered its own peculiar frustration here. For it, the resurrection, however affirmed or denied, did not constitute the object of faith. It was moral and religious fellowship precisely with the historical Jesus that was to be salvific; thus historical research was effectively liberalism's sacrament. When the results of this research proved in fact inconstant, the problem was therefore desperate. One proposed solution, appearing in several variants, was plainly ad hoc, yet has shaped discussion ever since: the invention of another sort of history than the normal sort, in which to find the salvific Jesus.[4] The *"Historie"* of Jesus, that is, what ordinary folk mean by history, may be unreliably reachable, but never mind, it is anyway the *"geschichtliche"* Jesus in whom we may believe. The *geschichtliche* person, whether Jesus or someone else, is the person *as* a factor in subsequent history, however that entity may be related to a patch of *Historie;* the *geschichtliche* person is what those struck by what is said of him make of him. And the *geschichtliche* Jesus is to be found in the New Testament, however unreliable the New Testament may be as *Historie.*

The notion harbors at least two fatal difficulties. For one, the actors of subsequent history, insofar as they too are historical entities of the real sort, must be equally indeterminate as time continues, so that *Geschichte* can never be known except for the moment. It is a short road from here to poststructuralism at its most nihilist. For another, the Resurrection is simply excluded: the real Jesus who might be resurrected will never be finished to be available for the event. Indeed, *"Geschichte"* is in fact a bowdlerized version of the resurrected life, thought to be going on now; it is a version of the Corinthian heresy. Nevertheless, it has from the turn of the century generally been assumed, if often subliminally, that our problem is some-

---

4. The following description is according to Kaehler, who set the language also for many who did not follow his particular proposal.

how located between the historical Jesus and a *geschichtliche* Christ of faith.

These escapes have been tried and have led nowhere. There remains, so far as I can see, one place where the controlling hermeneutical doctrines can be pressed, odd though it may at first seem to do it. I begin by proposing that the problem is not in fact between the historical Jesus and an ontologically different "Christ of faith." It is between a historical Jesus of scholarship and a historical Jesus of faith, between the successive proposals of the scholars and the account and picture that believers have rightly entertained of this man's actuality, intended to be located as much in the time and space of first-century Palestine as in that of the scholars.

If that is the real problem, then the first thing to notice is that faith's grasp of its historical Jesus is not founded only on the New Testament witnesses. The defining difference between the Jesus of faith and at least the usual versions of the historical Jesus is, I suggest, the former's larger basis of testimony and so of evidence to be weighed.

Besides the New Testament, there are two bodies of testimony to which believers have turned for information about Jesus. There is the Messianic witness of the Old Testament; and it does not matter to the following how we understand that witness to be made. And there is the spiritual tradition of the church. Thus the two phrases from Isaiah, evoking a "man of sorrows, acquainted with grief," and the church's iconography they have shaped, doubtless have more determined what believers think of as the historical Jesus than have any five chapters of the New Testament.

Dare we then bridge the gap between faith's historical Jesus and scholarship's historical Jesus by putting also, e.g., the Isaiah passage, in the scholars' pile of clues to be weighed? Might we argue on its evidence that the historical Jesus, as in fact a man of sorrows, could hardly have been a guru of the California type? Or might we even come from the other direction and weigh Bach's Passion-settings as evidence for how Jesus died? That he could not have died disillusioned or unmourned? Might the real historical Jesus, the one who actually lived back there and can be known to have lived back there, be a Jesus discoverable only from the whole Bible and from the church's Jesus-tradition?

Perhaps we should treat all witness to Jesus, including that from the Old Testament or the church's tradition, alike when it comes to historical evidential value. All would go on the table to be weighted. This relativizing of the testimony is possible with my proposed new sources just as for the generally accepted ones; Scripture's words and the church's words are at once identical with and different from the Word that Christ himself is; we call the relation "sacramental." Isaiah's or Paul's or Augustine's testimony speaks the Word of God; yet they may have gotten something wrong. Thus the Old Testament and churchly testimonies would be granted no more or less advance evidentiary weight than the New Testament. The inspiration of the Old Testament Scripture does not imply its "verbal inerrancy" any more than does that of the Gospels; and the range of infallibility extends no further in church teaching than in Paul's. If Mark's sequencing of events in Jesus' life can be corrected, so can a prophet's description of the coming Son of David or a great exegete's comment on a passage from John. *But then again, they may do the correcting.*

The proposal is of course preposterous — *unless* it is true that God is the specifically triune God, and that Jesus — just as the historical Jesus — is the second identity of this God, and that this God is the Creator. I have just listed two dogmas straight and given Cyril's construal of another. Our troubles with the historical Jesus — and the historical Paul and the historical whomever — were inaugurated by thinkers who exploited modernity's historical consciousness specifically and intentionally to escape "the yoke of dogma." But what if the church's dogma were a necessary hermeneutical principle of historical reading, because it describes the true ontology of historical being?

Because our other fathers, the church fathers, worshiped the specifically triune God, they understood the word of the Old Testament as the Word who is eternally with God and is God, and who has as the very same Word appeared among us "in these latter days"; they heard the testimony of the Old Testament as the voice of Christ, and indeed *could* not otherwise hear these texts. (For that matter, when they heard truth from "the Greeks," whether historians or poets or religious thinkers, they heard the same Word there.) And it is of course a commonplace of the theological tradition that the gospel-word in the church is Christ speaking. Now then — whose testimony to the historical truth about Jesus might the scholarly reader more want than that of the very man whose biography she or he is concerned for?

In the last paragraph I implicitly identified the Word, the *Logos*, with Jesus, and again readers may have thought to detect a leap. My argument indeed depends on a Christology like that of Cyril or Maximus or Luther. The voice of the man Jesus and the voice of the Logos are, in such Christology and in my argument, one divine-human act; precisely the man Jesus is the second identity of God and the second identity of God is the man Jesus. When the Logos or "the Christ" testifies to himself in Israel's Scripture or in the church, this is at once the man Jesus telling about himself, and the Logos telling about himself, and each telling about the other.

All this last is to be sure a collection of hard sayings for Christology of more Antiochene type. I will not here otherwise argue for the truth of the Cyrillian sort, than to point out that also other features of necessary Christian practice are badly supported by Antiochene Christology, or even by the almost-Antiochene standard Christology of the Western church; thus the real presence of the embodied Christ in the Supper has had in most of the West to be supported by ad hoc constructions independent of Christology.

If indeed the historical Jesus is the Logos, the second identity of God, then the testimony of the Old Testament to the coming Servant and the church's testimony to her Lord, are the testimony to himself of that same one person who the historical Jesus is. The testimony by which believers' grasp of the historical man Jesus is shaped can indeed be evidence for historical reconstruction. Only one step remains.

With that step to the doctrine of creation we return to Peter Brunner's own argument. The God whose Word is Jesus is the Creator, who creates by speaking. That is, the Word that is Jesus determines how things actually will be, are, and afterward will have been. There simply *is no* "history" independent of the Word and somehow behind it — which of course is why questers for a Jesus inhabiting such a sphere have not found one, and why the enterprise of knowing history in abstraction from this Word must always encounter events it cannot grasp.

The — of course unlikely — general adoption of this proposal would not end all argument about the historical Jesus. It would eliminate the difference in principle between scholarship's historical Jesus and faith's historical Jesus. But scholars by definition will continue to use historians' — in themselves commonsensical — tactics more rigorously than other believers. And no theory can protect the texts against loony or venal scholars or superstitious "ordinary believers." All tension between faith and the academy would hardly be eliminated.

Nor have we discussed *how* exactly we are to weigh such evidence as an Isaianic prophecy, or the Old Testament appearance of Israel as the Lord's Son, or a churchly tradition about Jesus' poverty. Part of the answer is, I would suppose, by the usual criteria of coherence with other testimony, toughness over against hermeneutical suspicion, plausibility within some general construal of temporal reality, etc. But use of these will be shaped in the one case by how we construe the general relation of the Old and New Testaments, and in the other by how we in general try to discern faithfulness in the church's developing tradition. Since these matters are themselves vigorously controverted, mere agreement on the point of this essay would not even terminate theoretical disagreement about the historical Jesus. But it might enable the arguments to be pursued with greater intellectual responsibility and theological relevance.

The Significance of the History
of Doctrine for Theological Study

JOHN H. LEITH

This essay is my inaugural lecture when I was installed as Professor of Historical Theology at Union Theological Seminary in Virginia, April 20, 1960. Publication today is justified, for the neglect of the history of doctrine is greater now than then in the writing of Christian theology as well as in the education of ministers. I came to the seminary following more than fourteen years in the pastorate. The lecture reflects this transition. It parallels Thomas Gillespie's move from many years as a pastor to the presidency of a seminary to educate pastors. The friendship of Thomas and Barbara Gillespie has enriched my life. Thomas has also been a bulwark of strength in undergirding the Christian and Reformed confession of the Presbyterian Church (USA). No other seminary president in recent decades has been his equal in classical Reformed and Christian witness.

The only appropriate word with which to begin an address on the occasion of one's installation as a professor in Union Theological Seminary is a word of gratitude. It is a privilege to share in the life of an institution which has played so significant a role in the history of our church. It is a privilege to have the comradeship of those who teach *in* and guide the affairs *of* this institution. It is especially a privilege to share in the education of those who study here and who will go out to be ministers of Jesus Christ in churches throughout the South. For these privileges I am deeply grateful today.

An inaugural address offers at least two options as to a topic. One is a study of some theological problem in its historical ramifications. The other option is the prior question, Why historical theology at all? Why should courses in historical theology be injected into an already overcrowded curriculum? This question is personal as well as academic. Why should one devote his life to the teaching of historical theology? Every Christian should be able to give some better justification for his daily work than the fact that it happens to be a pleasant way to make a living.

I have therefore chosen as our theme the question, What is the significance of historical theology in the training of a minister? The emphasis is on the word *minister,* the minister of a local congregation. Our primary concern as an institution of our church is the training of ministers. What does historical theology have to contribute to the making of good ministers of Jesus Christ in the Reformed tradition?

The foundation for all Christian theology is the revelation of God culminating in Jesus Christ and the witness to the resurrection of Jesus as attested in Scripture. The Bible provides the interpretative framework — creation, fall, redemption, consummation — within which Christian theology explicates the faith. The Bible also provides the language not only of theology but also of the believing, confessing community. All Christian theology acknowledges the Bible as the final authority.

Christian theology takes place in the church — the worshiping, believing, confessing congregation. Faith cannot be sustained apart from the work of the Holy Spirit in the fellowship of the believing, worshiping, witnessing community. The believing community sustains and is enriched by the individual believer.

Christian theology has been written historically in the active life of the church. In the ancient church, theology was written largely by bishops, in the medieval church by monks, in the Reformation by preachers, in the post-Reformation church by preacher-professors in universities committed to Christian faith. Theology since the Enlightenment has been written more and more in increasingly secular universities by professors who are more and more oriented by the professional guild. The goal of theology is less and less to edify, as Calvin insisted, and to equip the pastor of a local congregation to preach and nurture a congregation as a believing and worshiping community. The aim of theology is increasingly to impress the academic community by its intellectual sophistication.

Christian theology which is under the authority of Scripture and which takes place in the church has many other dimensions of less crucial importance. It is in dialogue with Christian experience, with culture, with living religions, with language, and with the claims of logic and the warrants that justify any assertion. Its end is edification and the explanation of the affirmations of Christian faith in intelligible words and sentences. In theology faith seeks intelligibility.

The central thesis of this presentation is that a thorough knowledge of the history of doctrine is essential not only for the work of the theologian but also for the Reformed pastor. Christian doctrine is the church's reflection upon the Christian revelation and the church's understanding of that revelation, less official than dogma and less general than Christian thought. Doctrine reflects Christian experience as well as intellectual activity. It finally must be confirmed in the experience of the Christian community. The history of doctrine does not replace revelation, but it does embody the depth and breadth of the Christian community's reflection on revelation. Every Christian theologian should ideally recapitulate in his or her life the whole history of doctrine. Human limitations set the parameters for this recapitulation. No theologian is ever truly catholic or ecumenical. But every theologian can hope that his or her exposition of a particular tradition contributes to a truly catholic theology.

The study of the history of doctrine is crucial for the theologian and for the well-being of the church for at least four reasons.

1. Historical theology is significant for the education of ministers because it is an aid to the recovery of a Christian memory.

The uprootedness of human existence is one of the tragedies of our time. People are bereft of roots in the past and become the victims of the tyranny of the present. In the words of Riesman's study *(The Lonely Crowd)* they are "other directed," because they have no inner direction and no tradition to give strength to their lives. Christians have rootage in the past because they belong to the great tradition of the people of God.

Yet it cannot be said that all who call themselves Christian have a really Christian memory, have a sense of belonging to a community whose roots go back through the centuries. This is a special temptation of American Protestants. Many are, in a bad sense of the word, twentieth-century Christians. Yet, as Professor Albert Outler has well expressed it,

It was in some sort of historical community that each of us heard the Gospel preached and at a time when we could not judge whether it was preached well or ill. Then, as we discovered the past of our own communion, and the past of other and disparate communions, we began to have some fuller measure of the common meaning of the Gospel we have heard and believed and the Gospel as believed and practiced by others.

In this respect, the discovery of our total Christian past is the means to a fuller initiation into the whole Christian family. Man is a creature capable of inheriting acquired characteristics not through his genes but through his traditions. Children are knit into family life by hearing the reminiscences of the family. It is the sense of this particular family tradition that makes its members truly kin, since the blood relation in itself is not sufficient to produce the feeling of truly belonging.[1]

A Christian memory is the recollection of the story of one's life as it reaches back through the ages. It is a thrilling fact this morning to recall that between each one of us and the events of the New Testament, indeed between us and Abraham and Adam, there is an unbroken succession of believing men and women who have heard the voice of the living God and in faith and love have obeyed. It is not without significance that early Protestant histories of the church as well as such confessions as the Scots Confession of 1560 trace the history of the church back to Adam.

Historical theology is *church* history, not the history of Christianity nor the history of theological texts. Professor Trinterud in his Presidential Address before the American Church History Society rightly said,

> The most crucial of these assumptions for the church historian is the assumption that the Church is a community of people redeemed by God in history through Jesus Christ. Apart from this assumption there would be no church history, but rather the history of the Christian religion.[2]

Historical theology is nothing more and nothing less than the recollection of the reflection of Christians through the centuries concerning their creation and redemption by God.

1. Albert Outler, *The Christian Tradition and the Unity We Seek* (New York: Oxford University Press, 1957), p. 41.
2. Leonard J. Trinterud, *Church History* 25, no. 1: 3.

H. E. W. Turner in his excellent book, *The Pattern of Christian Truth*, has well written, "All the major doctrines of orthodoxy were lived devotionally as part of the corporate experience of the Church before their theological development became a matter of urgent necessity."[3] Historical theology does not deal with beliefs in the abstract but with belief as it has been lived and confessed by the Christian community. The *Lex Arandi* is the *Lex Credendi*, which are in turn the source of Christian action, the *Lex Agendi*.

The life of the Christian community which historical theology seeks to recover is the life of the ecumenical church. It is also the life of the particular tradition and in our case the Reformed tradition. The two are not in conflict. For we can serve our own particular tradition best when we see and understand it within the ecumenical church, and we can serve the ecumenical church when we bring to it the treasures of our particular heritage. The recovery of catholicity in the theological enterprise is one of the pressing needs and bright hopes of the contemporary situation. In no small measure the theological achievements of the fourth and fifth centuries were due to the catholicity of the theological endeavor, a catholicity which from that point on was increasingly lost and which is only now being recovered.

Historical theology is the effort to take seriously the life of the church, the covenant community, through the centuries. It is hardly possible to take seriously the covenant community without taking seriously the covenant community's history. *The recovery of a Christian memory is nothing more than an awareness of the history of the church as the story of one's life.*

The question may be raised whether the "Scripture alone" of the Protestant does not make the living memory of the church a dispensable possession. The answer must imagine what our situation would be, if we were bereft of this living memory. Let us suppose that some holocaust in the third century had not only destroyed the Christian community from living memory but had also destroyed every known Bible. Then let us suppose that a Bible were found in some Dead Sea cavern. Now let us think through the possibilities and difficulties that would be involved in this newly discovered Bible becoming, apart from the living traditions of the

3. H. E. W. Turner, *The Pattern of Christian Truth* (New York: AMS Press, 1978), p. 474.

church, the center of a community of faith, worship, and action such as we know the Christian community to be today.

The historic fact is that the Bible was never alone in the theological work of Luther or Calvin. Recent studies have pointed out Luther's very great indebtedness to the traditions of medieval Catholicism. Calvin, fascinated as he was by the radical reformers, never succumbed to their anti-historical outlook. He could not bring himself to the point of saying that any whole segment of history of the church had been nothing but a great mistake, though he was certain that the church fell about the time of Gregory the Great. Yet he does not try to leap over the thousand years that intervened between the Reformation and Augustine, though it is with Augustine that he first tarries for long. He claims fellowship with such theologians as Aquinas and Bernard of Clairvaux. His mastery of the fathers and his appreciation of the ancient church are well-established facts. He deliberately worked as a theologian and as a worshiper in the tradition of the church.

Some radical sectarians have believed that they can get along without Christian history. In fact, they have insisted that salvation is to be found in the incredible historical gymnastic of leaping over fifteen centuries of church history to the New Testament. Even Protestants have sometimes fancied they could jump from the present to the New Testament with brief refueling stops in the sixteenth, fifth, and fourth centuries.

The plain fact, however, is that all Christians are more dependent on tradition than many have admitted. The discrepancies in interpretation, the idiom of theology, betray the tradition which is unconfessed. If the theologian does succeed in freeing himself from a Christian tradition, he will take his stance in an alien tradition. The Bible may be interpreted in terms *of* and *from* the viewpoint of the particular spirit of the age in which the interpreter lives, a spirit of the age which is bereft of the wisdom of what Christians have experienced through the centuries. The secular traditions of society may be substituted for the traditions of the Christian church, but no person can sit down traditionless to interpret the Bible.

Actually the church found very early in its history that the historical theology of the church as enshrined in the rule of faith was indispensable to the interpretation of Scripture. Irenaeus, Tertullian, and Athanasius all knew that the heretics could quote scripture. Therefore, they insisted that the Bible must be understood in the light of the church's rule of faith. And the church with the exception of certain sectarian groups ever since has insisted that the theology of the church as summarized in some rule of faith must be the guide to Biblical interpretation. It is a fundamental Protestant conviction that the living memory of the church stands under the authority of the Bible which is the concretion of the church's apostolic memory. It is likewise a fundamental Protestant conviction that the Bible is not alone. Hence the question is not the rejection or acceptance of one or the other, but the proper relation that must exist between them. The problem of the tradition and the traditions, or the Bible and tradition, which is now becoming one of the liveliest issues in theology, is a relevant concern for the person who wishes to speak the Christian message to people in our time.

2. Historical theology is significant for the education of ministers because history judges dogma and thus lays bare its real significance and meaning.

We never know the full meaning of any exegesis of Scripture or any theological reflection until we see it submitted to the test of time. There is a statement from the Old Testament which declares that the man who puts on his armor ought not to boast as the man who takes it off. (I suppose this means that any inaugural address is a very tenuous enterprise.) Surely this is true of the theological enterprise. Any cavalier treatment of older theologies which have stood the test of history is an amazing presumption. Professor James Orr of the old United Free Church of Scotland in a remarkably fine book, *The Progress of Dogma,* has put it this way, "The history of dogma criticizes dogma, corrects mistakes, eliminates temporary elements, supplements defects, incorporates the gains of the past at the same time that it opens up wider horizons for the future."[4] Of course, as Professor Orr well understood, history is no infallible judge of dogma. In Protestantism there is no infallible judge, but the historic wisdom of the Christian community as it has reflected upon the Bible is the best judge we have.

History judges dogma intellectually. In history an individual theologian's reflection upon the meaning of Christian redemption or a council's decree is subjected to the evaluation and judgment of many Christians in many different places and in many different situations.

History also judges doctrine morally and socially. James Orr speaks of

---

4. James Orr, *The Progress of Dogma* (New York: A. C. Armstrong & Sons, 1902), p. 17.

the correlation of doctrine with vital Christian experience and with its practical effects. John Calvin, who wrote his *Institutes* not only as a guide to the study of the Scriptures but also as an aid to piety, declared that a doctrine which did not edify was theologically unsound. Moreover, edification was one of the guiding principles of Calvin's worship. A preliminary principle which our Presbyterian forefathers attached to the Form of Government declared that "Truth is in order goodness; and the great touchstone of truth is its tendency to promote holiness."[5] The final expression and decisive test of a minister's scholarship are written in the life of the congregation.

We never know the full meaning of a Christian doctrine or of an interpretation of Scripture until we see it embodied in the life of the Christian man and in the life of the Christian community. As John Mackay has put it,

> The Christian revelation shall continue to have its crowning significance not in great systems of thought or in masterpieces of art, but in the renewed lives of plain people. Not in scholars and connoisseurs, not in poets and artists, persons who were enthralled and transfigured by the grandeur of the revelation, but in a community of believers, saints in the New Testament sense, men and women who heard and obeyed the Gospel of God, and were recreated in Christ Jesus, did the revelation of God reach the end which was also the beginning.[6]

History judges theology and exposes something of its meaning which can be found nowhere else, by laying bare its embodiment in the life of the Christian believer and in the life of the Christian community. For example, the real meaning of Arianism and the Nicene faith can be more clearly seen in their embodiment in the culture and in the imperial politics of the fourth century than in the theological tomes.

There is still a third way in which history judges dogma and that is by what H. E. W. Turner has called the instinctive judgment of the Christian community. Orthodoxy is established not simply by theologians, but also by ordinary Christians who are in no sense professional theologians. As Turner writes, "Behind the instinctive rejection of heresy there lay a kind of Christian common sense exercised at all its levels within the Christian Church, which is merely another name for the guidance of the Holy Spirit

5. *The Book of Order, PC (USA)*, G-1.0304.
6. John Mackay, *Christianity on the Frontier* (New York: Macmillan, 1950), p. 200.

leading the church into all truth and dividing to every man severally as he wills."[7]

Again this is no infallible judgment. But in the long run, as I think history indicates, the common sense judgment of the Christian community is more reliable than the judgment of theological faculties or church councils. In any case, it is through the common sense judgment of the Christian community rather than through the action of church councils that most Christian doctrines have been established, including that most crucial of all doctrines, the Nicene faith.

3. Historical theology is of significance in the education of ministers because it contributes to theological competence.

It develops theological competence by bringing to us the accumulative insights, methods, and conclusions of the Christian community as it has reflected upon the creation and redemption of God. We do not have to start from the beginning in the interpretation of the Bible or in reflection upon the significance of the Christian message.

Few if any theological problems or difficulties for faith which Christian people face today have not been faced in essential substance before. Few if any heresies which threaten Christian faith from within today do not bear a remarkable resemblance to Gnosticism, Arianism, Manichaeism, Pelagianism, or Deism and the various heresies of the centuries. Many of the issues which the church faces today and which many seek to evade are precisely the issues which the church found at Nicea or at Orange or at Worms that it could not ignore. Christian ministers who speak to intelligent Americans are greatly helped in this task if, through this knowledge of the Christian past, they can detect the incipient Gnosticism, Arianism, Pelagianism, or Deism of the present, and if they know the questions and issues which are frequently obscured in contemporary theology by language or the climate of opinion.

Historical theology contributes to theological competence by providing perspective for contemporary theologizing. History teaches few things as clearly as the blindness of particular cultures to truths which are obvious and clear in other situations. Errors can be so endemic in a particular culture that truths which are very obvious in other cultures cannot be recognized. Evil can be so pervasive in a society that good men are unaware of its existence.

7. Turner, *The Pattern of Christian Truth*, p. 498.

Herbert Butterfield in his book, *The Origins of Modern Science,* has pointed out how a climate of opinion prevented some of the greatest minds in the history of the human race from seeing certain things which are now obvious to any schoolchild.

> The supreme paradox of the scientific revolution is the fact that things which we find it easy to instill into boys at school because we see that they start off on the right foot, things which would strike us as the ordinary way of looking at the universe, the obvious way of regarding the behavior of falling bodies, for example, defeated the greatest intellects for centuries, defeated Leonardo da Vinci and at the marginal point even Galileo, when their minds were wrestling on the very frontiers of human thought with these problems. . . . It required their combined efforts to clear up certain simple things which we should regard as obvious to any unprejudiced mind, and even easy for a child.[8]

Historical theology ought to enable us to enter into conversation with great Christian minds of the past and thus should prepare us to engage our own age in conversation concerning the meaning of the redemption of God in history through Jesus Christ. History of doctrine increases our sensitivity to the nuances of theology.

4. Historical theology contributes to the training of ministers by telling the story of the Christian community's engagement with culture, in particular with the intellectual life of culture. This engagement is a twofold affair.

As Kenneth Latourette in his monumental study of the expansion of Christianity has pointed out, the Christian community influences the environment and is influenced by the environment. We neglect either aspect of the engagement at serious risk not only to our Christian life but to the soundness of our theology.

Culture always leaves its imprint upon theology. Paul Tillich has written that the form of theology is always cultural, if for no other reason than that theology has to use language which is a product of culture. The history of theology teaches the intrinsic datability of theological works. The accents and the idiom betray the cultural context. This is the reason today that European theology written in a European culture which experi-

---

8. Herbert Butterfield, *The Origins of Modern Science* (New York: Macmillan, 1957), p. 2.

enced an idealism, a romanticism, and a historicism more radical than anything in the intellectual history of America, and in the context of a political and economic history vastly different from that of America, cannot be simply repeated in America without either misunderstanding or irrelevance. It is a notorious fact that amateur Barthians are mistaken for fundamentalists, and sometimes not without reason.

Historical theology makes one aware of the cultural conditioning and the cultural idiom of all theology and of the necessity of translating every theology into the cultural idiom of one's own society.

Christian theology has not simply been influenced by culture; it has influenced and shaped culture. It has engaged culture for the sake of converting culture. In the past, great intellectual revolutions have not defeated Christian faith but have become the occasion for great new statements of the faith in terms of the intellectual climate. This was the great work of Thomas Aquinas and of Calvin. Today we need to learn from the past how the Christian community has dealt with cultural and intellectual revolutions, for we live in a day of cultural and intellectual revolution. At least three great cultural crises will increasingly be the cutting edges of theology during the ministries of those who now come to our seminaries.

The first is the scientific revolution which has wrought more drastic changes in our manner of thinking than anything else in human history. It has radically affected our way of looking at the world and human existence, and it raises a host of theoretical as well as practical questions for the Christian community to answer.

The second situation which challenges the Christian community is the increased contact with historic formal religions such as Islam and Buddhism and with new religions such as Communism. Increasingly the Christian community shall have to say a word about their significance in the providence of God and the responsibility of the Christian community over against them.

The third cultural situation which challenges the Christian community is the revolution which is taking place in the breakup of patterns of life and in the shaping of new patterns. Christian people have a right to expect from ministers and professors guidance and help in the theological understanding of the radical changes which are taking place, and guidance and help in obedience to Jesus Christ in the midst of the changes. The really critical test of theological teaching will not be found in classrooms, but in the embodiment of this teaching in the life of the church, especially in the life of the local congregation.

Adolf von Harnack, quoting Troeltsch, once declared, "One must overcome history by history,"[9] i.e., one must accept one's destiny, love it and transform it into something better. We study history in order to intervene in the course of history. Historical knowledge becomes an instrument of actions in the present. Harnack no doubt overemphasized the fact that man is in the world to act in it, not to contemplate it. And yet he said something which is profoundly true. Historical theology, and for that matter all theological learning, will in the end be a vain thing unless it comes to embodiment in human life. As John Mackay has put it, "The finality of Christian doctrine can never be purely speculative. Reformed thinkers are not interested in prying open the secrets of the universe in order to indulge a speculative bent. They theologize in order that divine truth may be more perfectly known, so that in turn the divine will may be more perfectly obeyed."[10] Historical theology, by reminding us of the way in which Christians have dealt with the crises of the past, throws light upon the role of Christians in the intellectual and cultural crises of the present.

I have tried to give four reasons why historical theology is significant for the education of a minister. It is an aid to the recovery of a Christian memory which is indispensable to an understanding of the Christian faith. It is the record of the judgment of Christian dogma by history which lays bare the meaning of dogma. It develops theological competence by making available the methods and conclusions of nineteen centuries of theological reflection, by opening up the perspective of the centuries and by training in theological conversation. It tells of the Christian community's engagement with culture during the past nineteen centuries and gives us some insight into our role as Christians amid the cultural crises of the twentieth century.

Historical theology is the record of the way the Christian community has understood the Christian faith and life and how it has proclaimed and witnessed to that faith and life. As such it is a guide and source of strength as we think through the meaning of Christianity and life today and proclaim it to the time in which we live. For this reason the history of Christian doctrine is of crucial importance for those of us in seminaries whose primary task is to educate students to become *effective* preachers and pastors in local congregations.

9. G. Wayne Glick, *The Reality of Christianity* (New York: Hayes and Rowe, 1967), p. 10, citing Harnack's quotation of Troeltsch.
10. Glick, *The Reality of Christianity*, p. 90.

Setting the Mind on Things Above: The Immediate Practicality of Theoretical Knowledge of God

BRUCE L. McCORMACK

> *So if you have been raised with Christ, seek the things that are above, where Christ is, seated at the right hand of God. Set your minds on things that are above, not on things that are on earth, for you have died, and your life is hidden with Christ in God. When Christ who is your life is revealed, then you also will be revealed with him in glory.*
>
> COLOSSIANS 3:1-4

This passage could pass for a motto for any genuinely Reformed theological existence. It is not simply the obvious fact that the Reformed laid so much stress, in their doctrine of the Lord's Supper, on the impossibility of dragging the ascended and exalted Lord's body down from heaven where it is "seated" at the "right hand" of God the Father (and the consequent need to seek the risen and exalted Lord where he may be found, viz. "above") which recommends this passage as one that reaches to the very heart of Reformed self-understanding. The note of setting one's mind on things that are above rather than things that are on earth was sounded, too, in their emphasis on the sovereignty of God in the planning and execution of human redemption. It was reflected in their Christology, in their efforts to preserve the Godness of God by denying every possibility of a divinization of the creature (through the affirmation of the so-called "extra Calvinisticum"). It was reflected in their understanding of faith, wherein they showed less interest in the fact that it was fiducial in nature (though they believed that as fully as did their Lutheran dialogue partners) than they did in the fact it was God's gift, efficaciously wrought in the human heart by the Holy Spirit.[1] It showed itself, too, in their treatment of justification, wherein their concern was far less with the faith that justifies (and playing that faith off against works) than it was with the fact that it is God who justifies by his grace, through faith.[2]

Interestingly, it was the "otherworldliness," if I may put it that way, of all Reformed thinking which made them such worldly people. For the radical distinction of God and the human, of things divine and things earthly, meant for them that the distinction of the creaturely into secular and sacral spheres was a frank impossibility. It was precisely in its secularity that the world was seen as belonging to God. And thus, every act of the human creature was filled with religious and ethical significance. The Reformed Reformation did not begin, as Karl Barth has observed, with the monk's question "How can I get a gracious God?" but with the more comprehensive question "What is the chief end of human life?"[3] And the answer to that question was that God has created us for knowledge of himself and has done so with a very concrete purpose in view. ". . . He created us for this [knowledge] and placed us in the world, that He might be glorified in us. And it is certainly proper that our life, of which He is the beginning, be directed to His glory."[4] Thus, even the this-worldliness of the Reformed was completely suffused, saturated, with other-worldliness.

"Set your minds on things that are above . . . for you have died." In the pages that follow, I want to reflect a bit on the significance of this fundamental attitude for a genuinely Reformed understanding of dogmatic (or, alternatively, "doctrinal") theology and its role in serving the nurture of a Christian life lived as service to God.

1. A point made by Karl Barth in his "Reformierte Lehre, ihr Wesen und ihre Aufgabe," in idem, *Vorträge und kleinere Arbeiten, 1922-1925*, ed. Holger Finze (Zürich: TVZ, 1990), pp. 239-40.
2. Barth, "Reformierte Lehre," p. 230.
3. Barth, "Reformierte Lehre," p. 239.
4. "Catechism of the Church of Geneva (1545)," Questions 1 and 2 in *Calvin: Theological Treatises*, ed. J. K. S. Reid (Philadelphia: Westminster Press, 1954), p. 91.

1. Theology is a "theoretical" discipline.

One of the more interesting debates to preoccupy the attention of medieval scholastics surrounded the question of whether theology was best understood as a "theoretical" or a "practical" science. Aristotle had laid the groundwork for this debate by distinguishing philosophy as a "speculative" science (whose end was truth) from the "practical" sciences (whose end was "work").[5] Building on this distinction, Thomas asks whether theology is not rightly considered a "practical science."[6] If a "practical science" is one "which ends in action," then it might well appear that theology must be a practical science, since theology culminates in the impact it has on human behavior — i.e., in morality. In his more considered response to this (superficially impressive) line of thought, Thomas says that theology is neither simply theoretical nor is it simply practical; it is both. And yet, it is both with the proviso that it is *more theoretical* than practical. And why? Thomas answered, ". . . it is more theoretical than practical, since it is mainly concerned with the divine things as they are, rather than with things men do. . . ." In the late Middle Ages, the great objection to this view was registered by Duns Scotus and his followers, with their emphasis upon the will (rather than the being) of God.

At the dawn of modern times, the Reformed scholastics (who took a lively interest in the question) tilted away from Thomas's view in the direction of Duns Scotus's. The position taken by Francis Turretin was typical.[7] "We consider theology to be neither simply theoretical nor simply practical, but partly theoretical, partly practical, as that which at the same time connects the theory of the true with the practice of the good. Yet it is more

5. See Aristotle, *The Metaphysics* II.1, trans. John H. McMahon (New York: Prometheus Books, 1991), p. 43.

6. Thomas Aquinas, *Summa Theologiae* Ia.1,4, ed. and trans. Thomas Gilby, O.P. (New York and London: Blackfriars in conjunction with McGraw-Hill and Eyre & Spottiswoode, 1964), p. 15.

7. Karl Barth's warning against false stereotypes of Protestant scholasticism on this point is well worth heeding. "It is true that H. Mulert (*Religion, Kirche, Theologie*, 1931, p. 28) and other modern authors claim that the orthodox regarded and pursued theology with rigid objectivism as *scientia de Deo et rebus divinis,* but this completely contradicts the tenor of the express declarations that are to be found in these theologians. . . . From the outset, Protestant orthodoxy suffered from a surplus rather than a deficit in the regard it paid to the religious subject [i.e., the human]." See Barth, *Church Dogmatics,* I/1 (Edinburgh: T. & T. Clark, 1960), p. 192.

practical than theoretical." Why more practical? Because theology involves a knowledge that "goes forth into practice and has operation as its object."[8] Just as medicine has as its object an operation (not merely the knowledge of how to cure diseases but the actual curing of them), the object of theology is to "impel" the human subject to "right actions" (centered in the worship of God). "There is no mystery proposed to our contemplation as an object of faith which does not excite us to the worship of God or which is not prerequisite for its proper performance."[9]

The great defect lying at the heart of the entire history of this debate, however, lies in the fact that it is altogether too *theoretical* (in a negative sense of the term which I will now describe). The procedure adopted is completely formal (and in that specific sense "theoretical"). It is of decisive importance to notice that the theologian is not actually engaged in the *practice* of doctrinal construction in joining this discussion, nor does he presuppose any material knowledge proper to the discipline of theology. What happens? The theologian takes up a vantage point *outside* the various academic disciplines, much as the Philosopher (i.e., Aristotle) did. All of the sciences (natural and humane) are viewed together, comparatively. Definitions are elaborated, and a classification is sought. Disciplines are grouped together as belonging to common types or kinds. The discipline of theology is then likened to one or more of the definitions acquired in this way. Where theology is believed to be in some respect like one kind of science and in other respects like another kind of science (as occurs in both Thomas and Turretin — albeit with differing results), an effort is made to coordinate the two definitions; to adjust one to the other in order to bring them into a meaningful relationship. The discussion is "theoretical" because it involves a conceptual labor that takes place in abstraction from the actual practice of dogmatic theology. This is no less true of Turretin (with his emphasis on the "practical") than it is of Thomas.

This is not to say that the question is an unimportant one. Nor is it to say that nothing can be learned from the answers given by a Thomas or a

---

8. Francis Turretin, *Institutes of Elenctic Theology*, vol. 1, trans. George Musgrave Giger, ed. James T. Dennison, Jr. (Phillipsburg, N.J.: Presbyterian and Reformed Publishing Company, 1992), p. 21.

9. Turretin, *Institutes*, vol. 1. The doctrines of the Trinity and the incarnation belong, apparently, to the latter class — doctrines less concerned with providing the believer with direct insight into what ought to be done than with orienting the believer towards the true God so that what is done will be done properly.

Turretin, that insights do not emerge which might be taken on board at the appropriate point, should a more adequate approach to the question be found. But the approach is inadequate because it fails to take into consideration the fact that what Calvin called the "knowledge of faith" (that which provides the "stuff" with which dogmatic theology works) is unique in kind. It is not a knowledge that can simply be brought into line with definitions which have emerged on the Philosopher's drawing-board. Should comparisons be made at all, the only appropriate place for such a task to be undertaken is in the *antilegomena,* not the prolegomena (in an appendix to dogmatics, perhaps). For before an adequate answer to the question can be advanced, we must first make clear to ourselves (at a minimum): (1) Who is the God who is known in faith? (2) Who is the human who knows this God? and (3) How does this God make himself known to human individuals? It is because the answers to these questions have a material content drawn from dogmatics proper that the scholastic's question (either "theoretical" or "practical" or a combination of the two) can only be addressed *after* doing the work of the dogmatic theologian.

Obviously, I cannot undertake to provide full answers to these material questions. What I can do is to set up some material "markers" that point beyond themselves to more fully elaborated doctrines of God and of revelation. First, then, who is the God spoken of in Christian dogmatics? Answer: the electing God who freely reveals himself to individuals when and where he deigns to do so. Because God is the Lord over the epistemic relationship he establishes between himself and the human knower, it is he and he alone who determines what form that relation will take. Second, who is the human who knows *this* God? The human who knows the electing God is the one who has been *made* the recipient of that knowledge by a sovereign and utterly efficacious act of God. The human who knows God has no control whatsoever over the epistemic relation that binds her to God. And, therefore, all of her activity in relation to this God can *only* take the form of a response to the prior divine action. Any activity of the human individual whose *content* is self-generated and self-normed can be of *no* interest for dogmatic theology — even if that activity be allegedly "moral" in nature. Only that activity which takes its rise in obedience to God's command — which, in other words, arises directly out of the epistemic/soteriological relation established unilaterally by God — can have a positive relevance for dogmatic thinking. The significance of that observation for our question here will soon be apparent. And, third, how does God reveal himself to human beings? On the "objective" side (that which is external to the human mind), revelation takes the form of the incarnation of God. On the "subjective" side (that which occurs *in* the human knower), revelation takes place preeminently (though not exclusively) through the illumination of the mind. And it is this last piece of material dogmatic content which is most pertinent to addressing the scholastic's question.

Faith, the faith that lays hold of God's promises in the gospel, is a form of *knowledge* — and that is of decisive importance for our question. Faith, as Calvin rightly held, comes about through hearing the Word. We may not, at this point, play the Personal Word (Christ) off against the words of Holy Scripture (as many modern theologians have been inclined to do). The Word, the Person Jesus Christ, communicates himself to us in and through the medium of words (in Scripture and in proclamation that is based on the exegesis of Scripture). And it is appropriate that he should do so, for he himself is — in a very real sense — *intrinsically verbal,* i.e., his person is linguistically communicable. It is no accident that the Evangelist John refers to him as the "Logos." He is Word; he communicates himself through words. Indeed we may say that the communication which occurs through words is a *rational* communication (as opposed to an irrational one).[10] We may do so without fear of falling prey to *rationalism* because we here understand human reason to be the apparatus which performs the role of *receiving* that rational communication; it does not generate its own norms or content.

Hence, the "knowledge of faith" is real knowledge. But its uniqueness rests, above all, in the fact that this is not a knowledge which can be acquired by the normal process of discovery, through the exercise of discursive reasoning. It is not a knowledge which humans could find or acquire on their own at all. It is a knowledge which must be *given,* moment by moment, by God. It is a knowledge which results from a sovereign, utterly effi-

---

10. Revelation, as Karl Barth rightly held, takes place preeminently in the sphere of human *ratio.* "Speech, including God's speech, is the form in which reason communicates with reason and person with person. To be sure it is the divine reason communicating with the human reason and the divine person with the human person. The utter inconceivability of this event is obvious. But reason with reason, person with person, is primarily analogous to what happens in the spiritual realm of creation, not the natural and physical realm. The Word of God . . . is a rational and not an irrational event. . . . [T]he encounter of God and man takes place primarily, pre-eminently and characteristically in this sphere of *ratio.* . . ." See Barth, *CD* I/1, 135.

cacious act of God the Holy Spirit — that "inner teacher by whose effort the promise of salvation penetrates into our minds."[11] It is a knowledge which, at bottom, is an act of mental comprehension, but which — because the effective source of this mental activity lies outside the human knowing apparatus — transcends *mere* mental comprehension. "When we call faith 'knowledge,' we do not mean 'comprehension' of the sort that is commonly concerned with things that fall under human sense perception. For faith is so far above sense that man's mind has to go beyond and rise above itself in order to attain it. Even where the mind has attained, it does not comprehend what it feels. But while it is persuaded of what it does not grasp, by the very certainty of its persuasion it understands more than if it perceived anything human by its own capacity."[12] To be persuaded! That, as Calvin rightly recognized, is an aspect which is common to all true knowledge (from whatever source). But the persuasion which is proper to the knowledge of God is not something that rests on proofs, on scientific investigation of data, etc. Persuasion, in this case, is completely dependent for its existence on the "internal testimony of the Holy Spirit." Calvin's conclusion: God is made known to the individual where and when the mind is illumined and the heart strengthened. "Now we shall possess a right definition of faith if we call it a firm and certain knowledge of God's benevolence toward us, founded upon the truth of the freely given promise in Christ, *both revealed to our minds and sealed upon our hearts through the Holy Spirit.*"[13]

Now notice: knowledge of God is a *theoretical* knowing in this precise sense: it is a knowing which occurs preeminently in the realm of human *ratio*. The "knowledge of faith" which provides theology with its material content is a knowledge which comes to us through the mind. But because the knowledge of God must be given to us, because we have no capacity in and of ourselves for acquiring it, therefore, it is a theoretical knowing which is eminently *practical*. It is a theoretical knowing which, in the very nature of the case, *transforms* the recipient of it. In giving himself to the human mind to be known, God reorients the mind, gives it a new direction, conforms it to himself (thereby overcoming, in some measure, what the Reformed tradition has called the "noetic effects" of sin). The

11. Calvin, *Institutes*, III.i.4.
12. Calvin, *Institutes*, III.ii.14.
13. Calvin, *Institutes*, III.ii.7 (emphasis mine).

note of "you have died" (as an essential presupposition to Christian living in Pauline thought) is applicable not merely to moral behavior but also, and even preeminently, to the life of the mind by means of which the reorientation of the individual takes place. For the one who has died, her mind has been "crucified," brought into subjection to Christ so that every thought might be taken captive to obedience to Christ (2 Corinthians 10:5).

We now begin to see how misleading the scholastic form of our question has been. In truth, theology is a theoretical discipline because it deals with a body of knowledge which has been given to theoretical reason. Most importantly, this theoretical knowledge is itself transformative ("be transformed by the renewing of your minds" — Romans 12:2). Thus, what the scholastic tradition (in both its medieval Catholic and its seventeenth-century Protestant forms) called the "practical" is actually *embedded in* the "theoretical" and may only be distinguished from it where the "theoretical" has been wrongly construed. And that is precisely what occurs when theologians allow definitions of the "theoretical" and the "practical" to be simply borrowed from philosophical (or, as is likely today, social scientific) evaluations of the various academic disciplines. The "theoretical" is understood as a different kind of mental activity from the "practical" with the result that (for those who construe the "theoretical" in this mistaken way) theology comes to be understood as a discipline in which the thinker abstracts him/herself from a *lived* relationship with God in order to contemplate "divine things" (articles of faith) coolly, dispassionately, in the stance of the natural scientist who collects and analyzes "data" in order then to organize it into a useful body of knowledge. The defenders of theology as a "practical" science, ancient and contemporary, have been right to protest against this reduction of theology to a merely academic discipline. But — and this is the crucial point which is widely overlooked today — the defenders of the "practical" have been too tainted with the root disease to offer effective protest! For they, too, proceed in a purely formal way to abstract the "theoretical" from the "practical" and to place them over against each other as mere concepts needing to be adjusted to one another — a little of this, a little of that, both "theoretical" and "practical," perhaps, but more of this than of that, back and forth, etc., etc. The "theoretical" — rightly defined! — *is* the "practical." No doubt, this answer will seem surprising in an age in which the "theoretical" stands so strongly under suspicion. But real deliverance from the ills which plague dogmatic theology today can only be purchased through a revitalization of the "theoretical" (in the genuinely Christian sense described above).

In sum: theology is a theoretical discipline for two closely intertwined reasons: because it is concerned with the knowledge of *God* and because it is concerned with the *knowledge* of God. To the extent that theology has lost sight of its primary concern (the knowledge of God), humankind has increasingly been made an *independent* subject of interest for theology (abstracted from the lived epistemic/soteriological relation out of which theology ought to be done) — and therein lies the real problem with an overemphasis on an abstractly conceived "practicality."

The dangers ought already to have been amply demonstrated in Turretin's writings. According to him, the "end" of theology is to be found in "the happiness of man." Although Turretin immediately proceeds to define this happiness in terms of a vision of God from which flows assimilation to him, the damage has already been done.[14] Where we are told that the "end" (or "goal") of theology lies in human happiness rather than the glorification of God, there we have before us evidence of a turn (subtle though it may be) away from the wisdom of the early Reformed.[15] "Set your mind on things that are above . . . for you have died" as the most basic piece of Christian wisdom has been replaced by concern for transformed human existence as an end in itself. Where that takes place, the attention of students of theology is diverted by the writers of it from God and redi-

14. Turretin, *Institutes*, vol. 1, p. 22.
15. This is not, of course, to make Turretin responsible for this development; on the contrary, his theology, taken as a whole, acted as a brake on a fundamental shift in orientation which had been emerging for some time prior to him. In the Puritan theology of a William Ames (first published in 1623 — some fifty-six years before Turretin's *Institutes*), we find a prototypical example of the impact which a concentration on human transformation (in considerable isolation from a concentration on its divine source) can have on how theology is understood. For Ames, "Theology is the doctrine of living to God." As such, it is more art than science. "Every art has its rules to which the work of the person practicing it corresponds. Since living is the noblest work of all, there cannot be any more proper study than the art of living." See William Ames, *The Marrow of Theology*, trans. John Dykstra Eusden (Durham, N.C.: Labyrinth Press, 1983), p. 77. The place of Ames in the history of Reformed dogmatics is not a question which can be explored here. For a discussion of that problem (and literature on it) see Karl Barth, *Die christliche Dogmatik im Entwurf*, ed. Gerhard Sauter (Zürich: TVZ, 1982), p. 115, note 22. Suffice it to say that this early seventeenth-century definition of theology manifests that "turn to the subject" which would remain characteristic of virtually the whole of modern theology through the end of the nineteenth century.

rected to themselves. It can never be good for human persons to have their attention diverted from the "things above." It cannot be redemptive to focus our attention more on issues of moral transformation (the acquisition of moral skills, for example, or the cultivation of moral habits of mind) than on the God who transforms us spiritually, the God who makes the human subject "capable" by grace of living a moral life in the Christian sense. As Luther liked to say, before we can have "fruit" (i.e., "good works"), we must have trees to bear that fruit. "First there must be a tree, then the fruit. For apples do not make a tree but a tree makes apples. So faith first makes a person, who afterwards performs works. To keep the Law without faith, therefore, is to make apples without a tree."[16] Faith makes a person who afterwards performs works; we Reformed would prefer to say that the justifying/regenerating grace of God makes a "person" who does works, but the point is well made nevertheless. But to be made a tree requires that we know God. If theology would, once again, become an enterprise which serves human redemption (rather than moralism), it must have the courage to become a *theoretical* discipline which concerns itself, above all, with truth.

We may tease out the significance of the foregoing for our time a bit further if we conclude with a brief discussion of the following question. What understanding of doctrine — and of doctrinal theology — is most commensurate with the description of theology as a theoretical science as we have been defining it here?

2. "Doctrine is the human word of the Christian which has passed through the crisis of the merciless reformation and purification of the Word of God attested in Scripture."[17]

The definition is Barth's and it is clear at a glance how much more robust it is than more recent talk of rules of grammar (the mastery of which facilitate the socialization of an individual into the faith of a community) or the thematization of a religious consciousness located in the depth dimensions of human being and existence. Mastery of rules of grammar and

16. Luther, *Lectures on Galatians, LW*, vol. 26, p. 255.
17. Karl Barth, "Reformierte Lehre, ihr Wesen und ihre Aufgabe" in idem, *Vorträge und kleinere Arbeiten, 1922-1925*, ed. Holger Finze (Zürich: TVZ, 1990), p. 223.

thematization have this much in common: they are both human activities which do not require a divine action in order to be possible. The human word of which Barth speaks, by contrast, is the consequence of a testing which takes place only where and when God witnesses to himself in and through the witness to him found in Holy Scripture. No doubt: human beings are also active participants in this testing. And it is always possible for sinful human beings to assume the primacy in this act of testing; to try to make themselves lords of the epistemic relationship with God. Indeed, apart from the *ongoing* exercise of God's sovereign grace, it is inevitable that sinful humans will do this. For those who truly understand who God is and who they are in relation to God, however, and are willing to live on the basis of this twofold understanding, constructive doctrinal reflection can only take its rise, moment by moment, out of the crisis of the life-giving judgment which the Self-witness of God through Holy Scripture brings to bear on that reflection. That human participation in this process has an ecclesial character is a subject for another place. What is crucial to point out here is that dogmatic theology draws its life from the experience of divine judgment ("you have died").

Doctrinal construction which is carried out under the conditions of divine judgment will not allow an artificial and wholly arbitrary distinction to be drawn between "practical" and "impractical" doctrines. Immanuel Kant's belief that the traditional doctrine of the Trinity is to be rejected because it transcends the bounds of practical reason (describing as it does what God is in himself rather than restricting its attention to what God is "for us" as the moral Ruler of moral beings) is only the best-known example of an approach to theology whose principal weakness, for the purposes of this discussion, lies in its treatment of the various doctrines as individual ideational units whose "practicality" may then be tested one at a time, in isolation from all the others.[18] To treat doctrines atomistically is to "kill"

18. [It is also true that the distinction Kant makes involving an alleged knowledge of God in himself (which is no knowledge at all) depends, in part, on the restriction of theoretical knowing to that which may be made known *publicly* (i.e., a knowledge which may be communicated to and shared by all men and women). That such a restriction has been shown not to apply to theological knowledge by Karl Barth (in his doctrine of revelation) is something I have tried to demonstrate elsewhere. See McCormack, "Revelation and History in Transfoundationalist Perspective: Karl Barth's Theological Epistemology in Conversation with a Schleiermacherian Tradition," *Journal of Religion* 78 (1998): 18-37.] For Kant's treatment of the doctrine of the Trinity see his *Religion Within the Limits of Reason Alone* (New

them; it is to withdraw them from the source of their life. For it is only as a whole, in their interconnected unity, that doctrines arise out of and belong to a transformative knowledge of God. If we seek to test each doctrine individually as to its "practicality," we will already have withdrawn ourselves from the *immediacy* of that epistemic/soteriological relation with God out of which theology ought to be done. We will have adopted a stance outside of the knowledge of God in order to analyze it, to break it down into constituent parts. And, inevitably, because we have stepped outside of a redemptive relationship with God, we will carry out this task of distinguishing and dividing in accordance with norms of our own devising. And so it is not surprising when the norm for testing the "practicality" of isolated and individualized doctrines turns out, typically, to take the form of assessing the "impact" of a given doctrine on outwardly observable human behavior.[19] Such an assessment is inviting because it gives the theologian (or, better, the "human scientist") a sense of being in control, of being the master of a field of inquiry which surveys nothing but manipulable and controllable data. What is especially lamentable in our day and age are the number of theologians who think themselves able to triumph over Kant on his own ground, testing the doctrine of the Trinity (for example) in terms of its impact on human behavior and finding that the doctrine does indeed impact human behavior in a positive way. Leaving aside the fact that Kant looks better and better the more theologians try to prove him wrong, the real error in all of this lies in the disengagement from the epistemic/soteriological relation with God in which genuinely Christian "practicality" is realized.

Setting the mind on things above lays upon the theologian the demand that his/her thought be *conformed* to the content of the knowledge given in divine revelation, a knowledge whose unified character is guaran-

---

York: Harper Torchbooks, 1960), pp. 129-38. Still, it remains true that Kant is using his distinction between God in himself and God "for us" as a norm for testing the viability of a doctrine, treated in isolation from that organically related body of doctrines which grants to it both its necessity and its meaningfulness.

19. There is, doubtless, more than a grain of truth in Sallie McFague's claim ". . . belief and behavior are more influenced by images than by concepts . . ." — today more than ever, we might add. See McFague, *Models of God: Theology for an Ecological, Nuclear Age* (London: SCM Press, 1987), p. 38. But given that Christian salvation aims at something much more profound than mere behavior modification, the pragmatism embodied in this piece of wisdom is scarcely defensible.

teed by the unity and singularity of the Person (Jesus Christ) who is its center. Theology which is carried out under this demand will be seen to consist preeminently in a twofold responsibility: viz. that of testing the various doctrines, first, as to their conformity to the witness of Holy Scripture (wherein the judgment of God is realized) and, second, as to their coherence with each other. Can such an exercise also become merely "theoretical" (in the negative sense of a disengaged, wholly "academic" enterprise)? Certainly. But because the demand which alone justifies this exercise (this *service*) is one that arises directly out of the epistemic/soteriological relationship with God, this understanding of doctrinal theology will always be superior to those which depend for their existence on stepping out of that relation as the first step. A "practical" theology which does not serve the knowledge of God in the way described (which does not demand of its "practitioner" that she set her mind on things that are above), will always be (in the only sense that finally counts) *impractical*.

The Hermeneutics of Imprecation

PATRICK D. MILLER

The testing place of theology is in its dealing with difficult issues. When tragedy and trouble strike or when things do not make sense in one's life or in the world generally, even those who have not bothered to think about the faith find themselves forced to become theologians, or to call upon theologians — often in the proper garb of the pastor. One way, therefore, in which theology serves the church is by taking up difficult matters of faith and life, to illumine both by thinking critically, historically, faithfully, and prayerfully about Scripture.[1] Some of these "hard" matters that confront Christian faith arise from the Bible itself. One of the most obvious is the *hostile and harsh attitude expressed toward one's enemies*, especially in some of the Old Testament texts,[2] notably the stories of the conquest of Canaan and the imprecatory, or curse, psalms. The second of these two genres, *prayers of imprecation*, is the case I am taking up here to see what possibilities lie before us for dealing with this difficult issue.[3] As

---

1. Exemplary of this fact is the way in which denominations set up councils and committees of theologians to deal with difficult issues, such as sexuality, abortion, the authority of Scripture, and the like.

2. One must be careful about assuming that this is only an Old Testament issue. The New Testament also has its expressions of hostility and curse toward opponents who are seen as the enemy, as one sees in some of the epistles and Revelation.

3. For a helpful effort to show how the "morality" of the conquest of Canaan may already have been an apologetic issue in the redaction of the book of Joshua, see now Lawson Stone, "Ethical and Apologetic Tendencies in the Redaction of the Book of Joshua," *The Catholic Biblical Quarterly* 53 (1991): 25-36.

an entree to the subject, I propose to take up one of the most familiar and most terrifying psalms of the Old Testament: Psalm 137.[4]

> 1 By the waters of Babylon,
>   there we sat down, yea we wept
>   when we remembered Zion.
> 2 On the willows[5] in its midst
>   we hung up our lyres.
> 3 For there our captors demanded
>   of us songs
>   and our tormentors mirth,
>   "Sing for us one of the songs of Zion!"
> 4 How could we sing the Lord's song
>   on foreign soil?
> 5 If I forget you, O Jerusalem,
>   may my right hand . . .[6]
>   May my tongue cling to the roof of my mouth,
>   if I do not remember you,
> 6 if I do not set Jerusalem
>   as the peak of my joy.
> 7 Remember, O Lord, against the Edomites
>   the day of Jerusalem,
>   how they said, "Tear it down! Tear it down!
>   Down to its foundations!"
> 8 O daughter of Babylon, you devastator![7]

4. The most recent extended treatment of the imprecatory psalms is Erich Zenger, *A God of Vengeance? Understanding the Psalms of Divine Wrath* (Louisville: Westminster/John Knox, 1996). This book includes a brief treatment of Psalm 137 and some broader hermeneutical reflections. A full treatment of imprecation in the Psalter would need to look at a number of other psalms, as Zenger does. In the more limited confines of this essay, I have chosen what may be the most difficult and disturbing of all the imprecatory psalms.

5. The tree may be a poplar that looks like a willow.

6. The text is doubtful at this point. The Massoretic Text has *tiškaḥ*, which would appear to mean "may you forget." This is dubious, and the versions have passive forms and the like. Other proposals, including transposing the last two letters of the root have led to a reading that is fairly common in the translations: "wither." Klaus Seybold has — candidly and accurately — acknowledged that it is unclear what happens to the right hand (*Die Psalmen*, "Handbuch zum Alten Testament" I/15 [Tübingen: J. C. B. Mohr, 1996], p. 510).

7. The form in the Hebrew is passive, but the active is more likely and is attested in some textual witnesses, though it may be *lectio facilior* in this case. See the discussion in

> Blessed shall be the one who pays you back
> what you have done to us.
> 9 Blessed shall be the one who seizes and dashes
> your children against the rocks.

The very familiarity of this psalm is somewhat surprising in that most of the psalms containing curses against the enemy — whether in large or small part — are not generally held in mind or get much attention in the teaching, preaching, and liturgy of the church, precisely because they are troublesome, a dimension of the Bible that we wish were not there. The *problem* of the curses is kept before us, or at least held in the back of our minds, but not the particular psalms. Psalm 137, therefore, is something of an exception.

This is an exceptional psalm for at least two reasons. The first is the power and poignancy of the first two-thirds of the psalm. The plaintive, despairing cry, "How can we sing the Lord's song in a strange land?" tugs at the heart strings and places this psalm in the life-and-death reality of exile.[8] Most of the psalms are difficult to locate in a particular historical moment. While referential openness offers rich opportunities for the hermeneutics of the Psalms,[9] this exception to that historical openness, where the voices of the oppressed singers of the psalm cry out from a particular situation of oppression well known to us, evokes a sense of understanding and empathy because we "know" what this psalm is about. In many other cases, we puzzle over the references of the imagery and the petitions. Here, however, the concrete situation is evident. We are drawn into solidarity with those who wept by the rivers of Babylon. The imagery of the willows on which were hung the harps and the picture of Babylonian tormentors taunting the Judean captives reinforce the emotional pull of the song. The reader is drawn into the story with all the sympathies on the side of the "we" who pray this lament.

Even the zealous response of the psalmists to the taunt strikes a

---

Leslie C. Allen, "Psalms 101–150," in *Word Biblical Commentary* (Waco: Word Books, 1983), p. 237.

8. This essay focuses on hermeneutical issues posed by Psalm 137. The reader is invited to consult the standard commentaries for exegetical details. The psalm may well come from the exile, but the very form of verses 1-3, and the repeated and emphatic "there" (*šām*) of verses 1 and 2 suggests that the speaker is looking back on captivity in Babylon from a later vantage point.

9. On the hermeneutical possibilities inherent in the historical openness of the Psalms, see Patrick D. Miller, *Interpreting the Psalms* (Philadelphia: Fortress Press, 1986), ch. 2.

chord in the reader-listener. The tenacious commitment not to let go of the memory of home is something known to many who are caught far from home and unable to return. The singing voice may be silenced in tears, but there is no forgetting. Not to be able to sing Zion's songs does not mean that Zion is ever forgotten. Memories of home keep this community going while it is in exile. The reader of the psalm knows that Zion is a *topos* for home, and every reader comprehends and joins with the community that is cut off from home but determined that as long as breath shall last, the particular memories of what it is like back there will be kept to the fore, held on to as the only treasure possible in a foreign land.

The second reason this particular curse psalm is so familiar to us when others are not is the powerful and terrible image of the babies being dashed against the rocks. It is a disturbing image in every way, a picture of violence at its worst: *killing, brutal killing, of the most innocent and defenseless.* The repulsiveness of the image paradoxically makes it stick in our mind. But this subject matter is not exceptional in Scripture. Brutal killing of babies and ripping open pregnant women appear not infrequently in Scripture (2 Kings 8:12; Isaiah 13:16; Hosea 10:14; 14:1 [Eng. 13:16]; Nahum 3:10; and cf. Jesus in Luke 19:44). Indeed, several times, this is an act or threat of *God*, and in Luke 19 Jesus announces the future crushing of Jerusalem *and its children*. Such texts, when encountered, also repel us, but they are not generally known and thus have not posed the problem that Psalm 137 does. So the hermeneutical problem with Psalm 137 is not confined to the subject matter even though such subject matter will always pose hermeneutical problems.[10] One must go further, therefore, with this text and explore other features of the psalm and our reading of it that pose the hermeneutical problem of this text.

For one thing, this is *poetry* in all its *power and evocative possibility.* Few accounts of the exile in Scripture are better known than this and none are able to resonate with a distant audience as well as this one. But one needs to be on guard at this point. The poetry of Psalm137 sucks in the reader inescapably, and it may not be possible to get back out. The second part of the psalm, with its familiar question at the beginning of verse 4 — How could we sing the Lord's song on foreign soil? — leads into verses that

---

10. As, for example, when we encounter texts that speak of the *ḥerem*, or ban, the utter destruction of the seven nations of Canaan, in some instances at the command of the Lord (e.g., Deuteronomy 20:17) or the Lord's servant Moses (Deuteronomy 7:1-6).

we may applaud. But we should not do that without realizing that they are also imprecatory, that is, a *self-imprecation*. The beginning of the curse form is already present in verses 5-6. These verses are an apostrophe to Jerusalem. The zeal and love for Jerusalem is what we hear. But the poet seems to be saying, in effect, "If I should forget you for a moment, let me be like a person with a stroke, unable to speak or move one side of my body." Empathy with the "we" and the "I" of the Psalm means a kind of identity with its vehemence that is disturbing, to say the least.

Another feature of the hermeneutical problematic of Psalm 137 lies in the combination of our *familiarity* with the text and the *incongruity* effected by the presence of the repulsive violence theme alongside other more compelling and attracting words of anguish in the face of oppression. The same happens in the reading and hearing of Psalm 139.[11] Unfamiliar and unused texts may have similar words, but their unfamiliarity means they do not pose the same kind of hermeneutical problem — for example, Psalms 10 and 109. Psalms 137 and 139, as we begin to read them, draw us in. At one and the same time, we are attracted and repelled. Only certain texts do that for us. Many of the violence texts of the Old Testament and other imprecatory psalms are simply objectionable and have little "play" for us. In the case of Psalm 137, however, a unified text engages our horizon in very contradictory ways. What is happening in that contradiction and how does this clash of attraction and revulsion happen? Is there any possibility that the unity of the text needs to be carried forward in our appropriation of it so that we also read the whole thing in some meaningful fashion? Or is it that the unity of the ancient text and the contradiction in our reaction are simply incompatible realities, and we have to explore the abrasiveness and friction between them? These are two quite different hermeneutical outcomes. The following observations seek to explore both of them.

We start with the recognition that the Old Testament itself seems to identify this as violence at its worst. The reader of this text — and others like it — cannot read it simply as one more example of a violence-ridden tribal society. The text itself lifts up this kind of act as the extreme form of the destruction of a community. (This is not individual violence; it is com-

11. I have suggested a way of interpreting Psalm 139 and its imprecations in *Interpreting the Psalms*, pp. 144-53. The remarks there about how the hatred of enemies and the imprecation against them are to be understood theologically supplement the hermeneutical suggestions made here.

munity violence.) Here, therefore, there is a sense in which the Scriptures serve not to perpetuate violence, as might seem to be the case by a surface reading and a surface hermeneutic. Rather, they contribute to the exposure and unmasking of violence.[12] The text mirrors the violence that is universal and exposes the violence that is a part of the society and of its God in the context of the announcement of a counter-society and a counter-God.[13] The discernment of such subtle but real exposure is, at least in part, the significance of René Girard's work, his identification of the violence that is so prevalent in the Old Testament and the implicit criticism that comes from its counter-voices and from the gospel.[14]

What I am suggesting is that within Scripture itself there are explicit and implicit criticisms of the inclination to violence expressed by the "I" of Psalm 137 that force a strong hermeneutic of criticism upon us, a critical hermeneutic that comes not from an external source but from the canon itself. That hermeneutic of suspicion is so strong that we have to ask if it is not the dominant outcome of the reading of the whole of these texts we call Scripture. That is, such a text as this is read in the light of other *texts* and of *the whole*. Those *other texts* include some that are similar to Psalm 137 in their disclosure of violence wished, announced, and enacted. As such texts — including some from the New Testament — mount up before us, they can expose the violence and make us uncomfortable with it.[15] Still

---

12. For an elaboration of the way the Old Testament works to unmask the human propensity to violence, see Norbert Lohfink, "Der gewalttätige Gott des Alten Testaments und die Suche nach einer gewaltfreien Gesellschaft," in *Jahrbuch für Biblische Theologie* 2 (1987), pp. 106-36. Cf., among other works by the same author, "Gewaltlosigkeit nach dem Evangelium angesichts der gesellschaftlichen Verankerung der Gewalt," in *Probleme des Friedens* (Frankfurt am Main: Pax-Christi-Bewegung. Deutsche Sekretariat, 1986); "Der 'heilige Kreig' und der 'Bann' in der Bibel," *Internationale katholische Zeitschrift COMMUNIO* 18 (1989): 104-12; and "'Gewalt' als Thema alttestamentlicher Forschung," in *Gewalt und Gewaltlosigkeit im Alten Testament*, "Questiones Disputatae," 96, ed. Norbert Lohfink (Freiburg: Herder, 1983), pp. 15-50.

13. Lohfink, "Der gewalttätige Gott."

14. The most famous of Girard's works is *Violence and the Sacred* (Baltimore: Johns Hopkins University Press, 1979). Among those works that have looked most closely at the Scriptures in the light of Girard's work, one may cite especially Raymund Schwager, S.J., *Must There Be Scapegoats? Violence and Redemption in the Bible* (San Francisco: Harper & Row, 1987).

15. Alternatively, the history of the church's use of such texts has also demonstrated the possibility that they may inure the community to violence. There is no guarantee that the hermeneutic being described at this point will operate automatically any more than is the case with any hermeneutical proposal.

other texts speak against the violence — including, prominently, some from the Old Testament, such as the Isaianic visions of peace and the absence of war and hostility (Isaiah 2:2-5 [Micah 4:1-5]; 11:1-9 [but note v. 4c]), the Psalmic vision of the Lord's destruction of the implements of war (Psalm 46:9-10 [Eng. 8-9]), the prayer for the peace of Jerusalem (Psalm 122) and wisdom's pragmatic approach to the enemy (Proverbs 25:21-22).[16] The *whole* of the canon presents the larger picture of God's way and God's purpose from the beginning to the end.[17] That whole, however, cannot be read simply in a linear development or progression. In the midst of the literature associated with the Second Isaiah, for example, where we read of the Suffering Servant who fulfills God's purpose as the one who bears the violence of humanity on behalf of humanity, we encounter Isaiah 34 and its account of the bloody sword of the Lord. And one of the texts that resonates most with Isaiah 34 is the Book of Revelation at the end of the New Testament.

In Psalm 137, we are drawn to the lament over human and communal suffering, the depiction of oppression, of persons exiled and tormented, of the loss of everything dear and meaningful. What the rest of the psalm does, at a minimum, is to ask if the clash or contradiction we experience in reading the psalm is the result of a sentimental appropriation of the first part so that we do not really know the depth of the psalmist's torment. To find the psalm as a whole both intelligible and meaningful requires that our romantic and sentimental appropriation of the first part be abandoned. These words have their power and truthfulness only within the devastating experience to which they point.

I have referred to the *memory* theme in the psalm (vss. 1, 5, 7) and particularly the memory of home, Jerusalem (vss. 1, 3, 5, 6, 7). It is especially in regard to that theme that one risks sentimentalizing and missing the force of that memory, so tenacious that it can evoke a self-curse against its ever being diminished (v. 5). It is indeed memory that keeps this community going, but it is one that also asks God to remember in judgment. And even though the terrible blessing/curse of the final verses is not an explicit invocation of divine action, it is borne on the waves of memory, the

16. It is worth remembering that Paul's famous words against vengeance in Romans 12:19-20 are built around quotations from the Old Testament that he appropriates for his teaching on the subject (Deuteronomy 32:35; Proverbs 25:21-22; cf. Proverbs 20:22; 24:29).

17. For a contemporary presentation of such an understanding of Scripture, see Kendall Soulen, *The God of Israel and Christian Theology* (Minneapolis: Fortress, 1996).

memory of what was done to Jerusalem and of Babylonians who are remembered only in the categories experience has provided: captor, tormentor, and devastator. That is the memory of rage, and the reader does not suddenly encounter it in the last verses. It is there from the beginning. The depth of that rage is even greater if, as is likely, this prayer was first articulated *after* the captivity in Babylon was over and is thus a "look back in anger."[18]

At the same time, one is free to ask — if not forced to do so — if even in awareness of the unity of the psalm and the way the end arises out of the beginning, one ought still to experience a contradiction, to ask if there is not a perduring abrasiveness between the two parts of the psalm so that once again criticism rather than retrieval is the last hermeneutical word. There are all sorts of things in Scripture, Christology, and the experience of the Christian community — Jesus' words about enemies and those who persecute you, Paul's words about vengeance in Romans 12, the meaning of the death of Christ, the experience of Christian martyrdom, the prayer of Stephen (Acts 7:60), and the like — that will not easily permit our dissolution of the contradiction effected by the psalm.

The hermeneutical problem posed by this text is in no small measure because it is a *prayer*. That is a large part of why Psalms 137 and 139 create a visceral reaction beyond that of other texts. Such horrendous prayer for the brutal killing of the children of one's enemies seems to defile the character of prayer itself.[19] But the *form* of the text, however much that form creates problems, may also be the only way in which the

---

18. The phrase is taken from the title of John Osborne's play.

19. In a seminary class on prayer in Scripture, I asked the members of the class to prepare their own imprecatory prayers. Three things happened most noticeably when the group met to discuss what they had written:

a. Many simply could not bring themselves to write such prayers.

b. The effort to do so and the effort to talk about or share the prayers they had prepared was an extremely emotional occasion.

c. Virtually everyone who attempted the task did not present a prayer of imprecation against his or her own enemies but offered prayers of rage and solidarity with others who had suffered, for example, women raped or abused. They were not personal supplications but intercessions in community and shared anger at the assaults that somebody had made on another person or persons. In this respect, I would regard their efforts as appropriate outcomes of their praying as Christians, that is, as those whose prayers for help are now primarily intercessory prayers for others in trouble and distress.

text can have any possibility *for us,* that is, is in any way capable of being appropriated. We can read reports of violence all through the Old Testament and be relatively unmoved by them. But here is a text that speaks in the first person (singular and plural), one that belongs to the prayer book and hymnbook of the church and thus invites our joining in. By its form the text blocks our distancing of ourselves from it. We may pass by other texts relatively easily. Here we are either drawn in to say these words or we have to make a decision to reject them. It is comparable to a congregation standing to recite the Creed. One has to do something with the text at that point. The participant is drawn into the community of recitation or must decide consciously to drop out of it. Such a sharp alternative does not confront us with every reading of Scripture in worship. But that is exactly why this text creates problems for the contemporary community. We are repelled by and wish to dissociate ourselves from an expression — blessings on a baby-killer — in a text to which we cannot otherwise sit loose and from which we cannot easily dissociate ourselves because to read it is to join in with the original speakers. The only simple way to respond is to cut that Gordian knot, as some hymnbook Psalters have done, and excise the final three verses of the psalm, allowing the congregation to appropriate the attracting and attractive part without having to face its outcome in a rage that already boils under the surface of the first part of the psalm.

Paradoxically it may also be the form of the psalm, that is, its character as prayer, that opens it to the contemporary reader of faith. For one can turn the whole matter around. Rather than asking if we could ever justifiably pray such a prayer as this, assuming that the issue is simply a matter of choice, of rational decision, we might better ask whether such *thoughts* as expressed here have any other permissible context than *conversation with God,* from whom no secrets are hid, from whom no rage or anger can be concealed. The unrestrained, justifiable but not justifiable, thoughts are let loose — but within a particular framework. In this sense, the rage and brutality are not allowed to go public.[20] They are real in this psalm, and there are terrible moments when they are real in human life. To pray such rage is

---

20. Compare the rage of many of the victims of the Oklahoma City bombing, who shouted and wept for joy at the conviction of Timothy McVeigh and testified in detail about the brutality of their children's deaths in order to try to convince the jury to sentence him to death.

at one and the same time to let it go and to hold it back. It is not now a part of our dealing with our neighbor-enemy. It is a part of our life with God.[21]

The prayer thus may become a vehicle for the inner fury of the oppressed, a way — to use the modern expression — of dealing with one's anger. There are other ways, as the Bible well knows (Genesis 4:7). But one should recognize that this is a fairly narrow range of hermeneutical possibility. It is precisely not a matter of universal applicability but of limited use, as the ferocity of the psalm gives voice to and channels the ferocity of the soul, turning the fallen countenance that has retaliation and murder in its eyes — or calls for execution — into a raging prayer that finally leaves the matter where Moses (Deuteronomy 32:35) and Paul (Romans 12:18-21) both tell us it belongs — in the hands of God.

Finally, I would suggest three things about the place of such a prayer as Psalm 137 in the worship life of the community, where our hermeneutical decisions come to life and expression:

1. The liturgical and musical expression of these thoughts can have its place in those traditions and practices where there is a *lectio continua* use of the Psalms. In such a regular ongoing reading of the whole Psalter, or at least large portions of it, the imprecations of Psalm 137 — and prayers like it — are placed in a larger context and not simply read or sung by themselves. They are abrasive pieces of a larger whole and not lifted up to a special place or made a point of focus by reading them by themselves. The rage is clear, but it is set in the context of all the psalms and the constant listening of the congregation to the images, the deep emotions, the hyperbole — to all the strong and intense language of the Psalms. Such a liturgical context appropriately relativizes the ferocity of the speaker and sets the contradictory responses of the contemporary hearer alongside other experiences of ambiguity, abrasive language, and unexpected or jarring movements of thought. The rest of the psalms give the reader a handle on the white heat of the psalm so that it neither burns unexpectedly nor is it suddenly dropped.

2. It is also possible that the *musical setting* of such a psalm can let the rage come forth and deal with it musically — hearing it, venting it, restraining it, and letting counter-tones have their say. One thinks, for example, of Leonard Bernstein's musical rendition of the raging of the nations

---

21. Jeremiah's laments are a classic example of such letting go of the rage and holding it back in imprecatory prayer that restricts the anger to the interior life with God.

against the Lord's anointed (Psalm 2) in the "Chichester Psalms." The rage is given full expression in the rapid repetition of *lāmāh rāgešû,* "Why do they throng tumultuously?" (Psalm 2:1) by the male voices, but they are finally overcome, controlled and muted by the single melodic counter-tenor's repeated *'adōnai rō'î lō' 'ehsār,* "The Lord is my shepherd, I shall not want" (Psalm 23:1). When the Psalms are set to music, the imprecatory elements are given a context — in music and lyrics — for hearing and appropriating them. That is what happens, for example, with Psalm 137 in the *Psalter Hymnal* of the Christian Reformed Church. The final line of the hymn makes just the theological move suggested above by drawing in from elsewhere in Scripture the words "Vengeance shall come from God our Lord." That is, the prayer for the destruction of Babylon and the brutal slaughter of its babies is placed under the recognition that such judgment belongs in the context of the loving and just purposes of God, albeit in this case with the emphasis on justice but knowing and assuming the proclivity of God, the leaning of God toward a loving mercy (Exodus 34:6-7; Psalm 30:6 [Eng. v. 5]; Isaiah 54:7-8). Vengeance is to be manifest only in God's vindication of God's purpose, not in our revenge against those who have hurt us.

3. When all is said and done, however, we still have difficulty singing "Babylon great, your seed be smashed" *(Psalter Hymnal).* The hymn's euphemistic rendition of the verse "Happy shall be the one who takes your little ones and dashes them against the rocks" does not help much. At this point, I remember that the Psalms are to be read as critically as any other part of the Scripture. The worshiping congregation receives these psalms from its Lord and in the context of his instruction and way. It cannot draw back from that. The words of rage in the psalms do not easily mellow into pleasant and uplifting hymns. So let them stay words of rage in the dialogue of the angry sufferer with God or in our angry suffering with others. Let us not easily baptize them into Christian prayer in those regular acts of worship through which the congregation expresses its faith in God and listens for a word from the Lord.

A New Anthropology from the Perspective of Theology

JONG SUNG RHEE

1. Four Spheres of Human Existence

Because of the variety of functions connected with what it means to be human, no total picture encompassing all the various products of human activity is possible. Rather, human writings (whether philosophy, fiction, science, psychology, history, religion, or poetry) all tend to focus on one or two particular aspects of human activity. This trend derives from human nature itself. Originally and fundamentally, human beings are related to four spheres of existence; that is, they live, act, make judgments, and believe in accordance with four innate functions, namely *logos, pathos, ethos,* and *mythos.*

In order to make my argument clear, I would like to explain those four elements or functions as follows:

Logos

Logos is a noun form of *legein* (Greek) meaning: (1) to pick out, gather, reckon, and recount; and (2) to say, speak, affirm, and to declare.[1] Hence,

---

1. George Abbott-Smith, *A Manual Greek Lexicon of the New Testament,* 3rd ed. (Edinburgh: T. & T. Clark, 1950), p. 265.

logos has two corresponding meanings: word or speech and the thing behind word and speech. Greek philosophy was more interested in the latter.
For instance, Heraclitus (sixth to fifth centuries B.C.) thought that "God is
the universal Reason *(logos),* the universal law immanent in all things,
binding all things into a unity and determining the constant change in the
universe according to universal law."[2] Plato speaks of the Divine Reason
(Demiurge–World Soul), which he sometimes called the Mind of God.[3]
The identification of *logos* with the divine is strengthened in Stoicism, a
popular philosophical school originated by Zeno (336-264 B.C.). According to Stoicism, "God is therefore, *ho logos,* the Active Principle which contains within itself the active forms of all the things that are to be, these
forms being the *logoi spermaticoi* (λόγοι σπερματικοί)."[4] *Logos* here is
rather to be understood as a working principle or law of things that happened rather than words spoken or written. *Logos* in the Jewish-Hellenistic
philosophy is understood as a working principle between God and man
and personified as the *logos* who is a mediator between God and man.
"The *Logos* is spoken of as the first-born of God, being πρεσβύτατος καὶ
γενικώτατος τῶν ὅσα γέγονε."[5] To a certain degree, the Jewish-Hellenistic
concept of *logos* influenced John the evangelist, and the concept from old
Greek philosophy has played a formative role in the concept of reason in
European philosophy further illustrated later in this article.

In Neoplatonism, reason *(logos)* is identified with *"nous"* (sometimes
translated "reason") and is treated as the second stage of its triadic system
(theory of emanation). Reason is not valued as important as the One ("to
hen"). Among the early Christian fathers, Tertullian particularly in some
of his moods passionately rejects reason, denouncing Greek philosophy as
the bridal gift of the fallen angels to the daughters of men and Greek philosophers as the patriarchs of the heretics.[6] But in general terms, the traditional Christian view asserts that a rational understanding of the world is
attainable, but only through the guidance of divine revelation. Augustine
furthered this idea by placing reason under the guidance of grace or revelation. He affirmed this position by saying: *"credo ut intelligam"* ("I believe
in order to understand"). John Scotus Erigena and Anselm, writing in the

2. F. Copleston, *A History of Philosophy,* vol. 1 (London: Search Press, 1946), p. 43.
3. Copleston, *A History of Philosophy,* p. 193.
4. Copleston, *A History of Philosophy,* p. 389.
5. Copleston, *A History of Philosophy,* p. 459. "The eldest and principal of all beings."
6. Alan Richardson, *Christian Apologetics* (London: SCM Press, 1947), p. 228.

early Middle Ages, treated reason as being as important as faith. According to Scotus, humanity has moved through three successive states with regard to truth: between original sin and the coming of Christ, reason was clouded by the consequences of error; from the event of Christ, reason is ready to accept the truth that God reveals to it in Holy Writ. Faith must now precede the exercise of reason and explore it rationally.[7] Anselm follows a similar train of thought in understanding the relationship between faith and reason by saying: one does not understand in order to believe, but on the contrary, one believes in order to understand *("neque enim quaero intelligere ut credam, sed credo ut intelligam")*.[8] According to Anselm, the order to be observed in the search for truth is therefore the following: first, believe the mysteries of faith before discussing them through reason; next, endeavor to understand what one believes. Not to put faith first is presumption; not to appeal to reason next is negligence. Both errors must therefore be avoided.[9]

There is another view in which Greek philosophy and Jewish law are understood as *"preparatio evangelica."* Clement of Alexandria was the forerunner of medieval scholasticism in this sense. Abelard, for instance, held that what had been revealed to the Jews by prophecy had been given to the Greeks by philosophy and that the doctrine of the Trinity had been taught by Heraclitus and Plato. According to C. C. J. Webb, Abelard began a process of rationalism in theology which culminated in Kant's attempt to confine "religion within the limits of the mere reason."[10] This trend has strongly influenced Heidegger and Bultmann, who treated reason as the main source and authority for making judgments on whether things are true or false, even whether there is a God or not. At the bottom of modern liberalism in theology and rationalism in philosophy, reason is the crown prince of all knowledge.

7. Etienne Gilson, *History of Christian Philosophy in the Middle Ages* (New York: Random House, 1955), p. 113. In the third state faith will disappear and be replaced by direct sight of Truth.

8. Anselm, *Proslogium* 1, 227; Gilson, *History of Christian Philosophy in the Middle Ages*, p. 129.

9. Anselm, *Proslogium* 1, 227; *Cur Deus Homo* 1, 2, 362.

10. C. C. J. Webb, *Studies in the History of Natural Theology* (Oxford: Clarendon Press, 1915), p. 231; quoted in Richardson, *Christian Apologetics*, p. 229.

Pathos

"πάθος," noun form of "πάσχω-πάσχειν," is translated in Latin *"passio,"* in English "passion," and in German *"Leidenschaft."* Aristotle included "πάθος" in his *"Organon"* and "πάσχειν" as one of the ten categories. In Christianity, particularly in medieval Christianity, passion was used in connection with the death of Christ as the substitutionary death for humankind. The meaning of the passion of Christ was emphasized and praised, adored, extolled, and glorified through music, paintings, and dramas. However, passion was treated for the first time philosophically by Descartes as a counterpart of volition which constitutes the world of human thought. According to him, "we may define them (passions) generally as the perceptions, feelings or emotions of the soul which we relate specially to it and which are caused, maintained and fortified by some movement of the spirits."[11] The passions, says Descartes, are "all good in their nature, but they can be misused, and they can be allowed to grow to excess." He warns of the danger of passion when it is not under control by spirit. "Because the passions can bring us to any kind of action only by the intervention of the desire which they excite, it is this desire especially which we should be careful to regulate, and it is in this that the principal use of morality consists."[12] In conclusion, Descartes affirmed the existence of two different types of substance, spiritual and material. In this sense of the word, he can be called a dualist, and he placed passion on the side of spiritual existence. By doing so, he treated passion as one of the important spheres of being human.

There are abundant illustrations, both tragic and happy, caused by excessive use of *pathos,* as Descartes warns. Marcus Antony's suicide (30 B.C.) upon hearing a false rumor of his lover, Cleopatra's, death; Emperor Nero's (supposed) setting fire to Rome in order to indulge his aesthetic tastes in its reconstruction both represent tragic excess of pathos; happy incidents include Hildebrand's antagonism against King Henry IV; Zinzendorf's *Herrnhut* project for persecuted Brethren; and Kagawa Toyohiko's Shinkawa slums project. All these events were good or bad ex-

---

11. R. Descartes, *Passions of the Soul,* 1, 2, quoted by Copleston, *A History of Philosophy,* vol. 4, p. 143.

12. Descartes, *Passions of the Soul,* 2, in Copleston, *A History of Philosophy,* vol. 4, p. 144.

amples and were brought about by the power of *pathos* innate in all human beings.

The majority of modern intellectuals feel uneasy with a modern culture dominated by militarism, racism, pollution, materialism, and alienation of all ideal human relationships. In the midst of such a secular, materialistic, and sexual culture, there is a strong desire to regain a more valuable society constructed by the motivations of love, compassion, and altruism so beautifully demonstrated by Tolstoy, Schweitzer, and Mother Teresa. Thus there is clear evidence that there is the second sphere of life of mankind which has been shown throughout the centuries.

Ethos

It is a generally accepted theory that humankind is naturally and substantially different from animals because humankind has by nature reason, affection, imagination, and wisdom. In addition, humans are able to make value judgments concerning things occurring around them and their own actions. Greeks called this value judgment *"ethos,"* which originally meant custom and which brings happiness, virtue, and wisdom (Socrates). Therefore, any conduct contrary to that which establishes happiness, virtue, and wisdom is not good conduct and is to be avoided.

Humankind has produced many sets of ethical teachings: the Code of Hammurabi, the oldest known set of moral teachings, originated in the seventeenth century B.C. in Babylon; the Torah in Israel in the fifteenth century B.C.; the Tao-teh-king, in which old Chinese metaphysics, ethics, and political theories were included, by Lao-tse in the sixth century B.C.; the *Shiking, Chuntsiu,* and *Yihking* by Confucius in the fifth century B.C.[13] Hinduism in India also has very old and valuable religious and ethical teachings called *The Hymns of the Rig-Veda* and the *Upanishads,* which constitute the last part of the *Rig-Veda* writings. Buddhism, the predominant religion of China, Korea, and Japan for more than fifteen centuries, is divided into two schools, the "Great Vehicle" and the "Little Vehicle." Both schools contain deep thought and well-systematized ethical codes.

A very carefully systematized ethical theory is found in Aristotle's

---

13. Four additional books were written or compiled by the disciples of Confucius.

Nicomachean Ethics named for his son, Nicomachus. Kant, the most significant ethicist in the Western world since Aristotle, made several important contributions to philosophical and moral sciences. He brought about a Copernican revolution in the field of epistemology through his critique of reason, postulation of the existence of God, acknowledgment of *"Ding an sich,"* and the assertion of the importance of the categorical imperative in the field of ethics.

Let us now turn our attention to Oriental or Asian writers on the question of ethical and philosophical teachings. After the death of Lao-tse, one of the oldest sages in China, his disciples compiled a book called Tao-teh-king which consists of two parts, entitled Tao and Teh, and has been divided by commentators into eighty-one short chapters. The first part is predominantly metaphysical, therefore often religious, and the second ethical and political. Tao is literally "way," and corresponds to words in many languages such as course, method, order, and norm. In Confucian literature, the word is used to designate "the way of Heaven," especially in its dealing with men and the moral order of the world. So, says Confucius, "If I hear the way in the morning, I would be very happy even if I die in the evening."

In the second part of Tao-teh-king, we can find the fundamental principle of ethics. Heaven and earth endure because they do not live of, or for, themselves. Nor are they prompted by benevolence: they treat all things like grass-dogs. This understanding of the universe is the norm for man, and should be made the inner law of his life from which conduct spontaneously flows. Then he not only *knows* the Tao, but *has* it; the cosmic principle is an ethical principle in him; his life is nature. This is the foundation of Taoist ethics and politics, which form the subject of the second part of the Tao-teh-king. In short, man should live like a baby, without ambition or a desire for wealth and fame; rather he should do nothing for achievement, but follow the natural order of life, which scholars call Wu-wei or quietism.[14]

Lao-tse's contemporary, Confucius, took a distinctively opposite direction regarding ethical teachings. He compiled the old Chinese literature sources and edited them. They are known as Shiking, Chuntsiu, and Yihking. In the school of Confucianism, four more "Books" came about which are treated as the standard teachings for those who want to become

14. G. F. Moore, *Studies in the History of Religion* (New York: Macmillan, 1912), p. 54.

learned and respected. They are called Non-uh, Meng-ja, Jung-yong, and Dehak in Korean.

The original and standard teachings of Confucianism, whether philosophical or religious, concern ethical teachings. There are countless commentaries and writings developed from them throughout the centuries. Confucius was not a speculative thinker; the problems of the origin of the universe, the nature of being, the one and the many, which engaged Lao-tse and the early philosophers of Greece, lay beyond the horizon of his mind. He was interested in the practical matters related to daily life. To him, God was essentially the moral order of the world, an impersonal being, often called Shang-ti, an order energizing the phenomena of nature as well as the course of history and the destiny of individual life.[15]

In this part, I have tried to show and explain that an ethical component was and is one of the dominant elements since humans adopted a communal lifestyle.

Mythos

According to Cornford, there is an inseparable relation and striking affinity between philosophy and mythology in the world of thought in Europe. Philosophy inherited from mythology and religion certain great conceptions — for instance, the idea of God, soul, destiny, law — which continued to circumscribe the movement of rational thought and determine its main directions. When we compare religion with philosophy, the former expresses itself in poetical symbols and mythical personalities, whereas the latter prefers the language of dry abstraction, and speaks of substance, cause, matter, and so forth.[16] Here we can find the fact that philosophy, therefore the *logos,* depended, and derived from mythology. The *mythos,* and more directly, mythology and the mythological worldview, is older than any philosophical worldview.

Since we have already examined how *logos,* reason, and philosophy have played an important role in our life and thought, let us now turn to

15. Moore, *Studies in the History of Religion,* p. 35. Mencius was a disciple of Ja-shi, grandson of Confucius. Mencius accepted most of Confucius' teachings and advocated the ethical ability of mankind and goodness of human nature.

16. F. M. Cornford, *From Religion to Philosophy* (New York: Harper & Row, 1957), Preface.

the world of *mythos* — mythology and the mythological worldview. There are abundant materials from which to choose mythological stories, but let us choose for our purpose one from Taoism.

Tao-teh-king is believed to be the collection of Lao-tse's teachings compiled at a much later time by his disciples and their followers. A key section explaining the purpose of life is found in the twenty-fifth chapter of the Tao-teh-king: "There was a Something, undifferentiated and yet perfect, before heaven and earth came into being. So still, so incorporeal. It alone abides and changes not. It pervades all, but is not endangered. It may be regarded as the mother of all things. I know not its name: if I must designate it, I call it Tao. Striving to give it a name, I call it great: great, I call it transcending: transcending, I call it far off: far off, I call it returning. . . . Man takes his norm from earth; earth from heaven; heaven from Tao; the Tao from itself."[17]

Confucianism exhorts one to hard effort to achieve a better life, better results, and a better reputation, but Taoism teaches the same purpose and accomplishment without exerting effort. It is the way of Heaven not to strive, yet it overcomes. It produces and sustains all, yet claims nothing for itself. Heaven and Earth endure because they do not live of, or for, themselves. This method of the universe is the norm for humankind. People should not merely take it as an example and pattern their conduct after it; they should make it the inner law of life, from which conduct spontaneously flows. Then they not only know the Tao, but have it. Thus, the cornerstone of Taoism is the doctrine of "not doing," inaction. In the depths of the Chinese philosophy of life and the world, there are two dominating currents: strong ethical teaching and strong not-doing-yet-overcoming-everything: Confucianism on one hand and Taoism on the other.

2. Our Findings

In the foregoing pages I have tried to explain the fact that there are four prevalent factors in the entire life of human beings regardless of race, tribes, countries, and civilization. They are human functions, activities, interests, and achievements established by *logos, pathos, ethos,* and *mythos* in all of human life. There are, however, some differences of interest, ability,

17. Moore, *Studies in the History of Religion*, p. 50.

and peculiarity according to individuals, societies, and groups of people and religions. In European history the dominant force of the development of civilization from the beginning is the logos motive.

Pathos, the second function or element of being human, has had an immeasurable influence on human history; we can say without reservation that all tragedies from Cain to Hitler were instigated, propelled, and driven by the impulse of pathos. When it is regulated by the power of *logos* and *ethos* it can bring about benevolent results, but when it is accelerated by an ill-motivated impulse of pathos, inescapable misfortune comes to us. This is the reason why Asian moralists and religionists teach that the most important thing for a happy, meaningful, and worthy life is to restrain oneself in order to obtain virtue leading to salvation or an enlightened world. They encourage one to follow the course of a hermit, whereas in Europe knowledge is more venerated.

As we have mentioned in the foregoing pages, there are two traditional teachings in China and Korea: Confucianism and Taoism. They represent two opposite schools of thought, Confucianism representing moralism, Taoism the way of mystics. The majority of Chinese and Koreans accept both teachings without hesitation and feel comfortable. While their teachings apparently conflict, the one emphasizing an ethical course of life and the other a reserved life or "doing nothing," at the bottom of their thought the two schools recognize the possibility of coexistence. Confucianism exhorts moral life for individuals and the nation, whereas Taoism has more interest in the individual obtaining the state of enlightenment before taking part in society as a leader. Herein is the main reason for the coexistence of these two teachings in China and Korea.

3. The Christian Message to the Contemporary World

There are many similarities between Christianity and other religions in their cardinal teachings, and therefore scholars of religious studies treat Christianity as one of the world's religions. However, after close examination, we can hardly deny or overlook the distinctive and peculiar nature that Christianity has maintained from the beginning. Three points in particular can be made:

a. All religions have their own creation stories and stories of divine beings with lives very similar to human life. Many gods and goddesses

marry each other and give birth to children. For instance, the twelve
Olympians made up a divine family. Zeus, the chief among the gods, drew
lots to apportion to each a share of the universe. The sea fell to Poseidon,
and the underworld to Hades. Zeus became the supreme ruler. He himself
is a son of Chronus. Stories about gods and the creation of humanity and
the universe described in other mythologies follow similar patterns.

Christianity too has a mythological description concerning the creation of the universe and the origin of humanity, but its contents are so
distinctive that they cannot be compared with other religious mythologies. In particular, the kingdom of Christ to be established after the Second Coming may be described mythologically. However, its nature is
completely different from other stories because it is the outcome, or historical conclusion, of the kingdom of God inaugurated on earth by Jesus
Christ through his incarnation. From the above observation, the fundamental difference between the Christian creation story and that of other
religions is that the mythological descriptions of other religions are ad-
aptations of human life and community, whereas the Christian
worldview is entirely dependent on what Yahweh God revealed and ex-
plained to us. In short, mythological descriptions of other religions are
the products of human experience and thought whereas Christian stories are given by God.

b. There are many man-made Creators of the universe, such as Zeus
in Greek mythology, Marduk in Babylonian mythology, Tao in Taoism,
Summum Bonum in Plato, and the One ("to hen") in Plotinus — all these
gods or supreme beings are without either ethical quality or ontological
foundation, but all are the products of human thought. By contrast, Christians believe in Yahweh, who is self-existent (Exodus 3:14), infinite in every
respect (Psalms 90:2; 102:12; Ephesians 3:21), immutable (Exodus 3:14;
Isaiah 41:4; Romans 1:23; Hebrews 1:11-12), and above all the only one
God (1 Kings 8:60; 1 Corinthians 8:6; Deuteronomy 6:4). If there are two
or more gods, none of them is absolute because this is a logical contradiction. Moreover, Yahweh God is ethically the final ground toward which all
ethical teachings and systems strive.

c. There are four spheres of human activities by which philosophy,
ethics, art, science, politics, and religions are formulated. They are the areas of *logos, pathos, ethos,* and *mythos.* Most philosophical schools, religions, sciences, educators, and mystics adopt and expand one or two of
them. For instance, Plato was very interested in the world of *mythos* and *lo-*

gos but not in *ethos;* Aristotle spent much of his time and energy formulating logic (philosophy) and ethics *(ethos)* but was almost ignorant about *mythos.* Confucius on ethics *(ethos)*, Lao-tse on mythos (mythos), Thomas Aquinas on dogmatics *(logos)*, Hinduism on the gods' world *(mythos)*, Islam on militant faith *(pathos)*, capitalism on worldly welfare *(pathos)*, and Communism on world rule by their ideal *(pathos* and *mythos)* — all exhibit this imbalance. Because of their one-sidedness or partial interest, their achievements did not or will not last long. Christianity, on the other hand, contains and concerns all four spheres, as well as their functions focused on the fulfillment of the will of God. Not all theologians and church leaders followed the same steps, but the most influential and admired leaders diligently and earnestly worked hard to imitate the life of Christ, in whom all four elements of life were well represented. Augustine was a man of *logos, ethos, pathos,* and *mythos.* The mythological aspect of his concern is beautifully described in the *Confessions* (IX, 10). Luther, Calvin, and Wesley also followed the same path.

However, Protestant orthodoxy and the Reformed tradition were interested more in the Bible (literally), and creedal statements of faith and apologetics. Accordingly, they succeeded in formulating the classical Protestant orthodoxy (Protestant scholasticism) in which ethics and eschatology were given a low profile. It is my understanding that the Bible teaches and clearly describes the four spheres in which human beings have existed throughout the centuries. The main reason for the success of Christian missionary work is the fact that missionaries presented the Christian message, not primarily via deep thought and well-systematized dogma or doctrines, but through the very simple message that Jesus Christ is the only savior of humankind and that those who believe in him will be saved and enter into the kingdom of God. But for the last four centuries, European churches have been more interested in the establishment of Christian civilization and the cultivation of human ability through which they intend to solve the problems of all time. As a result, in the twentieth century the European churches face rapid decline. While European theology is enjoying itself, it is intoxicated with logical speculation and academic achievement and has lost the vitality of the gospel and the hope for the ideal future life in the kingdom of God. The Bible as a whole and Jesus himself together with all the biblical writers emphatically, repeatedly, and picturesquely assure us that "Behold, the dwelling of God is with men, He will dwell with them, and they shall be his people and God himself will be with them; he will wipe away every tear from their eyes, and death shall be no more" (Revelation 21:3-4). In the twenty-first century, those Third World churches in which the movement of the Holy Spirit is very active will radiate forth the light of hope.

The True Subject of Christian Theology

GERHARD SAUTER

In order to characterize the subject matter of Christian theology, I propose, we have to name the decisive *characteristics* which make it possible to decide whether an assumption or argument fits with the constitution of Christian theology and draws attention to this constitution. That is, we discover the subject of theology in the sense of the reality, which gives form to theology and to doing theology.

"Subject" then does not imply the submission of theology to some philosophical or scientific definition of subjects, nor does it signify any matter of fact which could be described and established independently, and then serve as a "foundation" of theology. To avoid such a misunderstanding, I prefer the word "character" instead of "subject matter"; the character of theology is a profile or feature which cannot be mistaken for anything else and which enables us to recognize theology. You can compare it to the physiognomy of a person: A photograph may reproduce most of the details and yet it may miss the character. Conversely, a good artist is able to hit the point with a few lines, to draw the person, so that we can immediately recognize the face. In this respect, a good portrait is superior to any photograph, because the *coherence* of the lines is pointed out, the connections, which give *life* to the picture.

The physiognomy of theology is characterized by the being, self-manifestation, and action of God. To put it slightly differently: it is characterized by the theological answer to the questions: *"Who is God, that we might pray to him?"* — *"How does God address us, how do we encounter God?"* — *"Who are we in relation to God?"*

176

Theology is no recollection of dogmatical statements, but a vital body of language, rather an example of what Thomas Kuhn calls "normal science."[1] As with other sciences, theology is characterized by a constellation, a certain recurrent structure of words and objects. We have to draw this structure with a few statements in order to recognize it again and again in different circumstances and in different verbal sequences. We can demonstrate this by three paradigmatic answers to those fundamental questions stated above. These answers are related to the epoch-making approaches to the perception of the subject of theology. The first question "Who is God?" has been authoritative as a starting point for theology as talk of God in the Ancient Church.

The doctrine of the Trinity answers this first question and characterizes Christian talk of God as following God's coming: God is the Triune Identity,[2] Jesus Christ is God's self-manifestation — God in Christ, and as Spirit, God acts upon us and in us. We can discern the divinity of God — God *as God* — only by his self-manifestation (and in this sense, his revelation). On the other hand, it is impossible simply to *identify* God with the revelation and action of God — God acts in the creation, the reconciliation, and the consummation, and God manifests himself in *each* of these actions as Father, Son, and Spirit. God is One — and we can perceive and confess that God is One only from within that movement. This movement does not enable anyone to draw up a protocol; that is, to describe it from a distance.

We may use concepts to explain God's being, e.g., simplicity, but God will use these concepts in God's own way and thus say God's own word, breaking through all human knowledge of God. It is important that God uses our knowledge of God as a background for new insights which cannot be known in advance. But it is equally important for us not to stick to any such insight and then unfold its implications. A good example of such a wrong use of our knowledge of God may be Arian theology, stressing God's transcendence and eternity and oneness, which implies that the Word of God cannot be strictly divine. The doctrine of the Trinity leads us to a surprising modification of terms such as "eternity," "simplicity," and "immutability" — as soon as we ourselves are involved in God's movement.

1. Thomas S. Kuhn, *The Structure of Scientific Revolutions* (Chicago: University of Chicago Press, 1970).
2. Cf. Robert W. Jenson, *The Triune Identity* (Philadelphia: Fortress Press, 1982).

The second question reads: "How do we encounter God?" Thomas Aquinas has attempted to answer it. He explicitly discusses the subject of theology — *subiectum theologiae* — at a time confused by radical changes and disorientation. In the beginning of his *Summa Theologiae,* he introduces the "holy doctrine" as science *(scientia)* and asks whether or not God is the *subiectum* of this science.[3] Thomas rules out any philosophical definition of God's divinity, because God remains unutterable. God has disclosed himself in the creation, in the relation to God which characterizes all that is. Every creature is related to God and can therefore be articulated theologically. Three aspects of this determination are remarkable: (1) Thomas uses the term "subject," although he knows that God must not be mistaken for any given fact. Such a mistake is excluded (2) by the distinction between God and his creation. God makes this distinction by becoming objective in the world: the whole world is related to the Creator, and this relation discloses the distinction as well. It is (3) revealed by God — it is impossible for us to infer it. To discern the inner unity of the world, we need the articles of faith, a knowledge given by God; these articles are the principles of theological science.

Thomas seems simply to advance traditional authorities. The microstructure of his argumentations, however, shows a confrontation between metaphysical insights and biblical statements: a confrontation which articulates the world pervaded by God, but no theological reinterpretation of metaphysics. In this respect, the *Summa Theologiae* might be a standard even today.

It is necessary to examine whether Thomas sometimes simply draws conclusions concerning God from the given world. But apart from that point, the complexity claimed for theology is important. This complexity is based upon the fact that theology has to talk about God without being able to comprehend God — which holds especially for theological language. Theology as a science now gains a dramatic character. At the same time, theology is realistic: it has nothing to produce, and certainly nothing to produce by any stylistic charm. All this can be seen in the *Summa,* although it may seem dry and doctrinal.

3. Thomas Aquinas, *Summa Theologiae* I q.1 a.7 i. c.: "Illud est subiectum scientiae, de quo principaliter fit sermo in scientia. Sed in hac scientia principaliter fit sermo de Deo (dicitur enim theologia, quasi sermo de Deo). — Respondeo dicendum quod Deus est subiectum huius scientiae. [. . .] Quod etiam manifestum fit ex principiis huius scientiae, quae sunt articuli fidei, quae est de Deo: idem autem est subiectum principiorum et totius scientiae, cum tota scientia virtute contineatur in principiis."

Martin Luther has given an answer to the third question: "Who are we in relation to God?" Luther's terms may lead us to a concept of subject which avoids the difference between theology and medieval humanities. Theology and its subject may be *characterized* as the "In-Between" of God and humanity. The human being as part of the subject matter of theology is neither the person who has certain privileges (the subject matter of jurisprudence) nor the sick (as for medicine). Luther uses the scholastic concept of subject matter, but his characterization of theology modifies that concept: "The characteristic subject of theology is humanity who is guilty of sin and condemned, and God who justifies and saves sinful humanity. Whatever is asked or discussed outside this subject in theology is a misconception and poison."[4]

Of course, Luther does not want to assert that theology talks only and exclusively about the sinner and God the Savior who gives us his justice. The point of his determination is that true knowledge of human personality depends on a personal unity which God creates and addresses, and that true knowledge of God is constituted together with personal passion of God's acting towards us as Judge and Savior. We cannot talk of God in himself or human personality *as such*, nor about the relation of God and humanity, rather we can speak of the happening we are involved in, that God justifies and saves the person, whom we can perceive only and exclusively under God's judgment and promise of justification and salvation. John Calvin agrees with Luther in the beginning of the *Institutio* (I.1,1-2), when he underscores the insolvable connection between knowledge of God and self-knowledge.

What can we learn from these three sketches? The character of theology is outlined by *fundamental statements of theology*, which are related to each other and form a certain structure. We may call these statements *axioms* because it is not possible to get behind them; to give arguments in support of them already implies a misunderstanding. They are presupposed in all further statements of theology. The doctrine of the Trinity and

---

4. *Commentary on Psalm 51* (1532, printed 1538) in *Luther's Works*, American edition, 55 vols., ed. J. Pelikan and H. T. Lehmann (St. Louis and Philadelphia: Concordia and Fortress, 1955ff.), vol. 12, p. 311. — *Luthers Werke*, Kritische Gesamtausgabe, 66 vols. ed. J. K. F. Knaake et al. (Weimar: Böhlau, 1883ff.), 40/II, 328.17-20: "Nam Theologiae proprium subiectum est homo peccati reus ac perditus et Deus iustificans ac salvator hominis peccatoris. Quicquid extra hoc subiectum in Theologia quaeritur aut disputatur, est error et venenum."

Luther's description of the subject of theology have such an axiomatical character. Their quintessence is: God has acted and promised to involve us in his history with humanity. This — and nothing else — is the starting-point for Christian theology — and its certainty full of hope.

Axioms connect terms which are fundamental for a science. The axiomatic structure of theology, therefore, enables us to prove statements theologically. At the same time, this structure may be compared to other sciences, in order to discover parallels and characteristic differences.

The *first* parallel: *axioms are statements.* They outline the possibilities of theological arguments. At the same time, therefore, they mark the limits of language. In a certain sense, they are the borderline between language and reality. Insights and intuitive perceptions may "tune in" from beyond these limits. Axioms confront language with nonlinguistic reality — they force us to take into account the problem of "word and object" (Willard van Orman Quine): a fundamental problem for the philosophy of language and for philosophy of science as well. The discussion at this point has been extremely productive for the basic research in recent physics; the examination of the role of axioms in this context sheds light on the revolutions characterizing the history of science. This has been demonstrated by Thomas S. Kuhn and — with regard to the philosophy of language — by Hilary Putnam.

Alfred North Whitehead wants to distinguish between the immediate relation to reality and the reference of language — without deriving reference from basic experience. The distinction is rather meant to draw attention to the limits of language. Thomas Kuhn points out that axioms constitute reality for us — in contrast to the naive but still widespread idea of immediate sense data as the last resort for truth and reference. Of course, axioms do not constitute reality without what Hilary Putnam calls the "contribution of the environment."[5] Language, to be reliable, depends upon its environment. Reality has to "join in"; otherwise, language does not work and becomes useless and arbitrary. It is possible to argue for the absolutism of language, but language is the presupposition for perception, which depends on definable and irreversible connections of statements.

5. Hilary Putnam, *The Meaning of "Meaning"* in *Mind, Language, and Reality: Philosophical Papers*, vol. 2 (Cambridge/New York: Cambridge University Press, 1975), pp. 215-71.

The *second* parallel: *axioms indicate liability.* There are not only conventional answers to the question we ask. For us, axioms are the extreme tangents of reality itself. In this respect, they may be only relative, related to what they designate, but they are the constant framework for the further statements derived from them. Axioms enable us to find out the logical position of any single theological statement, to connect it to others and to formulate new hypothetical statements. Therefore, axioms are the starting-points for well-grounded argumentation, and they give perspective and depth to science.

Every science has axioms as *fundamental statements.* They differ essentially from intuitive insights — which may give important impulses for scientific discovery. Axioms contribute to a linguistic texture of correlated statements. The set of fundamental presuppositions records what appears irrefutable to every inquiry. Along these lines, Whitehead even talks of dogmas of physics: "In exactly the same way the dogmas of physical science are the attempts to formulate in precise terms the truths disclosed in the sense-perception of mankind."[6]

This indicates the point of comparison between sciences and, at the same time, the point where they may diverge characteristically. Axioms have a dogmatical status, because they define what is true. They do not, however, define truth as such. Nevertheless, they are the basis for further observations. Just for that reason we may call them dogmas, since a dogma is by no means an assertion which only claims to be valid.

As far as the truth of statements is concerned, dogmas and axioms have the same function.[7] Thomas Torrance seems to be right, therefore, when he reminds us of the fact that the term "dogma" formerly was not under the suspicion of a merely authoritative assertion. He writes: "Throughout the whole Church, in East and West, the emphasis upon *dogma* came to be upon well-grounded and agreed affirmation rather than arbitrary and individual opinion, and upon positive and constructive as opposed to skeptical or merely critical thought."[8] That was the use of the word in the writings of the Church Fathers: "In the strictest sense the doc-

6. Alfred North Whitehead, *Religion in the Making: Lowell Lectures 1926,* 3rd ed. (New York: Macmillan, 1927), p. 58.
7. John R. Carnes, *Axiomatics and Dogmatics* (New York/Belfast: Christian Journals, 1982).
8. Thomas F. Torrance, *Theological Science* (London/New York/Toronto: Oxford University Press, 1969), p. 339.

trine of the Holy Trinity is *theologia,* that is, theology in its purest form, the pure science of theology, or *episteme dogmatike*."[9]

Conversely, Michael Polanyi — as a contemporary scientist concerned with epistemological issues — uses religious or quasi-religious words, e.g., "belief," to characterize a kind of basic trust in reality.[10] Such a basic trust prevents the scientist from taking possession of reality rather than listening to its "self-explication," which the scientist cannot control as he controls scientific operations.

Of course, we have to consider the limits of the analogy. We do not propose to baptize scientific research. Conversely, faith is much more than a basic trust which agrees to given reality. The analogy between dogma and axiom also points to the divergence.

It is not possible to make one's choice concerning the axioms of theology in contrast to other sciences. In geometry you have to decide whether you accept the parallel postulate or whether you reject it. In the latter case, you have to replace Euclid's three-dimensional geometry. This was Albert Einstein's decision, which led him to the theory of relativity. This decision, however, does not affect everyday geometry. But in the framework of relativist physics, the new set of axioms is obligatory. You may choose the rule, but then you have to follow the rule. To accept mathematical axioms implies that for mathematical operations any further inquiry concerning the historical or conventional genesis of the numerical system is superfluous. On the other hand, it is typical for axioms that they open up scientific operations. For example, biology defines life by a set of parameters which are fundamental for planning and realizing experiments in order to acquire empirical observations. Thus they may be corroborated, although it is not possible to verify them by an experiment. The scientist who does not accept the axioms of biology does not make an arbitrary decision, but simply denies the possibility of the investigation of life. There may be reason for such a decision; science may be forced to modify or even to drop axioms. Such a decision, however, does not affect the validity of the axioms in relation to the knowledge discovered with the help of them.

9. Thomas F. Torrance, *The Ground and Grammar of Theology* (Charlottesville: University of Virginia Press, 1980), p. 158.

10. Michael Polanyi, *Personal Knowledge: Towards a Post-Critical Philosophy* (Chicago: University of Chicago Press, 1958), p. 271.

Why, though, is it impossible to make one's choice concerning the axioms of theology? There have been — and are today, especially in the United States — attempts to reject the doctrine of the Trinity. But can we learn from such rejections, for example from Friedrich Schleiermacher,[11] that they reject the axiomatic structure of theology characterized above and exchange it for another set of axioms — say, according to philosophy of religion — as Schleiermacher did?

Sciences are comparable because of their axiomatic structure, but they differ from each other in the microstructure of their axioms. The constitution of an axiom cannot be evident from the historical genesis of certain — though fundamental — insights.

Let us look to theology: The encounter with Jesus of Nazareth was overwhelming, because he preached God's coming and pointed to God's presence in his practice. The apostles' faith was confirmed at Easter; the cross on Golgotha had been a shock for them, but this shock was transfigured into the confidence that Jesus Christ remains present in their lives. All this does not exhaust the statements of Christian theology concerning God in Christ: the incarnation and the essential likeness of Jesus Christ and God. Another example: the Jews talk of God as Savior. It may be possible to trace back such a predicate to the experience of liberation in the Exodus — certainly a crucial event in the history of Israel and the Christian church and a starting-point for the narrative of liberation. But the narrative does not answer the question: Who is the subject, who acts, who enables us to tell a story which is more than fiction?[12]

A fact has been created: unexpectedly and surprisingly, contingent and not deducible from all former experiences and all of the expectations which sprang from these experiences. To articulate such a fact immediately implies God-talk, because such a fact implies God's self-manifestation. This articulation, therefore, gets a profile and makes it possible to recognize God in comparable situations. This is the outer surface of theological thought in the making: persons have to change their way of talking about God. Now they call God the Liberator — with respect to the Exodus — and they call God the Lord who acts in the life, death, and resurrection of Jesus.

11. Friedrich Schleiermacher, *Der christliche Glaube,* 2nd ed. (Berlin: G. Reimer, 1830/31). ET: *The Christian Faith,* ed. H. R. Mackintosh and J. S. Stewart (Philadelphia: Fortress Press, 1976).

12. Cf. Gerhard Sauter, *"Exodus" and "Liberation" as Theological Metaphors in Eschatological Rationality: Theological Issues in Focus* (Grand Rapids: Baker, 1996), pp. 27-53.

Such a talk of God essentially points to God and is totally dependent on God's coming and his presence, because it cannot establish itself. The physiognomy of Christian theology sketched above is a good illustration: it outlines the event which we can recognize as God's encounter with us, but it cannot prognosticate that event. It outlines a certain *movement*. Thus, the axioms of theology are constituted *dialectically*.

In order to comprehend this, let us start with the score, the possibility of all theological language. The question, whether and for what reason people talk of God, is answered by Christian theology with the twofold statement: we are not able to talk of God — we are forced to talk of God, we are not able to evade it. That is true even in the case of the man from whom Jesus demands faith and who cries, desperately and at the same time beside himself: "I believe, help my unbelief!" (Mark 9:24). Unbelief must not be mistaken for the subjective impossibility of faith, which implies that we have to take the risk of a jump into the faith. Unbelief is nothing other than sin — we have to remember Luther's definition. God-talk is completely pervaded by the dialectical movement of sin and grace, unbelief and faith, a movement which outlines the mystery of faith: a change of place wrenching us from our terrible self-reference, which even prevents us from discerning our sin. Luther has stated it bluntly: "And this is the reason why our theology is certain: it snatches us away from ourselves and places us outside ourselves, so that we do not depend on our own strength, conscience, experience, person, or works but depend on that which is outside ourselves, that is, on the promise and truth of God, which cannot deceive."[13]

The dialectics of faith rule out any subjective foundation of theology. The self, especially the self confessing "I believe," is not a fixed point of reality and certainly not the central point of the universe. At most, the self can discover tensions and polarities, a field and framework for interaction with reality. Dialectics, then, becomes reduced and twisted — a permanent transcendence and at the same time a search for the self.

After the acid-test of the scientific critique of knowledge, scientists and philosophers cannot follow such a movement of the self. "Self" and

13. Martin Luther, *Lectures on Galatians* (printed 1535), Galatians 4:6, in *Luthers Werke* 40/I: 589.25-28: "Atque haec est ratio, cur nostra Theologia certa sit: Quia rapit nos a nobis et ponit nos extra nos, ut non nitamur viribus, conscientia, sensu, persona, operibus nostris, sed eo nitamur, quod est extra nos, Hoc est, promissione et veritate Dei, quae fallere non potest."

"world" are related dialectically — an insight which essentially gets over the Cartesian vis-à-vis of subject and object which has been fatal for the notion of scientific discovery. Every single act of perception is a transitional moment in the stream of events summarized by the word "world." Each part of the world, then, can be fixed only approximately and coarsely (one thinks here of Albert Einstein and Werner Heisenberg).

All this certainly leaves behind a mere subjectivism and self-referential subjectivity, but it does not hit the mark as far as the movement of faith is concerned. This movement is limited by another dialectic which includes it. God takes humanity in Jesus Christ, accepts even death, enters the world without being absorbed. God becomes objective in the world, but that immediately implies the distinction between God and world. God transforms the cosmos, because the cosmos, including God, can no longer move itself and rest on itself. God's presence limits the cosmos, each time anew by God's revelation, which is characterized by the dialectical congruence of disclosure and concealment in the mystery of God's presence. God acts in God's *own* way: the revelation contradicts all human self-interpretations of the world, all projections which emerge when we read and shape the world in order to project our personality into the world. The divine contradiction, however, implies the possibility of recognizing and expecting God's presence, and at the same time implies that it is impossible to predict the encounter, to infer it from our interpretation of the world.

This dialectical movement points towards God's *essence*. Or rather: to the *necessity* of dialectical talk of God, which we cannot exceed, because God-talk is bound to God's *self*-manifestation, which dialectically ties together judgment and salvation. This is the ultimate dialectical structure of Christian theology and its statements concerning God the One, who alone unites what we cannot bring to a synthesis. This may be illustrated by the biblical attributes of God: power and love — justice and mercy. Of course, God is not simply erratic and unpredictable, but God's actions are different — in order to lead us to the ultimate unity, which essentially disappears as soon as we try to conceive it. To experience this unity implies the suspension of our split world of values — neither a synthesis nor a *complexio oppositorum*. The dialectical movement of our talk of God resists all attempts to conceptualize God, to define God as *omnitudo realitatis*, as the whole of reality. Einstein has put it in his way: "The Lord God is clever, but not tricky." We can read this sentence — in German! — in the lounge of the former Department of Physics at Princeton University.

185

The dialectical structure of God-talk takes us back to the starting-point, to the question: How can we talk of God? To address God, in complaint, request, petition, and thanks, moves us towards God's own movement into the world. Our language is not able to represent God, but it can give an outline and point to the traces of God's movements. The dialectics of theological language, then, is the movement of faith, so that we reach the point where we have to start. This belongs to the characteristics of dialectical structures, which must not be mistaken for the circular movements of the self-centered self.

Therefore, we find the ultimate and encompassing dialectics of theology as soon as we talk of God. This dialectical movement is *asymmetrical*: it is initiated by God and we are involved, but our part is no counterbalance. This dialectical asymmetry has been stated in Micah 6:8: "You have been told. . . ." Karl Barth was right, when he characterized the First Commandment as theological axiom.[14] God's word contradicts our monologues; we are made listeners, involved in an asymmetrical relation which is no dialogue, though we may answer and even address God as a friend.

Theology has to state what we must say "for God's sake," because we would have to be silent otherwise. To put it differently: theology states what we can keep secret only at a heavy price — the denial of God.

This is the testimony exacted from all who take over the task of theology. In theology we weigh the *price* of confessing or denying God. We have to follow God's distinction of what is essential for the faith and what has to be excluded. Theology cannot replace the testimony of faith, but it may be helpful if we have to *argue* for the faith. All the knowledge and all the experience in theological ways of thinking, acquired and corroborated over the centuries, may be helpful as soon as we articulate our faith, in order to *convince* other persons rather than to persuade them.

Doing theology, therefore, we must not exact less from ourselves than from all who confess "I believe." Moreover, we have to accept another task which belongs to our profession: we have to account for the answers to indismissable questions — and for answers which must be excluded because they produce fatal contradictions.

14. Karl Barth, *Das erste Gebot als theologisches Axiom* [1933], in *Theologische Fragen und Antworten: Gesammelte Vorträge*, vol. 3 (Zollikon: Evangelischer Verlag, 1957; 2nd ed., Zürich: Theologischer Verlag, 1986), pp. 127-43.

The question of the subject matter of theology is indismissable. Theologically, the question is answered by the set of axioms, so that the dialectical constitution of the axioms at once structures theology as a whole.

Theological statements define what we must say "for God's sake," because otherwise we would have to be silent. Therefore, certain other determinations of theology are excluded. For instance: theology cannot explain the world — otherwise theology will lose its character. Of course, in the history of Christian theology there *have* been many attempts to give a theological explanation of reality as a whole. But what was the price? Similarly, theology cannot answer the question of the true meaning of the world; it is not possible to connect meaningful experiences and actions in order to make theology a theory of meaningfulness.[15] All this concerned, theology must not take into account anything which might change its dialectical constitution and replace it by polarities or abstract relations. Otherwise, theology will be perfidious. Finally, we must exclude any ultimate foundation by human reason, which is intended to prove theological statements. Theology, then, will necessarily lose its own character, because it is integrated into some other set of axioms. This aspect is just the point where the axiomatic foundation of theology converges with the general discussion in the theory of science. Therefore, theology may enter this debate in a productive way.

15. Cf. Gerhard Sauter, *The Question of Meaning: A Theological and Philosophical Orientation,* trans. and ed. Geoffrey W. Bromiley (Grand Rapids: Eerdmans, 1995).

An Exegetical Analysis of 1 John 1:7

EDUARD SCHWEIZER

The blood of Jesus cleanses us from all.

1 JOHN 1:7

My wife and I have been guests of Princeton Theological Seminary so often that it has become, though in a transient way, time and again our home. The theme of this Festschrift "theology as servant of the church" is certainly well chosen as a characterization of this school and its president. I will try to reflect on this motto, looking at the New Testament and choosing the problem of a modern (or postmodern) proclamation of the expiatory sacrifice of Jesus as an example. Today, some declare that this is the absolute (perhaps, even the unique) center of the New Testament; others reject it as an obsolete atavism. May the New Testament help us to understand in what way the suffering and dying of Jesus "for our sake" touches, encourages, and warns our church today. And may my modest and short exegetical analysis give, at least, a bit of pleasure to the one who is honored by this Festschrift.

1. The Social Dimension of the Passion of Jesus

The first part of the gospel tradition, in which the story of Jesus has been told in a continuing sequence of episodes is, as far as we can see, the passion of Jesus.[1] This section is, from the beginning, remembered and told in biblical language. The main point in this statement is the fact that this is not a secondary result of proper theological reflection, but that it was done in the way as a matter of course. It went without saying that the words of scripture molded all remembrance of Jesus' suffering and death. In our earliest gospel, in Mark, there are still traces of this molding. In a natural way, he and his traditions speak of what happened to Jesus in the same way the Psalms have spoken of so many suffering righteous ones. There is only one verse (15:34: "My God, my God, why hast thou forsaken me?") which might be easily identified by the reader with Psalm 22:2 (RSV:1),[2] though Mark does not refer to the scripture. It is the formulation that Jesus took over in his last cry. It might also be that the report in 15:24 that the soldiers under the cross "divided his garments among them" reminded some readers of Psalm 22:19 (RSV:18). In all the other examples, the reference to the biblical texts is almost hidden.

This shows that Psalm 22 was a prominent part of scripture to evoke reflection on the passion of Jesus. Whereas Mark and Matthew report the "dividing of the garments" of Jesus, John goes further; in 19:23-24 he mentions the scriptures explicitly and quotes also the second half of Psalm 22:19. He therefore distinguishes the "tunic" (without seam, he adds) for which the soldiers "cast lots," from other garments, which they divided by "making four parts, one for each soldier." V. 8 (RSV:7) of the same Psalm 22 provides the phrase "wagging their heads" to Mark 15:29 (and Matthew 27:39). This phrase is lacking in Luke, but at the same place within the story of the crucifixion (Luke 23:35 parallel to Mark 15:29), he found in the very same verse 8 (7) of Psalm 22 the phrase "stood by watching" and "scoffed at him." Even more interesting is Psalm 69:22 (21): "They gave me gall for food and for my thirst they gave me vinegar to drink." It has probably influenced the form of Mark 15:36 (a bystander fills a sponge with "vinegar . . . and gave it to him to drink"). This is also told by Matthew in 27:48. He, however, read the Psalm verse totally and distinguished a first drink of "gall" in 27:34 from the second one of "vinegar" in 27:48. Surely, Mark also knew of a first drink (15:23), but he speaks of "wine mingled with myrrh," where the word "mingled with myrrh" might be due, at the

1. It is the only part, the structure of which is roughly the same in all four gospels.
2. I always quote the reference of the Hebrew text, though the Septuagint is more important.

most, to a vague reminiscence of Psalm 69:22. The background of Mark 14:18 might be Psalm 41:10 (9): "who ate of my bread," but only John (13:18) quotes it directly and defines it as a reference to the scriptures. The phrasing of Mark 14:34 is reminiscent of Psalm 42:6 (5), 12 (11), and 43:5, as we find it in the Septuagint.[3] Finally, Psalms 38:12 and 88:9 seem to have influenced the wording of Luke 23:49.

What in this meticulous (and a bit tiring) analysis is theologically important? I think that we learn by it that at a very early stage (the earliest perhaps), before any theological reflection arose (which started only in the later gospels), Jesus was seen as the one who fulfilled what the psalms illustrate. Primarily, this was not used at all as a proof of his messiahship. A very early part of the church detected that in the life and death of Jesus, God entered into solidarity with all the suffering righteous ones lamenting in the psalms, not understanding his way and shouting to or against him. Jesus consummates that long history of human misery, and in him God himself comes to every one who still suffers on earth.[4]

Result 1: God's love towards a suffering mankind has no end, not even in the most desperate situation. In Jesus it has become flesh. For the first narratives, this was an unreflected truth. Later theological reflection led to more detailed views, still focusing on God's unlimited solidarity with all suffering human beings.

2. Its Influence on Social Attitude

According to Mark's gospel, Jesus predicts his coming suffering and death three times (8:31; 9:31; 10:32-34). He does so three times in the context of a total misunderstanding on the part of his disciples of his way in lowliness (8:32: Peter; 9:32-34: the disciples fighting over who would be the greatest; 10:35-37: James and John desiring the best seats in heaven) and of his own call to a new structure of social life (8:33-37: losing one's life for the sake of others; 9:35-37: becoming servant of all; 10:42-44: "it shall not be so among you . . ."). The basis on which such a new life comes into being is "the Son of man . . . giv-

---

3. Omitted by Luke. John 12:27 shows, perhaps, the influence of the second verb *(syntarassein)*!

4. A man who was tortured in one of the South American prisons told us that everything broke down in his inner life except the knowledge that Jesus has been there too; it was only this knowledge that kept him throughout the night.

ing his life as a ransom for many" (10:45) or in the (probably more original)[5] version of Luke 22:27: Jesus "the one who serves." One could quote dozens and dozens of New Testament passages in which the message of Christ's suffering and death continues into a description of or a call to a new behavior towards all our fellow-people within and outside the church. One of the most appealing examples is, from my view, the very center of the first letter of Peter, around which the whole epistle revolves: 2:11–3:17,[6] surrounded by christological and ecclesiological statements showing from where all power, strength, and love flow. It is in the everyday actions of the "little ones" (Mark 9:42; Matthew 10:42; 18:6, 10, 14), of the church members no one pays attention to, of the slaves and the women, that the church lives as "the chosen race, the royal priesthood, the holy nation, God's own people declaring the wonderful deeds of the one who called us out of darkness into his marvelous light" (2:9)! And so it is, because "Christ also suffered for us, leaving us an example, that we should follow in his steps" (2:21).[7]

Result 2: Jesus' passion calls and enables his followers to create a new world with new, often inverted social structures.

3. "Ransom for Many"

"Ransom" has become, in a large way, a metaphor for "redemption." In the time of the New Testament, the original commercial situation has, long ago, been transgressed. Numbers 3:12-13 (cf. 8:17-18) speaks of the Levites as "ransom"[8] for all firstborn in Israel, who actually belong to God. This is

---

5. Cf. J. Roloff, "Anfänge der soteriologischen Deutung des Todes Jesu (Mk. X.45 und Lk. XXII.27)," *New Testament Studies* 19 (1972/73): 38ff.; *diakonein* means primarily "to serve at table," and this suits the situation after the meal in Luke 22 (cf. also 12:37!). According to John 13:2, Jesus washed the feet of his disciples, strangely enough, during or after the meal, not before it. This might be a reminiscence of an early tradition that Jesus was, after his last meal with his disciples, serving them.

6. Old-fashioned and obsolete in details, as it may be, its main message and its trend as a whole are most important, in modern times as always.

7. Cf. the exegesis of this passage in my commentary *Der erste Petrusbrief* (Züricher Bibelkommentare 1998 [in print]). The phrase "to follow in (his) steps" is also to be found in Philo (*Virtues* 64, using the same Greek words).

8. In the Greek text of the Old Testament, the same word is used as in Mark 10:45, though in the plural. For the idea that the blood of a martyr brings salvation to all generations in Israel, cf. Jubilees 7:35 (cf. also *Sibylline Oracles* 3:311-13).

certainly not a deal of a businessman in his trade. *God* elects a tribe in Israel to live closer to him than other tribes and redeems in this way all first-born. According to Luke 2:24 God accepts even "a pair of turtledoves" instead of the firstborn son (though he might be a son like Jesus!). A businessman acting like God would have to declare himself bankrupt very soon! Furthermore, the days of offerings are festival days full of joy in Judaism as in the Hellenistic world.

Result 3. A sacrifice is no payment to God; it is a sign given by God's grace, which reminds us of our shortcomings and helps us to express our gratefulness for God's unbelievable mercy.

4. The Blood of Christ

Many people today accuse Paul of having invented a blood-of-Christ theology. This is doubtless wrong.[9] On the contrary, if Paul has "invented" a new theological approach, it is a theology of reconciliation. This term appears eight times (noun and verb) in his undisputed letters and only there in the whole New Testament (Romans 5:10-11; 11:15; 2 Corinthians 5:18-19[10]). This is a term that has no roots in sacrificial language. It belongs to the diplomatic vocabulary of civil and military leaders who work for an agreement or an armistice with the opponent.[11] The area which the word covers is good and peaceful living with fellow beings. The background is the human striving for social betterment on a large scale. Paul uses it for God's relation to mankind, and exclusively so that *we* have to be reconciled, never God. When a pigheaded child runs away from its mother into the dark and cold garden, after a while, the mother goes to her scared and freezing child and reconciles it by inviting it back into the warm kitchen, asking, perhaps, whether it would not help her to bake the cake. She doesn't ask to be reconciled first; *she* is the reconciling part that solves the problem, exactly as God and God alone is reconciling us, not waiting for our attempts to reconcile with him (Isaiah 66:13, cf. 60:41).

9. The term "blood (of Christ)" is rather typical of the letter to the Hebrews and other post-Pauline writings.

10. In a general sense also in 1 Corinthians 7:11.

11. Cf. C. Breytenbach, "Versöhnung — eine Studie zur paulinischen Soteriologie," *WMANT* 60 (1989); also J. Blank and J. Verbick, eds., *Sühne and Versöhnung, Theologie zur Zeit*, vol. 1 (Düsseldorf: Patmos, 1986).

Wherever Paul speaks of the blood of Christ, it seems to be traditional language that he takes over. This is certainly true of the liturgy of the Lord's Supper (1 Corinthians 10:18; 11:25-27), but Romans 3:25; 5:9 seem to be traditional too. What is the origin of the term "blood" that occupies such a central place in the celebration of the Lord's Supper? According to Mark, Jesus said: "This is my body/This is my blood of the covenant" (14:22, 24), where the genitive "of the covenant" combined with "my (blood)" is rather awkward.[12] According to 1 Corinthians 11:24-25, the cup is not equivalent with the blood of Jesus, but with "the new covenant in my blood." I think that this formulation is closer to what Jesus pronounced on the last evening of his earthly life. It was written down about twenty years earlier than Mark wrote his formulation; and, accordingly, Mark's more parallelized version is suspect of being a further development[13] (cf. modern liturgies and already John 6:56). Be this as it may, both versions agree in describing the blood of Jesus as "the blood of the covenant." This is the language of Exodus 24:8-11: "Moses . . . threw the blood of the covenant . . . upon the people"; he ascends the mountain with "seventy elders," who "saw the God of Israel, and there was under his feet as it were a pavement of sapphire stone, like the very heaven." There "they beheld God, and ate and drank." Their experience was an eschatological experience, as it would not be given to any earthly being before the Last Day. Thus, the blood of the covenant was a kind of symbol or, rather, pledge of God for a truly new world coming to them. This linguistic origin is not the sphere of expiatory sacrifices, and this is also true for the paschal lamb.[14] The blood of the covenant is rather a symbol or pledge for an inviolable treaty, in which both parties declare: what happened to this animal shall happen to me if I ever break this covenant. To be sure, over time the idea of an expiation may also have be-

12. There was a long discussion of the problem whether such a double genitive ("the blood of me of the covenant") would be possible in Aramaic; it seems that some (rare!) examples of such a construction can be alleged (J. A. Emerton in *Journal of Theological Studies* 15 [1965]: 58-59).

13. This does not apply to its vocabulary ("for many" is, probably, older than "for you" in 1 Corinthians 11:24).

14. Its background is *"apotropaeic."* Even the lamb of Isaiah 53:7 = Acts 8:32, which is "led to the slaughter," is combined with the obviously equivalent metaphor of "the lamb before its shearer" (not including its death!). *Amnos* (Isaiah 53:7) is also used in John 1:29. Revelation 5:6 speaks of the "ram" or "(male) lamb" *(arnion)*.

come influential, but it shows, at least, that the meaning of a sacrifice that guarantees the stable faithfulness of God towards his covenanters is much larger and not limited to an expression of his expiation on grounds of an offering.

This agrees with the social context of 1 Corinthians 11. Such a context is already visible in the formulations of the words of institution themselves, which connect the *new covenant* with the cup, not the blood of Jesus. The covenant has created a new reality of social togetherness. This is the special emphasis of this report of the last supper of Jesus; its meaning focuses on the *present* gift of God for the life of the celebrating community. Paul urges his readers to correct their "unworthy manner" of "eating the Lord's Supper" — by "waiting for one another" (vv. 27, 20, 33). In no way does Paul accuse the Corinthians of any lack of high Christology or of sacramentalism. What was wrong with them was negligence in their treatment of their brothers and sisters. In Mark and Matthew, the emphasis lies rather on the death of Jesus (in the *past*) in which God covenanted to love us, long before we knew him. The additional verses in Luke (especially 22:16-18, cf. 22:30) underline the *future* fulfillment of eating and drinking at Jesus' table in his kingdom.

Result 4: The blood of Christ is expiatory, but also guarantees God's covenant and, therefore, urges and enables us to live as those who have been freed for a new life with God and with all our fellow Christians and fellow citizens. The words of institution of the Lord's Supper can be emphasized in very different ways.

5. Back to "the Blood Poured Out for Many" (Mark 14:24)

There is no doubt that the metaphor of expiatory sacrifice is to be found in several layers of the New Testament. It marks the central message of the New Testament, insofar as it proclaims the *"extra nos"* ("outside of us," as the Reformers stated) of God's action, which happened in a uniquely concrete way, not in a rhetoric of mediation, but in his Word that became flesh (John 1:14). That God is our salvation and our peace is the basis of all our faith and our belief. Our lives and our actions depend on his gracious gift, not on a reward for our works. However, this can become true for us and in us in the model of being healed by God's solidarity or enabled to start a different way of life, or of recognizing God's mercy in gratitude without end, or of enjoying the wellness of an authentic community around the table of the Lord.[15]

The very early (earliest?) creed in 1 Corinthians 15:3-5 is rooted in Judaism. It thinks in temporal (historical) terms of God's saving history *(Heilsgeschichte)*, focusing on the most urgent need of those who confess it: to be saved in the last judgment by forgiveness of our sins and to be resurrected to an eternally blessed life. The creed[16] in 1 Timothy 3:16, "confessed" by the church as "the mystery of our religion," is of Hellenistic-Christian origin, focusing on their most urgent need: earth and heaven, heaven and earth, earth and heaven[17] have come together again. This is what the small congregations of Jesus sang without fatigue, telling themselves and everybody who heard them: God is no longer far away in an unreachable paradise (as the Greek gods on Olympus), separated by a brazen sky, against which all prayers and all laments rebound. Hellenistic Christians might have been closer to modern Christians than to Jewish Christians who thought of sin in terms of moral shortcomings. They might have better understood what sin really is by experiencing the remoteness of God, the absence of God in their lives.

Result 5: Therefore, "the blood poured out for many" is our only salvation, indeed. But in what way this becomes true for us must by necessity be expressed, thought of, and practically experienced in modern language as the truth of today, which enters the totality of our lives — our brains as well as our bellies, and our will as well as our senses.

---

15. This is very rarely true in our celebrations of the Lord's Supper, where the people who communicate either usually come to the front of the church, one behind the other, or stand in a semicircle. Sitting around a table might be more important than we think.

16. It may have been a confessing hymn.

17. The structure a-b / b-a / a-b is also that of Proverbs 10:1-5, 26:6-10, and some other passages.

The Reconciliation of Mind:
A Theological Meditation upon the Teaching of St. Paul

THOMAS F. TORRANCE

In Christ all the fullness of God was pleased to dwell, and through him to reconcile to himself all things, whether on earth or in heaven, making peace by the blood of his cross. And you, who once were estranged and hostile in mind, doing evil deeds, he has now reconciled in his body of flesh by his death, in order to present you holy and blameless and irreproachable before him.

COLOSSIANS 1:19-22

I appeal to you therefore, brethren, by the mercies of God, to present your bodies as a living sacrifice, holy, acceptable unto God, which is your spiritual worship. Do not be conformed to this world but be transformed by the renewal of your mind, that you may prove what is the will of God, what is good and acceptable and perfect.

ROMANS 12:1-2

In these statements, St. Paul stressed the fact that we are alienated or estranged in our minds, and indeed are hostile in mind to God. This is a basic New Testament conception which was deeply resented by the rational culture of the ancient classical world of Greece and Rome, and which the rational culture of the medieval world and the rational, philosophical, and scientific culture of our modern world have found very difficult to accept. This applies not least to "evangelical Christianity" today, which on the whole still seems to work with what may be called an "unbaptized reason," for it does not seem to have thought through sufficiently the transformation of human reason in the light of the Word made flesh in Jesus Christ. Hence the *mind* of the church and the *mind* of society are not inwardly formed by the Gospel — they remain basically unevangelized. The reason for this is that we have not taken seriously this New Testament emphasis that the mind of man is alienated at its very root. It is in the human mind that sin is entrenched, and so it is right there, the Gospel tells us, that we require to be cleansed by the blood of Christ and to be healed and reconciled to God.

According to the teaching of the Bible, man has been created in mind as well as body out of nothing. We must not forget that a creaturely human mind has "being." This is a fact which, interestingly, our neurologists, brain-scientists and psychiatrists have been coming to recognize. Some of them speak of the mind as constituting a "fifth dimension," and others refer to the "ontology of mind." The mind is ontologically real — it has being. What they do not often recognize, however, is that it is deep in this mental being that our humanity is twisted and distorted, and indeed, to use Old Testament language echoed here by St. Paul, is "desperately wicked." We do not find in St. Paul, any more than in the Old Testament, any body/soul or body/mind dualism, for, as James Denney used to express it, man is the body of his soul and the soul of his body, or the body of his mind and the mind of his body, a unitary whole. It is as such that man has fallen and become alienated from God, and as such needs to be redeemed.

Now the mind of a human being constitutes what the Greeks called the *hegemonikon* or the governing principle, for it is the mind that governs or directs our behavior as human beings. Thus where modern people tend to refer to the will as the determining factor in human behavior, the Greek Fathers traced everything back to the mind. It is a mistake to think that they were not interested in the will and did not therefore stress the freedom of the will as modern people do, because they laid this emphasis upon the mind as the governing element in human nature. The Greek Fathers realized, however, as perhaps few people do today, that although we may have free will, we are not at all free to escape from our self-will. That is why they put their finger on the twisted state of affairs in the depths of the human mind. It is in the heart of our mental reality which governs and controls all our thinking and culture that we have become estranged from the truth and hostile to God. And it is right there, in the ontological depths of the human mind, that we desperately need to be redeemed and healed.

As I have indicated, the rational culture of the ancient classical world found this very difficult to accept, so that inevitably difficult problems arose whenever the Gospel began to take root and find expression in Greek life and thought. Thus we find cropping up fairly early within the church an insidious heresy that came to be known as "Apollinarianism." It took its name from Apollinaris, a very clever theologian, who refused to believe that in his Incarnation, the Son of God took upon himself our alienated, twisted mind, because it was in that mind that sin had become rooted and entrenched. If Jesus had taken our alienated mind upon himself, so argued Apollinaris, he must have been a sinner, in fact an original sinner. And so he held that the Son of God became incarnate in our human existence in such a way that in Jesus, the human mind was displaced by the divine mind. It was therefore some sort of neutral humanity that the Son of God assumed, and not the actual humanity in which we sinners all share.

However, the Fathers of the Church found this conception of the Incarnation to be evangelically and soteriologically deficient. If at that point, in the heart of our mental being, we are not redeemed and cleansed by the blood of Christ then we are not really saved at all. If in the fundamental controlling principle of our human mind, we are untouched by the Incarnation and the Atonement, then we are no better off than the pagan Greeks. And so the Christian church insisted that we must take very seriously the fact that in the Incarnation, the Holy Son of God assumed our fallen, enslaved human nature, our twisted, distorted, bent mind, *but* that in assuming it right from the very beginning, our Lord converted it, healed it, and sanctified it in himself. In taking from us our fallen human nature upon himself, instead of sinning in it as we all do, Jesus condemned sin in our carnal mind, and was himself wholly without sin. And so by living out a life of perfect holiness and purity in his mind, he sanctified and healed our human mind in the whole course of his incarnate and redemptive life from his birth to his crucifixion. He carried our mind into the very depths of his agonizing and atoning struggle on the Cross — he descended into the hell of the utmost wickedness and dereliction of the human mind under the judgment of God, in order to lay hold upon the very root of our sin and to redeem us from its stranglehold upon us. Yes, it was not only our actual sins, but it was original sin and original guilt that the Son of God took upon himself in Incarnation and Atonement, in order to heal, convert, and sanctify the human mind in himself and reconcile it to God.

There is extant a fragment of a second-century theologian, Irenaeus, which I like to think of in this connection. In it there seems to be a suggestion that the Incarnation may be understood in the light of the incident recorded in the Gospel when Jesus touched a leper, and, instead of becoming leprous himself, he healed the leper. In the western world today one hardly ever comes across a leper. I used to pass a leper colony when I went to school every day as a boy in China. That was long ago, but I have never forgotten the horrible emaciation of face and hand and limb in leprous flesh. If I sense what Irenaeus had in mind in that tantalizing fragment, it was that Jesus had taken what Irenaeus spoke of as our leprous humanity upon himself, but that instead of becoming a leper himself, he healed and transformed our "leprous" human nature and restored it to be like the flesh of a newborn child. But let us not forget that it was our diseased *mind* that our Lord assumed for our sakes. In assuming it, however, far from sinning himself or being estranged and alienated from the Father, even when he penetrated into the fearful depths of our alienation — "My God, my God, why have you forsaken me?" — he converted it from the very bottom of our disobedient human being, from the roots of our estranged mental existence, into perfect oneness with the mind of God — "Father, into thy hands I commend my spirit." In the Epistle to the Colossians, as in the Epistle to the Ephesians, St. Paul thought of that atoning reconciliation as embracing heaven as well as earth, for all things invisible as well as visible need to be cleansed by the blood of Christ and reconciled to God and even be renewed in "the spirit of our mind." Reconciliation in Christ applies to the invisible mental life of human being!

It was in order to conserve this biblical teaching that great Patristic theologians in the early church enunciated as a fundamental principle, *"The unassumed is the unhealed"* (Gregory of Nazianzus), or *"What Christ has not assumed has not been saved"* (Cyril of Alexandria). They reckoned that the Church would be soteriologically and evangelically deficient if it refused to take seriously that Christ took our fallen mind upon himself in order to redeem and save it. That is a truth which I first learned from my beloved Edinburgh teacher, H. R. Mackintosh, who had himself been profoundly influenced by the Christology of these Greek Fathers. But it was only when I studied Karl Barth's account of this doctrine that its truth broke in upon my mind in a quite unforgettable way. I refer to that section in the *Church Dogmatics* I.2, where Barth expounded the mystery of the Virgin Birth. Overwhelmed by the immense significance of what our Lord had done all for our sakes and in our place, I fell to the ground on my knees trembling in awe and wonder at the sheer miracle of God's grace in the birth, life, and passion of Jesus — the miracle that foul, wicked, depraved humanity, twisted in upon itself, had been appropriated from us by the Son of God, and been cleansed, changed, redeemed, and sanctified in him.

There we have to do with the inner heart of evangelical theology — the transforming of the human mind in such a way that it is no longer conformed to the patterns of this world but brought through renewal into conformity to Christ, through the communion of our mind with the mind of God in him, and its assimilation to the holiness and truth of God incarnate in Jesus. That is far from being easy, but it is something which fidelity to the Gospel will not allow us to avoid. It was because Karl Barth, for example, took this so seriously that he spent so much of his life thinking out in the light of God's self-revelation in Christ what the renewal of the human mind means, and what knowledge of the truth as it is in Jesus implies for the transformation of reason, intelligibility, and objectivity in Christian theology. Karl Barth was above all an evangelical theologian who spent his life in evangelizing the human reason, whereas the great majority of Protestant and Roman Catholic theologians still operate, I am afraid, with an unregenerated and unbaptized reason, and thus avoid the agonizing experience of working out conformity to Christ in the ontological depths of their minds.

Sometimes the inner conflict in which people find themselves can be very sharp, as I learned as soon as I began to teach Christian theology, so that I regularly made a point of alerting students to what was involved. I used to tell them about a friend of mine who went up to Basel to study music when I went there to study theology with Karl Barth. In those years before the war, there were two of the world's greatest musicians in Basel, Adolf Busch and Rudolf Serkin — it was with the latter that my friend Edgar wanted to take piano lessons. Serkin looked at his hands and asked how old he was. When he said that he was twenty-seven, Serkin shook his head and told him that he was too old for him to take on, and declined to enroll him. But Edgar hung about and when Serkin found that he had an unusually keen "understanding for music," he sent him to a friend in Salzburg who gave him exercises for six months on end, until the muscular functioning of his hands was transformed. I recall his talking to me afterwards about the drawn-out pain and agony of that experience. But it had been worth it, for when the muscles in his hands had been sufficiently restructured, Serkin at last took him on — and in due course Edgar became a distinguished musician, and indeed a composer, himself.

In recounting that story to my young students I used to say to them, "Something similar may well happen to you in these classes, for as you let the truth of the Gospel have its way with you, you will find the very shape and structure of your mind beginning to change." That is indeed what the Gospel is about, a *metanoia*, a radical repentant rethinking of everything before the face of Jesus Christ. No better account of theological method has been given than that which Jesus gave to his disciples when he said: "If any man would come after me, let him deny himself and take up his cross and follow me." That is what repentant rethinking means: you cannot separate evangelical theology from that profound experience of the radical changing and transforming of your mind that comes through dying and rising with Christ.

There often came a point in my classes when I felt that the students wanted to throw their books at me, as the inner struggle between the Gospel and the frame of mind they brought to it became intense. Let us make no mistake about it: divine revelation conflicts sharply with the structure of our natural reason, with the secular patterns of thought that have already become established in our minds through the twist of our ingrained mental alienation from God. We cannot become true theologians without the agonizing experience of profound change in the mental structure of our innermost being.

"Let this mind be in you *(touto phroneite),*" as St. Paul wrote to the Philippians, "which was also in Christ Jesus." The early Greek Fathers gave a great deal of thought to that injunction. They cultivated what they called "the apostolic mind" *(phronema apostolikon),* for it was only through the mind of the Apostles embodied in the holy scriptures that the church could be imbued with the mind of Christ *(phronema Christou)* himself. That is precisely what a faithful theology is about, the assimilation of the mind of the church to the self-revelation of the Father through the Son and in the Spirit.

Thus a regular question raised by Christian theologians, concealed behind all the great debates in the early centuries, was whether they were really thinking *worthily* of God in accordance with the mind of Christ Jesus, as it has been imprinted by the Holy Spirit in the apostolic foundation of the church and expressed in the apostolic scriptures. All through those early centuries as the gospel was carried from end to end of the Mediterranean world, Christian theology played a major role in the evangelizing of nation after nation, for it was only as the mind and culture of people were brought into conformity to the mind of Christ that the church could put down permanent roots in the soil of humanity. As in the New Testament, preaching and teaching *(kerygma* and *didache)* were always interwoven with each other, so in the remarkable growth and expansion of the church after New Testament times, theological and evangelizing activity always functioned inseparably together. By its intrinsic nature an evangelical theology is an evangelizing theology, for it is concerned with the winning and transforming of the human mind through conformity to the mind of Christ Jesus — not simply the minds of individual human beings but the mind of human society and culture in which individual human beings exist.

What does this have to say to us today about what we call "evangelical Christianity"? We have been concerned with evangelizing men, women, and children as individual human beings, calling for repentance and personal decision for Christ as Lord and Savior, and rightly so. But have we been concerned with the evangelizing of the *mind* of the society in which these people live? If not, how can a Christian church put down roots in an unevangelized society and remain genuinely Christian? I believe this is where evangelical Christianity today has failed terribly. By and large, as far as I can see, even the mind of the church, let alone the mind of society, is still secular in that it shares the mind of the secular society within which it exists. We have Christian people, but do we really have a *Christian* church? We have people who profess to believe in Christ as Lord and Savior, but do we have a church that is so imbued with the mind of Christ that its members individually and as a community think *instinctively* in a Christian way?

I have been wonderfully blessed with a mother and a wife who have a profoundly Christian, and indeed a remarkably theological, *instinct.* My mother had little academic training in theology, but her life and her understanding were so tuned in to the mind of Christ that she knew at once where the truth lay and was quick to discern any deviation from it. This is also very true of my dear wife, who is imbued with an unerring *theological instinct*, evident again and again in her reaction to ideas put forward by preachers or teachers. At the end of the day that was the test I used to put to my students, as I read their essays and examinations or listened to them in the chapel. "Has this person a genuinely theological instinct or not? Is his or her thinking spontaneously and naturally governed by the mind of Christ?" That is much more important than being theologically learned, much more important than being able to offer a formal academic account of some doctrine or historic debate in the church. What really counts in the end is whether a person's mind is radically transformed by Christ and so spiritually attuned to the mind of Christ, that he/she thinks instinctively from the depths of his mental being in a way worthy of God. As Athanasius used to insist, we must learn to think strictly "in accordance with the nature" *(kata physin)* of God the Father as he is made known to us through the Son and in the Holy Spirit, that is, in an essentially godly way *(eusebos)*. To think like that from a center in God himself, in accordance with his essential nature revealed in the Incarnate Son, is, he claimed, what *theologia* strictly is. If any one does not think in that way, but thinks from a center in oneself, governed by the devising of one's own reason, then one is bound to think of him in an unworthy or irreligious way *(asebos)* — which Athanasius designated *mythologia*. Either you think from out of a mind centered in God through union with the mind of the Lord Jesus, or you think from out of a mind centered in yourself, alienated from God and inwardly hostile to the Truth incarnate in the Lord Jesus, that is, in a way that is finally governed by the unregenerate and unbaptized reason.

The transformation of the human mind and its renewal through assimilation to the mind of Christ is something that has to go on throughout the whole of our life — it is a never-ending discipleship in repentant rethinking as we take up the cross and follow Christ. That is why we cannot be theologians without incessant prayer in offering ourselves daily to God through the reconciling and atoning mediation of Christ; and that is also why we cannot be evangelists without being theologians whose minds are constantly schooled in obedience to Christ. It is after all with our minds that we worship God and it is only with our minds that we can preach the Gospel and evangelize the world. Is that not, in part at least, what St. Paul was concerned with in the two verses from the twelfth chapter of his Epistle to the Romans, "I appeal to you therefore, brethren, by the mercies of God, to present your bodies a living sacrifice, holy, acceptable to God, which is your spiritual worship *(logike latreia).* [By *logike latreia,* however, St. Paul meant not just spiritual but *rational* worship.] And be not conformed to this world but be transformed by the renewal of your mind, that you may prove what is the will of God, what is good and acceptable, and perfect." Notice the distinctive way in which St. Paul interrelated the renewing of the mind with the offering of the body as a living sacrifice and with rational worship. It is not with disembodied minds that we have to do here, but with the created unity of mind and body in which the human self is constituted. While stress may be laid upon the transformation of the mind and its assimilation to Christ, it is the whole human self that is involved. The transformation the Apostle called for is so deep that it evokes out of the rational self an instinctive judgment about what is good, acceptable, and perfect before God. That is to say, in the way I have been expressing it, we are called to be transformed in such a profound way that there develops within the depths of our rational being a *theological instinct* in virtue of which we are able to make true theological judgments. Without such a theological instinct we are little more than people with secular minds loosely clothed with a Christian profession. A genuine *theological instinct* of the kind St. Paul has in view cannot be gained apart from a constant self-offering in rational worship to God, for it is through that inner relation between prayer and the transforming renewal of our minds, that we may be so tuned in to God that we fulfill our service in the rational way acceptable to him.

In his scientific autobiography, Werner Heisenberg tells us that again and again when the mathematics of quantum theory proved to be as difficult as they were intricate, he would go away for three or four weeks at a time to play the piano or the violin in order, as he put it, to tune in to the "Central Order" — the name he used in that context for God. When his whole being was tuned in to that Central Order he would come back to find his mathematical equations working out more easily. It is something similar that happens in theological activity. Through study of the holy scriptures, through meditation and prayer we tune in to the mind of God incarnate in Jesus Christ, the Source of all rationality, until our own minds, healed, renewed, and sanctified in him, are instinct with his Truth — then it is that we may preach and teach the Gospel, and find it transforming the lives and minds of people and the society to which they belong.

Hungarian Greetings to the President of Princeton Theological Seminary!

KÁROLY TÓTH

S ince its foundation at the beginning of the previous century (1812), Princeton Theological Seminary has been paying ever increasing attention to the sister churches in Central Eastern Europe, and more specifically to the Hungarian-speaking Presbyterian (Reformed) churches of the area. During this more than one and a half centuries, the Seminary has developed into a powerful Presbyterian institution and is functioning today as one of the most respected educational institutions of the Presbyterian churches in the United States. At present, some 1,000 students are preparing for pastoral ministry and scientific theological work respectively at Princeton Theological Seminary. They include a great number of students from the developing countries of Asia, Africa, and Latin America, as well as scholarship students from Central and Eastern Europe, and so from the Hungarian language area as well.

Princeton Seminary's interest in the Hungarian-speaking Reformed churches increased particularly in the years following World War II. Characteristic of this process is that Princeton Seminary, thanks to the peculiar and wise openness of the ecumenical movement and the Reformed World Alliance, has always been guided by presidents whose interest in the churches of Central Eastern Europe never ceased. It can be said that this policy is unbroken, to which the presidencies of such professors as John MacKay in the 1950s, James I. McCord in the 1970s, and now Thomas W. Gillespie, testify. All of them, especially Dr. Gillespie, embody the talents and blessings of their predecessors. After having been an effective local pastor, Dr. Gillespie is now a recognized biblical scholar and capable leader of eminent church institutions. All three recent presidents are honorary doctors of the Reformed Theological Faculties in Budapest or Debrecen. That is why the fifteen years of presidency of Dr. Thomas W. Gillespie is gratefully commemorated in Hungary as a token of a century-long fraternal relationship between Princeton and Hungary, and between the American Presbyterians and the Hungarian-speaking Reformed Christians.

We refer here to the largest Presbyterian Church in the very center of Europe, the Reformed churches worshiping God in Hungarian. By very cautious reckoning, there are more than three million Hungarian-speaking Reformed believers living within almost one block of the Danube basin. For your information: more than fifteen million Hungarians are living all over the world, almost eleven million of them in present-day Hungary and nearly four million in the neighboring countries, the rest mostly in diaspora in Western Europe or North America. We speak, therefore, of about three million Hungarian Reformed believers. The intensity of their religiosity is another question, its forms being surely very different, and it would certainly be interesting to analyze this problem.

We have to demonstrate the sorrowful peculiarities of these churches and to affirm that the Hungarian Reformed believers — in spite of all misfortunes afflicting them during the centuries — are still serving with undiminished energy and are bearing witness to Jesus Christ, the Lord of the church. This testimony is being carried out in our days in rather special ways, because a large number of our church members still feel themselves belonging to the one Hungarian Reformed Church, yet in consequence of the Treaty of Versailles (1920) are shut out of the present mother country and must live in various postwar states.

After the fall in 1918 of the Austro-Hungarian monarchy, which was chiefly responsible for the First World War, historical Hungary was most severely afflicted by international punishment: according to the terms of Versailles, two-thirds of the area of the country were annexed to the surrounding new states (Czechoslovakia, Romania, Yugoslavia), and about one-third of our population was lost.

But in spite of all these afflictions, the Hungarian Reformed believers have proved to be the preserving element of the nation and are in this way serving and bearing witness — together with our church in the mother country — to our belonging to one another, in Transylvania, the present

Romania, as well in the north, the present Slovakia, and in the south, the present Yugoslavia and Croatia. The oddity of the situation is that even Austria, in spite of sharing blame for the war, was also given a small piece of land from the western territory of Hungary.

At this point, we have to cast a glance at two peculiarities in the situation of Hungarian Reformed believers in our days:

1. The Presbyterian (Reformed) Church in Hungary for more than four and a half centuries has been a basically democratic church. The three million Reformed believers live in a representative church order developed gradually, the main requirement of which is the harmonious cooperation of separate autonomous church bodies. Here, however, we have to state immediately that this democratism has the disadvantage of a centrifugal force, protesting always against any centralized government. The local congregations enjoy a strong autonomy. The community of twenty to thirty parishes, the seniorate (their total number is twenty-seven), is similarly autonomous. The greatest church bodies, the church districts, are composed of several hundred congregations. The same autonomy is also in force in the national church, whose situation is further complicated and aggravated by the often grievous conditions of the Hungarian Reformed believers living in the five neighboring states. And beyond all that, several regions since the Reformation have developed certain peculiarities whereby the whole of the church is made somewhat multicolored.

2. The second important thing is that the Hungarian-speaking Reformed Church is the only Presbyterian Church in the world with an episcopal system. This peculiarity raises serious questions, because it means that all the autonomous church bodies are jointly governed by ministers and laymen. The development of this system is due to the constant struggles our church has had to fight since its official foundation at the Synod of Debrecen in 1567, the description of which would go beyond the limits of the present paper.

In the past decade (1988-1998), the Hungarian Reformed Church underwent a change whose great significance and many implications *we are now unable to assess in their entirety.* The whole of the Hungarian Reformed Church is characterized by the conscious or unconscious conviction that *a continuous process of transformation is necessary.* We are convinced that we have to work for a change into something better and better. In the struggles of the past centuries, but particularly in the years after World War II, our church was kept alive by the hope that a more just politico-economic system capable of further development would evolve after Western models in this area too.

Instead of this, however, our nation was inevitably thrust into a politico-economic system by the big "behemoth" or "leviathan" (Book of Job, chapters 40–41), our Eastern neighbor, the former Soviet Union. Our church was forced into opportunism and continuous limitations, sometimes even by false theological motivation in order "to save what could be saved." During the four decades of the reign of a ruthless atheistic system, the Reformed churches of the area suffered two main blows: (a) in consequence of the liquidation of the peasants and smallholders called "kulaks," they lost their social and economic basis; and (b) through the elimination of the ecclesiastical schools (the network of which had by the twentieth century extended to the whole of Hungarian national culture), they lost a strong spiritual basis. In the 1950s, after the general nationalization of ecclesiastical schools, the ancient College of Debrecen was the only educational institution left under the management of the Hungarian Reformed Church.

The faults and deficiencies of the Soviet system soon came to light. This began in Berlin (1951) followed by Budapest (1956) and Prague (1968), and parallel with them, the well-known events in Poland. The result of all this was that, by the middle of the 1980s, those outside the churches who had believed in the possibility of reforming the "socialist" system, rejected this dream. From 1989-1990 on, the liquidation of the entire Soviet-type system became inevitable. This happened in Hungary just as in the rest of the "socialist" countries, leaving free scope for the activity of the Christian churches. And the churches did take advantage of this possibility, even if incalculable and critical situations were made thereby.

This profound and radical turn of events took the churches by surprise. Today this can be seen mostly in the fact that no uniform theological and ecclesiological answer can be given to the question: *Which necessary things have priority over the others that need to be done?* A further difficulty is caused by the fact that the churches often fall victim to a certain kind of nostalgia, to the embellished memory of the past. But which past should be chosen? One might think of the reform era of the 1840s, or the age of the monarchy (1867-1919), or the Horthy regime (1920-1945), or the few years of democratic transition (1945-1948). The chaotic mentality is further complicated thereby.

It is therefore very difficult, if not impossible, to resist these nostalgic temptations. In consequence of the unexpected gain of our national liberty, we are in danger of mistaking our nationalistic feelings and the nation itself for the kerygma, the message of God's Word. The partly justifiable sense of nationalism raises further difficulties.

Although the local congregations avail themselves of all possibilities, the main effort of the national church in this last decade has been the restoration of the former system of church schools and ecclesiastical education. What has been achieved so far, however, is a mere fragment of the network of schools with which the churches served the nation between the two world wars. After the relevant resolutions passed in the early 1990s, the system of schools run by the churches at present amounts only to 4-5 percent of all public education in Hungary. The churches are, of course, unable to meet their obligations either financially or by providing the necessary teaching staff. They need massive support on the part of the democratic state.

A critical remark is very appropriate here: as I have said already, the local congregations availed themselves of the religious freedom and its fruits attained in consequence of the turn for the better in 1989-90. In my opinion, however, the greatest omission of the church is that it has not made use of the last ten years for the establishment of new congregations, for the development of the existing ones, and for church growth. The congregations swollen under the pressure of circumstances were not divided, and thus did not multiply in order to encourage the growth of the church. This would have undoubtedly demanded very great efforts, but in default of this the missionary movement has involuntarily been left to the "converting activity" of various and ubiquitous sects. The correction of this fault is a difficult but urgent task, the more so, because the communist regime enforced the gravest restrictions in this area. This reminds me of the words uttered by a present politician of ours who said that the old regime has not hindered the development of any new system by overtly opposing it, but by its more or less covert appearance in the new one. Innumerable instances could be mentioned for this, which, however, must be dispensed with at present.

In the last ten years, a new system of democratic institutions and a new form of economy have developed. What help can be given in this situation by the American Presbyterians, and by Princeton Theological Seminary? First of all, we have to make it clear that we are in great need of all kinds of help: spiritual, moral, mental, and others. Therefore, we are very grateful that the Seminary has not ceased to look with loving eyes upon us, has in the most difficult times invited and still invites, and acts as host to our students and professors, regularly sends delegates to our church and takes lively interest in the life of our church. Regrettably, scholarship students could not be sent to Princeton at the height of the Cold War (1950-55), but immediately afterwards, Hungarian students again began to arrive in Princeton.

We also ask our Presbyterian brothers and sisters in America to beware of the opinion that by gaining our liberty, everything has been solved, so we are "no longer interesting." Today more than ever, we desire their attention, interest, and patience; and we ask them never to forget the difficulties of our national and ecclesiastical life, but kindly follow it with great attention.

The greatest help Princeton Theological Seminary can give us, and all the Hungarian Reformed believers in the Carpathian basin, is that they never forget that their political, social, and theological knowledge is always desired. We ask you to remind us constantly of the primary importance of being directly guided by the Holy Scripture with regard to the past and present age. What did God want to tell us through the four decades of trials, and what are we challenged to by God's Word today? These questions can only be answered in a patient wrestling together with the problems. Almighty God has preserved our church in all trials and difficulties of our history. Why? Obviously, because he wants us to bear witness to his saving grace. It is in performing this testimony that we shall need your help in the future too. With many thanks for what we have received so far, we further expect the words of love and warning from Princeton.

Doctrine and Preaching:
The Task of Theology as Servant of the Church

LEANNE VAN DYK

This essay rests on a scarcely concealed, yet perhaps not widely shared, presupposition. I am presupposing that it is a good thing to preach doctrine; indeed, that preaching doctrine is part of the task of pastoral ministry and part of the learning, growing, maturing experience of the congregation. Furthermore, I assume it is the task of the doctrinal theologian to engage in doctrinal exposition primarily for the life of the church. Doctrinal theology, then, exists primarily not for the sake of its own inner coherence or comprehensiveness. It certainly not does exist for feeding the voracious appetite of academia and its highly specialized guilds. It exists to serve the church in all its ministries, including proclamation, education, pastoral care, and mission.

Karl Barth carefully articulates the relationship between dogmatics, or doctrinal theology, and proclamation. He reminds all dogmatic theologians that dogmatics is secondary; proclamation is primary. He says that "dogmatics cannot wish to be an end in itself."[1] Rather, it "has to investigate and say at each given point how we may best speak of God, revelation and faith. . . ."[2] In typical fashion, Barth then goes on to warn even the

---

1. Karl Barth, *Church Dogmatics*, I/I (Edinburgh: T. & T. Clark, 1960), p. 84.
2. Barth, *Church Dogmatics*, I/I, p. 85.

best-intentioned dogmatic theologian that such a responsibility is, none-theless, a *human* responsibility. "It (dogmatics) should not think that it can lay down what God, revelation, and faith are in themselves. In both its investigations and its conclusions it must keep in view that God is in heaven and it on earth, and that God, his revelation and faith always live their own free life over against all human talk, including that of the best dogmatics."[3]

This essay, then, takes seriously both the affirmation of the relation-ship between dogmatics and proclamation — or theology and preaching — and the warning of Barth. The affirmation — that theology must serve preaching — is the primary presupposition of this essay. The warning — that theology must not suppose it has the final word on God and God's ac-tivity in the world — must give these reflections their proper modesty and provisionality.

In addition to the above presupposition, a disposition informs this essay. I care about preaching; I care about doctrine and I am convinced the two can be fruitfully related. As a teacher of Christian doctrine, I think about how to communicate doctrine and what practical, pastoral, and homiletic difference it makes.

Finally, an observation also informs this essay. It is an observation well stated by Robert Hughes and Robert Kysar in their recent book, *Preaching Doctrine for the Twenty-First Century.* "No longer can we assume that our congregation knows the tradition of its denomination," they write. "No longer can we take for granted a fundamental understanding of the basics of the faith. Something like a doctrinal defoliation has oc-curred."[4]

These two authors locate the source of this defoliation both in the church and the culture. The church has abdicated its responsibility in in-struction in the faith — in catechesis. The culture, too, has stripped off the leaves and flowers of theological interest and knowledge. These cultural factors are familiar to those of us committed to the church; they read like a list of viral symptoms: consumerism, individualism, media saturation, re-sistance to authority, suspicion of tradition, and radical secularization.

Cultural pressures are not the only explanation for doctrinal defolia-

3. Barth, *Church Dogmatics,* I/I, pp. 85, 86.
4. Robert Hughes and Robert Kysar, *Preaching Doctrine for the Twenty-First Century* (Minneapolis: Fortress Press, 1997), p. 1.

tion. Another consideration is the issue of language — of words — even, of specific words. How is it that Christian words like grace, salvation, Jesus — how is it that these words can be ever alive, ever fresh, ever real? Novelist Walker Percy ponders this issue as well with respect to the task of writing fiction. He says, "Language is a living organism and as such is subject to certain organic ailments. In this case, it is the exhaustion and decrepitude of words themselves, an infirmity which has nothing to do with the truth or falsity of the sentences they form. The words of religion tend to wear out and get stored in the attic. The word *religion* itself has a certain unction about it, to say nothing of *born again, salvation, Jesus*. . . . And it doesn't help that when religious words are used publicly, at least Christian words, they are often expropriated by some of the worst rogues around, the TV preachers."[5]

Also culpable in the unctuous use of classic Christian words are television and film portrayals of Christian believers. Rarely is such a portrayal authentic; it is usually grossly caricatured and often negative. These caricatures and dreary misrepresentations of Christian faith perhaps add to the organic ailment of religious language.

Walker Percy goes on in his analysis of the difficulty of using religious language and concepts in writing fiction. Referring again to the TV preachers, he says, "They are proclaiming the same good news he (the novelist) believes in, using the same noble words, speaking of the same treasure buried in a field, but somehow devaluing it. If these are the fellows who have found the treasure buried in a field, then what manner of treasure is it? . . . He (the novelist) feels like Lancelot in search of the Holy Grail, who finds himself at the end of his quest at a Tupperware party."[6]

Percy's sharp criticism of the TV evangelists illustrates vividly an intriguing problem not only in Christian fiction but also Christian proclamation. How does a Christian novelist or preacher authentically affirm the grace of God in Jesus Christ when those very words are like whited sepulchers? Once more, Percy remarks, "Of course, just because Jimmy Swaggart believes in God doesn't mean God does not exist. But it doesn't make life any easier for the novelist."[7] The very words needed to proclaim

5. Walker Percy, "Why Are You a Catholic?" in *Living Philosophies: The Reflections of Some Eminent Men and Women of Our Time* (New York: Doubleday, 1990), pp. 167-68.

6. Walker Percy, *Signposts in a Strange Land,* ed. Patrick Samway (New York: Farrar, Straus and Giroux, 1991), p. 177.

7. Percy, *Signposts in a Strange Land,* pp. 159-60.

the gospel are, at best, exhausted, words that no longer have the energy and muscle to do their job. They are, at worst, actually reversed, so that the authentic and true meaning of words like grace, salvation, God are lost in the thick fog of misuse, caricature, and stereotype. The authentic good news of these classic Christian words needs to be reclaimed and poor imitators or pretenders decisively retired.

This excursion into Christian fiction writing raises precisely the same problem as that faced by preachers in writing sermons. Preachers, too, wish to use words like grace, sin, virtue, and hope in their full, flowering, Christian sense. Yet it is just these words that are defoliated or exhausted. The challenge of preachers in service to the *Word* is to find ways to recover these classic Christian *words.* Doctrine can — and must — be part of that effort to preach effectively, authentically, and truly.

Before an analysis and recommendation of the relationship between doctrine and preaching, some initial discussion is necessary on doctrine itself. Two important books illustrate the relevant issues in relatively brief scope.

The first is George Lindbeck's *The Nature of Doctrine,* which takes up precisely what the title of the book states — a discussion of the *nature* of doctrine. Lindbeck suggests that doctrine is a sort of grammar of the community, "that is, as idioms for the construing of reality and the living of life."[8] Doctrine, on this view, is essentially a communally authoritative rule to order the life and practice of the community. The subsequent enormous response to Lindbeck's seminal book demonstrates both the potential and the problems to such an approach. This theory of doctrine has the advantage of a keen cultural and contextual awareness. Doctrine fits a context; it has a *milieu;* it takes its place in the context of a larger cultural reality. This view, however, has the difficulty of adjudicating the issue of truth claims.[9] In a famous illustration, Lindbeck claims, "The crusader's battle cry 'Christus est Dominus,' for example, is false when used to authorize cleaving the skull of the infidel (even though the same words in other contexts may be a true utterance)." Lindbeck's nuanced and careful argument for the model of doctrine as "regulative," similar to the grammatical rules of a

8. George Lindbeck, *The Nature of Doctrine: Religion and Theology in a Postliberal Age* (Philadelphia: Westminster, 1984), p. 18.
9. Lindbeck himself acknowledges this problem. He says, "It seems odd to suggest that the Nicaenum in its role as a communal doctrine does not make first-order truth claims, and yet this is what I shall contend" (p. 19).

language, attempts to solve this primary difficulty. Here it is possible only to note the problem.[10]

The second book on doctrine considers not the *nature* of doctrine but its *function*. Alister McGrath considers this issue in his book, *The Genesis of Doctrine*.[11] There are four functions of doctrine, according to McGrath.[12] There is, first, the function of doctrine as social demarcation. Because Christian communities are social entities, doctrine has a social function. For example, the early Christian church defined itself doctrinally as distinct from the official religions of the Roman Empire. Early doctrine was frequently polemical because self-definition was required to avoid assimilation and to resist annihilation. The doctrinal character of the Radical Reformation or early New England Puritans or the Karl Barth of August 1, 1914 — the day many of his revered teachers issued a manifesto of support for the Kaiser's war policy — all these examples and countless more illustrate the function of doctrine as a social locator.

Second, McGrath suggests doctrine as interpretive narrative. "Doctrine," says McGrath, "provides the conceptual framework by which the biblical narrative is interpreted. It is not an arbitrary framework, however, but one which is suggested by that narrative, and intimated (however provisionally) by scripture itself."[13] The biblical narrative is primary and the doctrinal interpretive framework secondary. But the biblical narrative invites and allows such interpretive structures. Thus, doctrine is not a sort of sediment that inhibits the biblical narrative. Rather, scripture and doctrine enrich each other in a sort of hermeneutical spiral. Doctrinal reflection can inspire new readings of a text. The biblical narrative can explode the tidy boundaries of doctrine and reform it.

McGrath's third function of doctrine is as an interpretation of experience. Far from being abstract, speculative, or removed from human experience, doctrine can speak to human experience and illuminate it.

---

10. The two alternatives Lindbeck identified to his regulative model were, first, the propositional model — one which proposes a hard realist approach to doctrine, that is, doctrine as statements of what is really the case and, second, the expressivist model — one which proposes the function of doctrine as noninformative symbols of attitudes, affects, or orientations.

11. Alister McGrath, *The Genesis of Doctrine: A Study in the Foundations of Doctrinal Criticism* (Oxford: Basil Blackwell, 1990).

12. These four characteristics are found in chapter 3, pp. 35-80.

13. McGrath, *The Genesis of Doctrine*, pp. 58, 59.

McGrath notes, "It is the sheer elusiveness of human experience, its obstinate refusal to be imprisoned within a verbal matrix, which underlies the need for poetry, symbolism and doctrine alike."[14]

Finally, McGrath offers a fourth function of doctrine: as truth claim — a statement of what really is the case. He suggests a number of different understandings of truth which give it a richness and depth helpful in thinking about doctrine. First, there is the view of truth which finds its root in the Greek word *aletheia*. The root of the word in combination with its prefix means to reveal or uncover. Truth is disclosure; it is revelation. Second, there is the view of truth which finds its root in the Latin word *veritas*. The connotation here is a precise and accurate rendering of what actually happened. Third, there is the view of truth which finds its root in the Hebrew word *emunah*, which connotes trustworthiness and faithfulness. With these linguistic insights McGrath suggests that doctrine functions as truth claim in that it discloses the living God, a God who freely and graciously reveals divine love and mercy. In addition, doctrine functions as truth claim in that it gives an accurate account of God, humanity, and God's dealings with humanity. This accurate account is characterized by wide variation in numerous different contexts, to be sure, but the veracity of the doctrine underlies the variations. Furthermore, doctrine functions as truth claim in that it points to a personal relationship with a faithful, trustworthy, and utterly reliable God.

Such an understanding of the truth claims of doctrine immediately connects with the task of preaching. Preaching strives to reveal the gracious and loving God; it seeks to give an accurate account of God's relationship with the created world, and it is motivated by the call of pointing always to the relational God who is slow to anger and abounding in steadfast love and mercy.

With this brief survey of the function of doctrine and its claims to truth, a sharper focus on doctrinal preaching is possible. A number of characteristics or sensitivities which doctrinal preaching ought to have are enumerated by Robert Hughes and Robert Kysar in their recent book on doctrinal preaching. These characteristics, with examples on how they might take shape in a sermon, now follow.

First, doctrinal preaching must attempt the framing of experience, an overall interpretive structure. Such interpretive structures exist, implic-

14. McGrath, *The Genesis of Doctrine*, p. 68.

itly or explicitly, for all human experience. For Christian believers, that interpretive structure is the Christian gospel. But often, congregations do not have the ability or experience to make that structure concrete and specific. Hughes and Kysar remark that "the doors and windows, the walls and the roof, the electrical outlets and the lights of a building are meaningless unless they are joined together by a basic framework. On that framework each of the individual parts finds a place and a use — each makes sense when integrated together through the framework. It is the framework of life that is missing for a lot of our listeners."[15] Doctrinal preaching must supply the overall frame of meaning for our congregations.

The second and third characteristics of doctrinal preaching identified by Hughes and Kysar can be combined. Doctrinal preaching must have, second, concreteness or specificity and, third, be imaginative or empowering. Here the challenges for the preacher are several. She must find vivid illustrations and examples to give the doctrine that emerges from a specific biblical text concreteness and specificity. Such illustrations and examples are found in good literature, in novels, short stories, plays, and film. Literature that powerfully, poignantly, and truly illuminates the human experience is the terrain the doctrinal preacher searches. Furthermore, the preacher searches the newspapers, the popular press, and the scholarly journals, in an effort to be alert to cultural markers and events as a means of drawing a contrast — a contrast between cheap modern analogues to the gospel and its authentic claims and character. Finally, the preacher brings listeners into the world of the Scripture and invites them to make that world their own. These are the efforts that make a sermon doctrinal in a concrete, vivid, and imaginative way.

The parable of the Prodigal Son, for example, is a biblical text that powerfully illustrates the doctrine of justification. The biblical story itself, the resources of the doctrine of justification, and the best illustrations and analogies one can find make up a doctrinal sermon that, perhaps, may reach a self-conscious adolescent longing for a word of absolute unconditional acceptance. This understanding of justification meets a powerful and primary need of people at all stages of development.[16]

15. Hughes and Kysar, *Preaching Doctrine for the Twenty-First Century*, p. 11.
16. This is the primary definition of justification that Calvin offered in the *Institutes:* "Therefore, we explain justification simply as the acceptance with which God receives us into his favor . . ." (3.11.2).

In preaching the doctrine of justification, the preacher can point out that accepted people thrive and flourish. Babies who are cuddled and loved grow up and embrace the world right back. Children who are not measured by performance but treasured for their place in the home have a far better chance of self-confidence and happiness. Adults who find unconditional acceptance in a friend or spouse experience the sort of security and comfort rare in our competitive, success-driven world. Acceptance and yearning for it are common human experiences that can help bring a classic Christian doctrine to life.

Concreteness and specificity can be exemplified in a sermon on justification by finding a story of unconditional love and acceptance. The short story by Wendell Berry, "Pray Without Ceasing," is such an account. The story is of Thad Coulter, who killed his best friend in broad daylight on the main street of town because the friend would not lend him a large sum of money. Thad is arrested and jailed.

Overcome by shame and horror, Thad sits in his jail cell and longs for his own death. But then he receives a single visitor, his daughter Martha Elizabeth, who had walked many miles to see him. When Thad looked up and saw her, he covered his face with his hands. It was not his guilt and shame that made him cover his face. There was that, too, in his soul, so thick and deep it choked him. But what made Thad cover his face was something else.

"In that moment, he saw his guilt included in love that stood as near him as Martha Elizabeth and at that moment wore her flesh . . . surely God's love includes people who can't bear it."[17]

The narrator of the story says, "People sometimes talk of God's love as if it's a pleasant thing. But it is terrible, in a way. Think of all it includes. It included Thad Coulter, mean and drunk and foolish, before he killed Mr. Feltner, and it included him afterwards."[18] The unconditional acceptance of Martha Elizabeth for her father — an acceptance fully cognizant of Thad's crime yet able to gaze at him and take him in — that acceptance makes concrete and vivid God's acceptance of us in justification.

In addition, the cheap modern equivalents to justification can be contrasted with the genuine Christian reality. In our secular culture, acceptance

---

17. Wendell Berry, "Pray Without Ceasing," in *Fidelity: Five Stories* (New York and San Francisco: Pantheon Books, 1992), p. 50.

18. Berry, "Pray Without Ceasing," p. 49.

and righteousness are calibrated by standards of wealth and popularity. Brand-name shoes, late-model cars, peer groups, bank accounts, vacation homes — these are the standards of acceptance. A sermon on justification can concretely illustrate such a contrast and call the congregation to a genuine confidence in their unconditional acceptance through Jesus Christ.

Other doctrines that can be preached in ways that are concrete and imaginative include the doctrines of sin and grace. Here the cheap modern equivalents to these classic Christian doctrines are important to identify. Grace, if it means anything in our secularized culture, means a quick and easy pardon or a sentimental flourish. Sin has come to mean a sort of naughty excess. A dessert can be sinful, but there is enormous resistance to acknowledging that the human heart is sinful. Preaching about sin and grace needs to get the relationship between sin and grace right, both the depths of sin and the heights of grace. Preaching sin without grace is judgmental. Preaching grace without sin is a radical thinning out of the gospel. It is to render the Christian gospel oddly superfluous or unnecessary. One preaches grace effectively partly by including the reality of sin. One preaches sin effectively partly by including the radical need and dramatic effectiveness of grace.

Preaching on virtue runs into deep cultural resistance as well. The words virtue and virtuous, instead of referring to qualities of character and life that authentically mirror our union with and imitation of Christ, often connote miserly fastidiousness or dreary legalism. This doctrine, too, must be reclaimed in creative and effective doctrinal preaching. Fortunately, there is a wealth of vivid contemporary examples that can support such a goal. Some of the best illustrate the depressing *absence* of virtue. Compelling examples of genuine virtue are harder to find.

One angle on virtue development that can be well illustrated in a doctrinal sermon is anger control. The virtue lists in Colossians 3, Ephesians 4, Galatians 5, and Romans 12 all emphasize the importance of anger control as an essential Christian virtue. This is because anger is a community-destroying, relationship-damaging, and person-poisoning state. In a sermon on one of these virtue lists, or perhaps the story of Nathan and David in 2 Samuel 12, the different kinds of anger can be discerned. When anger destroys self, other, or community, when it rises up to justify one's self or protect one's pride or power, anger is sinful. But when one gets angry at the humiliation of another or injustice toward others, then anger is appropriate.

219

Neil Plantinga gives an example of a situation in which anger would have been fully justified. "In Montgomery, Alabama, in the forties, city fathers wrote municipal bus regulations to minimize proximity of black and white passengers. One of the regulations prohibited blacks from walking through the bus to their own section since, to do so, they would have to pass through the white section and might accidentally make body contact with white passengers. Thus, in a demeaning alternative, blacks would pay their fare at the front, exit the bus, walk its length outdoors, and then reenter the vehicle at the rear. Inevitably, certain white bus drivers amused themselves by driving away before their black passengers could reboard. Of course, the trouble here was not that blacks got angry at such humiliation, but rather that whites did not."[19]

Such a vivid and painful story powerfully summons appropriate, righteous anger. But anger is often sinful; it is this kind of anger that we are told to "put off" in the New Testament virtue lists. This kind of anger is often a mask or disguise for something else, usually envy or resentment. The stunning portrayal of envy in the film *Amadeus,* which tells the story of the court composer Salieri's poisonous envy of Mozart's talents, displays the fertile links between envy, anger, and self-destruction.

Other virtues, or their lack, are illustrated in literature, biography, autobiography, newspapers, and congregations. One thinks of Douglas MacArthur for an illustration of pride or of Jimmy Carter as exemplifying both integrity and occasional vindictiveness.[20] One thinks of Sister Helen Prejean, in *Dead Man Walking,* who displays compassion and blunt honesty in her advocacy for both death-row inmates as well as victims and their families. One remembers remarkable families who display hospitality and acceptance in their adoption of physically or emotionally impaired children. One recalls godly individuals in each congregation who counter fear with love, hatred with forgiveness, bitterness with trust. There are the daily, common, often unnoticed acts that bring the virtues of Christian living into vivid outline.

19. Cornelius Plantinga, Jr., *Not the Way It's Supposed to Be: A Breviary of Sin* (Grand Rapids: Eerdmans, 1995), p. 166. This story comes from Taylor Branch, *Parting the Waters: America in the King Years, 1954-1963* (New York: Simon and Schuster, 1988), p. 14.

20. As Douglas Brinkley points out in his recent biography of Jimmy Carter, *Jimmy Carter: The Post-Presidential Years* (New York: Random House, 1998), Carter was remarkably magnanimous in his commitment to human rights and health but could also display petty anger and vindictiveness. Frequently, of course, vices and virtues exist in one and the same person.

The fourth characteristic of doctrinal preaching, which summarizes the other three, is that it must translate tradition. If our theological tradition has been lost, if doctrine has been defoliated, it must be reappropriated, reclaimed for the church in this context at this time. Sermons that concretely and imaginatively expound and explain a central Christian doctrine and demonstrate how this doctrine fits into an overall interpretive structure — these sermons translate tradition.

Ellen Charry's recent book on the pastoral function of Christian doctrine, *By the Renewing of Your Mind,* is a comprehensive examination of the pastoral and formative function of Christian doctrine. She traces the person-forming and virtue-crafting function of Christian doctrine in the long tradition of the church. Starting with the scriptures, she then explores the thought of Athanasius, Augustine, Anselm, Thomas Aquinas, Julian of Norwich, and John Calvin. Each of these Christian writers saw doctrine — the articulation and explication of Christian claims — as having strong pastoral implications. She states her thesis quite plainly, "The point is simply that as these major shapers of the Christian tradition formulated, reformulated, and revised Christian doctrine, its moral, psychological, and social implications were uppermost in their minds."[21] Doctrine — and thus doctrinal preaching — has a shaping role, a formative role; it is to invite believers to be transformed by knowing God and giving him honor and glory.

Charry is not suggesting a merely instrumental role of doctrine, a role solely of formation. Her point is that besides the realist claims made by Christian doctrine, it is *also* person-forming, virtue-enhancing; it is an invitation to authentic life with God. And this, surely, is the task of pastors and teachers — to invite people to authentic life with God. Doctrinal preaching, in its role as proclamation, education, pastoral care, and mission, serves this primary call of the Christian pastor and teacher.

21. Ellen Charry, *By the Renewing of Your Minds: The Pastoral Function of Christian Doctrine* (New York: Oxford University Press, 1997), p. 233.

Order and Ardor

DAVID B. WATERMULDER

"Be aglow with the Spirit," was the title of President John Mackay's farewell address to the members of the graduating class of Princeton Theological Seminary in the spring of 1954. Thomas William Gillespie was one of those students, being awarded the Bachelor of Divinity (now designated as the Master of Divinity) degree.

Using as his text the words of the apostle Paul in Romans 12:11, Dr. Mackay declared, "Ours is a very passionate generation, a generation all aglow. We witness the clash of rival passions. We have fanaticism and we have faith. . . . In the attempt to squelch fanaticism we run the danger of extinguishing faith. . . . Spiritual *ardor* is the essence of the Christian life. . . .

"Remember this: there is something beyond churchmanship in all its forms, more important than anything that is related to ecclesiastical *order*. There is something that goes beyond theological orthodoxy, important though it is that your doctrinal ideas be sound. There is something also beyond ethics. That something is an inward fire, a glow, the presence of the Holy Spirit."[1]

Over the years, Dr. Mackay returned to the theme of *Order and Ardor* many times. "What is obviously needed is a transcendent frame of reference," he wrote back in 1943, "a great luminous idea, a central sun of some kind that would light up our cultural scene."[2]

---

1. *Princeton Seminary Bulletin* 48, no. 2 (October 1954).
2. John A. Mackay, *Heritage and Destiny* (New York: Macmillan, 1943), p. 63.

Dr. Mackay concluded his words to the graduating class of 1954: "'Be aglow with the Spirit.' If you are going to be true to Christianity's deepest tradition and be able to match this hour, maintain the Spirit's glow."

The contrast between order and ardor, and the way the one has influenced the other, is one of those convenient ways of understanding the plight and promise of the church in the last half of the twentieth century. During that time, each of the three presidents of Princeton Seminary has wrestled with the ways a genuine *ardor* for the faith might best be expressed in the often rigid precincts of academic and ecclesiastical *order.*

John Alexander Mackay served as the seminary's president from 1936 to 1959. He might be described as the great ecumenist with the glint of the World Council of Churches in his eyes long before it became a reality in 1948. He fervently talked about "ecumenics" long before most Protestants knew what the term meant. A man far ahead of his time, he dreamed of a world order where the church of Jesus Christ would play a pivotal role, and where the new Princeton Seminary which he was establishing would be a significant leader to usher in the new day. Those who knew him only slightly might have thought that his visionary concerns made him seem *austere,* but those who worked closely with him over the years would have said that *awesome* came closer to defining the man.

When he was succeeded in the presidency by James Iley McCord in 1959, books with such titles as *The Organization Man* and *The Man in the Gray Flannel Suit* described the compulsive ambition that seemed to fuel the nation's leaders for whom process and method and organization were "the way to go." McCord was first of all a brilliant and astute scholar, but he also was a perceptive organization man who devoted both of these skills to the continuing development of the seminary. In his early years as president, he worked closely with Eugene Carson Blake, the most influential member of the Seminary's Board of Trustees and perhaps the man who best symbolized Protestantism throughout the world. McCord devoted some of his time and remarkable talent to the various committees and commissions of the World Council of Churches, the World Alliance of Reformed Churches, the Council on Theological Education, and other groups, while at the same time applying his formidable gifts to the expanding concerns of Princeton Seminary.

As he roamed over the academic and ecclesiastical landscape, those closely associated with him sometimes used the word *political* to describe his statesmanship, but to those who knew him well, he was also intensely *practical* as his leadership became felt in all areas of the theological and ec-clesiastical world. Among his many accomplishments was the founding of the Center of Theological Inquiry in 1978. A recent brochure describes the Center as "an independent research institution . . . Christian in purpose, it is ecumenical, inter-religious, interdisciplinary and international in char-acter."

Then came a president fresh from the world of the parish, the pres-bytery, and the dramatically changing American culture. Dr. Mackay's concern about the relation of *order* to *ardor* may not have been the pre-dominant concern of those directing the bureaucracies of the ecclesiastical world, but Thomas Gillespie was experiencing first-hand the growing con-cerns of church members who sought a less-structured church that re-flected the more informal lifestyle around them.

For many of the hundreds of *pastors* who have graduated from Princeton Seminary, the fact that Gillespie was a pastor ("cultivate the shepherd's heart," Mackay used to say) almost instantly made them feel at home with him. Certainly all three presidents — Mackay, McCord, Gillespie — developed cordial relationships with the Seminary's gradu-ates, just as all three made remarkable strides in building up the faculty and strengthening the Seminary's academic stature. But it was almost sec-ond nature for Gillespie to resonate with the pastor and to seek to blend *order and ardor* and, as he heard when he received his diploma in 1954, to "be aglow with the Spirit." *Personable* is a way that many people might de-scribe him, but *pastoral* may more adequately catch the winsome nature of the man.

Now, as we anticipate the dawn of the twenty-first century, we ask the same question: What does it mean to be "aglow with the Spirit"? As we wrestle with the ways a genuine ardor for the Christian faith might be ex-pressed within the sometimes rigid confines of ecclesiastical and liturgical order, how do we effectively blend order with ardor?

Every pastor is aware of the changing role of the parish church within a culture that no longer looks to the church for guidance or direction. "All sorts of Christians are waking up and realizing that it is no longer 'our world' — if it ever was," writes William Willimon. Earlier in this century "Chris-tians could deceive themselves into thinking that we were in charge, that we had made a difference, that we had created a Christian culture."

As that notion of our world draws to an end, Willimon continues, we may discover "that the church, as those called out by God, embodies a social alternative that the world cannot on its own terms know. . . . The demise of the Constantinian world view, the gradual decline of the notion that the church needs some sort of surrounding 'Christian' culture to prop it up and mold its young, is not a death to lament. It is an opportunity to celebrate."[3]

Willimon's "opportunity to celebrate" is another way of stating Paul's admonition to "be aglow with the Spirit" and Mackay's plea for a transcendent frame of reference. Even the World Council of Churches emphasized the need for *ardor*. "Come Holy Spirit — Renew the Whole Creation" was the theme of its seventh assembly in 1990. Commenting on this theme, Princeton Professor Daniel Migliore cites a number of reasons for this resurgence of interest:

> Viewed in broad cultural perspective, the new interest in the Holy Spirit is a protest against depersonalization and bureaucratization in both modern society and the church. It is a protest against the domination of form over vitality, structure over purpose, external authority over free consent. When questions are settled simply by quoting passages from the Bible or citing the doctrines of the church, this is rightly judged by many people as but another instance of the ethos of control and coercion. To know God as Spirit is to experience God as a liberating rather than coercive power.
>
> The new interest in the Holy Spirit may also be seen as a hunger for a deeper faith, for a new relationship with God, for the experience of love and friendship, and for the spiritual resources to deal with the personal and corporate crises of our time.[4]

Dr. Mackay's plea in 1954 for "spiritual ardor" was uttered at a time when "organized religion" seemed to be flourishing and the churches were growing. Now, over fifty years later, the established "mainline" churches (denominations) are not only growing smaller in a nation that is growing larger; they are part of the religious establishment that simply has lost meaning for an increasingly large segment of our population.

3. Stanley Hauerwas and William Willimon, *Resident Aliens* (Nashville: Abingdon, 1989), pp. 17-18.

4. Daniel L. Migliore, *Faith Seeking Understanding* (Grand Rapids: Eerdmans, 1991), pp. 166-67.

The Center of Theological Inquiry, mentioned earlier, has sought to confront these problems by drawing together select groups of scholars from around the world who seek to answer these five central questions:

How can science and faith inform each other?

What can people of faith do to help create supportive communities in a pluralistic, fragmented, and violent age?

How can the followers of different religious traditions comprehend, respect, and work with each other?

How can faith help us know how best to live, given the rapid pace of change in technology, medicine, ideals, and values?

How can a renewed faith help us to express and understand meaning rich enough for human life together?[5]

These questions become all the more pertinent as America faces the next century with a new wave of immigrants. The magazine *Business Week* cites these government statistics: "During the next decade . . . nearly a million immigrants are expected to arrive in the U.S. every year. Most, both legal and illegal, will continue to come from Latin America and Southeast Asia, but every foreign land will be represented. So will every level of skill, education and talent: new arrivals will make up hotel beds, start their own shops, and pursue pathbreaking medical research. . . . By 2006, in fact, immigrants will account for half of all new U.S. workers; over the next 30 years, their share will rise to 60%."[6]

A telling question for Protestants — and in particular for Presbyterians — is whether this new wave of U.S. citizens is of any concern to them. Will carefully honed liturgies which are prized so highly have any meaning to these new citizens, or should the established denominations and churches seek to accommodate the new arrivals by relating to the way *they* express their faith? Must ardor give way to liturgical order? Will being "aglow with the Spirit" — the ardor — be allowed to fuse with or overcome the rigidity of ecclesiastic order? Will "church government" allow for flexibility in the way churches function as they seek to adapt to "foreigners who do things differently" — people who now are fellow citizens?

5. "Fusing Faith and Reason," Center of Theological Inquiry, 50 Stockton Street, Princeton, NJ 08540.

6. *Business Week*, August 31, 1998, p. 76.

"The unity of the church is not to be found primarily in the structures, offices, doctrines, or programs," writes Professor Daniel Migliore. "It is a distinctive unity rooted in new fellowship with God through Christ in the Spirit. The unity of the church is a fragmentary and provisional participation in the costly love of the triune God. Unity in the love of this God cannot possibly mean lifeless uniformity or deadening sameness. The unity of the church is a unity of love that enters into relationship with others and finds identity in relationship."[7]

Questions about structure and form and what is meant when we speak of the unity of the church come to mind when we recall the way the Protestant establishment has responded in the past. In tracing the history of the Protestant church in late nineteenth-century America when the last great wave of immigration took place, church historian Martin Marty reports that "Protestantism had prospered in town-and-country America, among northwest European and British immigrants who adjusted easily to the covenants of the Republic. Now, suddenly, America was becoming an increasingly urban and industrial scene. Protestants did not know how to minister to the millions of new arrivals in crowded cities or to the workers in the new factories. The Protestants realized that industrial change brought into being a new victim class of the poor and overlooked. Could the churches find in their own tradition ways to understand, motivation to serve, techniques to be effective?"

By the end of the nineteenth century, writes Marty, the old "Protestant empire" was considerably weakened. With attempts to relate to the new arrivals "the divisions came to be 'conservative' versus 'liberal,' 'traditional' versus 'progressive,' 'resistant' versus 'adaptionist' in character. The house divided was less able to define the terms to which non-Protestants had to relate. The Protestants' divisions also left the opening for new secular schools of thought and churchless ways of behavior to develop."[8]

Coupled with the difficulties of the Protestant churches to relate to people of different ethnic and cultural backgrounds is the violent change that has taken place in America's cities. One is tempted to say, "Same song, next verse!" as we trace the inability of the denominations to rise above their differences and allow ardor to triumph over order. And when we ob-

7. *Business Week*, August 31, 1998, p. 201.

8. Martin E. Marty, *Pilgrims in Their Own Land* (Boston: Little, Brown and Company, 1984), pp. 298-99.

serve how many divisions there are *within* the particular denominations today, one wonders whether Mackay's yearning for "a central sun of some kind that would light up our cultural scene" will ever become a reality.

The question becomes more crucial when we see what has happened to the established ("mainline") Protestant churches in America's cities. The following membership statistics from the Presbytery of Philadelphia (the first presbytery in the United States, established in 1706) should raise many questions about the capability of the churches to minister to the masses (or to anyone other than "their own kind," for that matter). These figures are for the Presbyterian Church (USA), but somewhat similar statistics for most, if not all of the other major denominations could be reported for their churches in America's larger cities.

Year	Number of Churches	Number of Church Members
1960	196	111,282
1980	162	71,086
1997	151	46,951

These numbers show the dramatic decline: forty-five fewer churches and 64,331 fewer members in the last thirty-seven years. Of these 151 churches in the Presbytery of Philadelphia, 64 are located within the city limits of Philadelphia. They have a total membership of approximately 8,400 members. Most of them are in the "inner-city" areas where new and different populations have supplanted the old Protestant hegemony. The remaining number of church members — over 38,000 — come from churches in the surrounding suburbs or the outlying areas of Philadelphia.

How do we react to these numbers? They are nothing new to the pastors and workers in the inner-city churches who face hosts of problems that the pastors and leaders in the suburbs and the "average" American communities know little about. What is very clear is that it is almost meaningless to measure (statistics) the inner-city churches by the same criteria we use for the churches in the towns, communities, suburbia and exurbia of America.

In this regard, many people may have been "hooked" on *order* (ecclesiastical) and have not discerned *ardor*. The real question we need to ask is how we may "be aglow with the Spirit" as we work with people for whom proper ecclesiastical order is the last thing that would ever occur to them.

For the past fifty years the Presbyterian Church (USA) has been grappling with the problem of "the urban church," and remarkable innovative attempts have been made to resolve it, with little more success than the mayors and school superintendents of our major cities have had. Some of the denomination's most dedicated and committed pastors have poured out their lives in trying to find effective ways to serve the citizens in the inner city. In many ways, tackling the problems of "the inner-city church" has become the new missionary frontier of the church.

As many Executive Presbyters might tell us, it is time for us to begin to measure the inner-city church in new and different ways. What, for example, do the above statistics tell us about the relation of order to ardor? Certainly we are neck-deep in ecclesiastical order when the same measurement is used for inner-city churches that is used for suburban and exurban churches. We do not measure the effectiveness of our missionary work abroad this way; why do we continue to categorize the inner-city church by the same measurements we use for the other churches?

Perhaps the day has come when we should stop counting the individual inner-city churches by their gains and losses, and begin to measure their meaning in terms of spiritual *ardor* — the number of people who are being served and who are nurtured in their understanding of the God who has come in Christ.

Is it ecclesiastical order that is dictating to us when we think that at least one pastor should be attached to each church? Do our statistics (ecclesiastical order) measure the vitality of those churches by the number of "new members" received and the "receipts" reported each year? How do our statistical reports measure those churches that are strategically located in areas of great need? They may be ministering to the community in myriads of ways — with soup kitchens, neighborhood programs, and other activities. And they also have services of divine worship.

In Jesus' parable, the "righteous" ask, "Lord, when was it that we saw you hungry and gave you food, or thirsty and gave you something to drink? And when was it that we saw you a stranger and welcomed you, or naked and gave you clothing? And when was it that we saw you sick or in prison and visited you? And the king will answer them, Truly I tell you, just as you did it to one of the least of these who are members of my family, you did it to me" (Matthew 25:37-40).

How many ways there are to be "aglow with the Spirit" without being institutionalized in doing so! Some presbyteries have sought to put groups of such churches together in clusters so that they can become more effective in their neighborhoods. It would be a triumph for the Spirit if many small urban churches were linked together in these clusters. Each cluster — staffed by a minister of the Word and Sacraments, an Educational and Music minister/director, along with two or three skilled professionals — would minister to the physical as well as spiritual needs of the people in the surrounding area.

Many "new approaches" to the church's witness in the inner city are being tried by those close to the inner-city problems. Especially in such situations, *order* is essential to manage and direct a well-equipped ministry. But even more essential than order is the spiritual *ardor* which requires a ministry to the whole person — body, mind, and soul.

In the early days of the twentieth century, the Protestant church in America was aflame with the foreign missionary endeavor. Church members responded to the call to establish churches, schools, hospitals, and extensive programs in distant lands. As we approach the twenty-first century, could not a similar enthusiasm arise for a bold, comprehensive mission in America's cities? It would require working with other denominations and parachurch groups. If Christ's command to "Go therefore and make disciples of all nations" (Matthew 28:19) applies to distant places, doesn't it also apply at home? And doesn't it require new and different ways for the churches to minister? If that were to happen, then *ardor* would determine what *order* was to do, and *order* would fulfill the demands of *ardor*.

> The old order changeth, yielding place to new;
> And God fulfills himself in many ways,
> Lest one good custom should corrupt the world.[9]

*   *

At a recent meeting of the Board of Trustees of Princeton Theological Seminary, President Gillespie shared a "dream" with the members of the Board. He and Barbara had recently returned from visits in distant lands with our Christian sisters and brothers, many of them graduates of the seminary. In some of the places they visited, he said, the educational resources — particularly the libraries — are woefully inadequate.

Wouldn't it be wonderful, he mused, if we channeled some of Prince-

9. Alfred, Lord Tennyson, *Morte D'Arthur*.

ton Seminary's vast resources to these third-world seminaries? We could devise ways to install computers in their libraries which would be equipped to use all the resources of the seminary's Speer and Luce libraries, thereby giving our fellow Christians abroad access to the same remarkable resources that are available to anyone studying here in Princeton.

That was an example of *ardor* — Christian ardor — which would have to rely on *order* — Christian order — to achieve its goal. Were that to happen, Dr. Mackay would be proud. "Be aglow with the Spirit," he would say.

Biblical Theology and the Authority of Scripture

MICHAEL WELKER

1. What Is "Biblical Theology"?

"What is biblical theology?" This question is not easily answered, for "biblical theology" has been variously understood:

- as a branch of the theological disciplines of exegesis, systematics, or practical theology; or
- as a complex interdisciplinary theological program that takes up the impetus of the Reformation and of the Second Vatican Council; or
- as the regulative idea of a theology in accordance with the Bible, that is, a scripturally appropriate theology; or
- as the idea of a theology found in the Bible, and its — at least latent — realization.[1]

---

1. For a distinction between the two key ideas, cf. G. Ebeling, "The Meaning of Biblical Theology," in *Word and Faith* (Philadelphia: Fortress Press, 1963), pp. 79-97; J. P. Gabler, *De iusto discrimine theologiae biblicae et dogmaticae regundisque recte utriusque finibus* (1787), relevant portions translated and published by J. H. Sandys-Wunsch and L. Eldredge, "J. P. Gabler and the Distinction between Biblical and Dogmatic Theology," *Scottish Journal of Theology* 33 (1980): 133-58; cf. also R. Smend, "Johann Philipp Gablers Begründung der Biblischen Theologie," *Evangelische Theologie* 22 (1962): 345-57.

Translated by Arnold Neufeldt-Fast, Ph.D., Kitchener, Ontario.

These four concepts are connected with each other in a variety of ways. On the one side, this gives the impression of conceptual confusion; but on the other side, this brings with it inner- and inter-disciplinary tensions which can be very constructive and fruitful.

"Biblical theology," whether understood as a branch of the theological disciplines or as an interdisciplinary theological program, is always confronted not only with the suspicion of conceptual unclarity, but also with the following never ending problem: if "biblical theology" is to be understood as "theology" in the sense of an abstracted or ultimately ascertainable, comprehensive framework for thought and conviction,[2] that is, in the sense of a specific system, then it is impossible. This type of biblical theology would contradict not only the variety and vitality of the biblical witness and record, which developed over a 1500-year period; above all, it would obstruct the vitality of the revelation of God to which the various biblical records testify from their particular perspectives.

There is a theological and scientific consensus — outside of a few exceptions — that it is misleading to "abstract from the Bible some concealed historical or conceptual system, an economy of salvation or a Christian view of things. There can be no biblical theology in this sense, either of the Old or New Testament, or of the Bible as a whole."[3] But if "theology" is understood not as talk of God in a comprehensive, fully developed framework for thought, but rather as "God-talk" that is genuinely capable of development with regards to content, comprehension, and subject matter, and is accompanied by certainty and directed towards truth, which, however modest and fragmentary, serves to strengthen the certainty of faith in the development of the knowledge of God[4] — then talk of a biblical theology appears to limit itself to the trivial insight that the biblical texts are filled and saturated with theology. In so far as all ponderable Christian theology ultimately claims to have biblical warrant and to be in accordance with scripture in one sense or another, there appears to remain no obvious place for the concept of a biblical theology. The expression "biblical theology" appears either to

2. For the larger theological concept presupposed here and in the following, cf. M. Welker, "Theology in Public Discourse Outside Communities of Faith?" in *Religion, Pluralism, and Public Life: Abraham Kuyper's Legacy for the Twenty-first Century,* ed. Luis Lugo, intro. by Max L. Stackhouse (Grand Rapids: Eerdmans, forthcoming 2000).

3. Karl Barth, *Church Dogmatics,* vol. I/2, trans. G. T. Thomson and H. Knight (Edinburgh: T. & T. Clark, 1978), §§19-21, 483.

4. Cf. note 2 above.

propagate a theologically and scientifically problematic notion of unity or a system,[5] or, however, to stress the simple fact — but with a skewed emphasis — that the biblical texts speak of God in a qualified manner and that Christian theology is oriented scripturally.

Yet between these two extremes, which make all talk and further development of biblical theology skeptical, the notion of biblical theology has gained a sharpened profile in the course of the twentieth century as an inner disciplinary and interdisciplinary programmatic concept and a concept for reform. Already in the 1920s and 1930s, opposition to the critical-historical study of the Bible intensified with the reservations that it "divides up the Bible into disconnected layers, emphasizes too strongly the similarities between the Bible and its cultural environment, overemphasizes the developmental process, and forgoes the task of delivering an actual theological interpretation of the Holy Scriptures."[6] This opposition and the endeavor to develop alternatives came to be understood (in part) in terms of the programmatic and reforming concept of "biblical theology." Beginning in the 1970s this programmatic and reforming concept has been taken up with increasing vigor by systematic theology as well, and employed finally to characterize interdisciplinary theological approaches for thought and research.[7]

5. For a critique of this view, cf. J. D. Levenson, "Why Jews Are Not Interested in Biblical Theology," in *Judaic Perspectives on Ancient Israel,* ed. J. Neusner et al. (Philadelphia: Fortress Press, 1987), pp. 281ff.; D. Ritschl, " 'Wahre,' oder 'neue' Biblische Theologie? Einige Anfragen zur neueren Diskussion um 'Biblische Theologie,'" *Jahrbuch für Biblische Theologie* 1 (1986): 135-50.

6. J. Barr, "Biblische Theologie," in *Evangelisches Kirchenlexikon,* vol. 1, ed. E. Fahlbusch et al., 3rd ed. (Göttingen: Vandenhoeck & Ruprecht, 1986), pp. 488-94, 489.

7. In this regard, cf. the following journals and series: *Biblical Theology Bulletin* (1971-); *Overtures in Biblical Theology* (Philadelphia: Fortress Press, 1977-); *Biblisch-Theologische Studien* (Neukirchen: Neukirchener Verlag, 1977-); *Horizons in Biblical Theology* (1979-); *Ex Auditu: An Annual of the Frederick Neumann Symposium on Theological Interpretation of Scripture* (Princeton, 1985-); *Jahrbuch für Biblische Theologie* (1986-); also, cf. esp. F. Mildenberger, *Biblische Dogmatik. Eine Biblische Theologie in dogmatischer Perspektive,* vols. 1-3 (Stuttgart: Verlag W. Kohlhammer, 1991-1993); Ch. Schroeder, "Macht und Gerechtigkeit: Ansätze des nordamerikanischen Forschungsprojekts 'Bible and Theology' zur Neukonzeption einer Biblischen Theologie," *Jahrbuch für Biblische Theologie* 11 (1996): 183-96; W. Schweiker and M. Welker, "A New Paradigm of Theological and Biblical Inquiry," in *Power, Powerlessness, and the Divine: New Inquiries in Bible and Theology,* ed. C. L. Rigby (Atlanta: Scholars Press, 1997); B. Oberdorfer, "Biblisch-realistische Theologie: Methodologische Überlegungen zu einem dogmatischen Programm," in *Resonanzen: Theologische Beiträge Festschrift für M. Welker zum 50. Geburtstag,* ed. S. Brandt (Bovenden: Foedus Verlag, 1997), pp. 63-83.

2. Biblical Theology as a Brand
of the Theological Disciplines

Above all in the Anglo-Saxon world, biblical theology in the twentieth century has been understood as a branch of the exegetical disciplines (Old Testament and New Testament), which — in contrast to those branches oriented towards history and the history of religions — attempts to bring out the theological messages of the biblical texts. In this regard biblical theology attaches special importance to the "unity" of this message, also to grasping the "unity" of the Old Testament, of the New Testament and of both testaments,[8] and to understanding and presenting the uniqueness and special nature of the biblical message(s) over against the religious-historical contexts. Given this project, biblical theology is thrust out of the exegetical context and is faced with problems such as developing various concepts of "unity" in view of a multitude of texts and traditions, justifying them over against the historical and historically proceeding subdisciplines, as well as the problem of conflating concepts as: "middle of the scripture," "unity of the testaments," and the "*proprium* of the biblical message." Moreover, biblical theology is faced with the question regarding the connection and difference between the theological disciplines,[9] as well as with the problem of distinguishing itself from a biblical theology that comes out of systematic theology and occasionally out of practical theology as well. Finally, biblical theology is faced with the challenge to clarify the differences between the church and Israel in their understanding and interpretation of scripture.[10]

The term biblical theology, however, is also used as a designation for a subdiscipline or specific presentation of systematic and dogmatic theology. In this regard the programmatic concept of biblical theology does not simply represent a rhetorical claim by theology as scripturally appropriate in

8. Cf. H.-J. Kraus, *Die Biblische Theologie: Ihre Geschichte und Problematik* (Neukirchen-Vluyn: Neukirchener Verlag, 1970); M. Oeming, *Gesamtbiblische Theologien der Gegenwart. Das Verhältnis von AT und NT in der hermeneutischen Diskussion seit Gerhard von Rad,* 2nd ed. (Stuttgart: Verlag W. Kohlhammer, 1987).

9. E. Jüngel, "Das Verhältnis der theologischen Disciplinen untereinander" in *idem, Unterwegs zur Sache: Theologische Bemerkungen,* 2nd ed. (Munich: Chr. Kaiser Verlag, 1988), pp. 34-59.

10. Cf. B. Janowski, "Biblische Theologie I," *Religion in Geschichte und Gegenwart,* 4th ed., vol. 1 (Tübingen: J. C. B. Mohr [Paul Siebeck], 1998); E. Zenger, ed., *Die Tora als Kanon für Juden und Christen* (Freiburg: Herder, 1996).

contrast to philosophical theology or other theologies with a looser or hardly comprehensible connection to the scriptures. Already Schleiermacher had considered the internal differentiation between a scientific *(wissenschaftliche)*, symbolic, and "scriptural" dogmatic, the latter of which he also called a "biblical dogmatic." Likely with the work of W. M. L. DeWette in mind,[11] Schleiermacher connected to this notion the concept of a dogmatic in which "the reference to Scripture predominates throughout."[12] In contrast to a systematic-theological approach which "stresses individual passages torn out of their context" in order to support one's own idea, construct, or train of thought, he recommended "a large-viewed use of Scripture" which takes "account of larger sections, and these particularly fruitful ones, so as to exhibit in the trains of thought of the sacred writers those same combinations on which the dogmatic results also are based."[13] Yet more significant than impulses from the history of theology[14] is a whole syndrome of developments — which have problematized many well-rehearsed forms of systematic theology — that have increasingly heightened interest in differentiating and developing a biblical theology in the last third of the twentieth century.

The decreasing formative influence of the confessional writings, together with the intensified effort towards constructive ecumenical understanding, as well as the decreasing formative influence of philosophical theories — both in terms of delivering capable models for thought as well as in their cultural-diagnostic competence — have generated a stronger fundamental orientation of systematic and also practical theology in the historical, cultural, and social sciences. This has occurred without regard to the differences in weight or influence between the German- and

11. Above all, see: W. M. L. DeWette, *Die Biblische Dogmatik Alten und Neuen Testaments, Oder kritische Darstellung der Religionslehre des Hebraismus* (1813) in *idem, Lehrbuch der christlichen Dogmatik* (Berlin: G. Reimer, 1831).

12. F. E. D. Schleiermacher, *The Christian Faith*, vol. 1, ed. H. R. MacKintosh and J. S. Stewart (New York: Harper & Row, 1963), §27, 116; cf. also the work by Oberdorfer, "Biblisch-realistische Theologie," noted above (fn. 7).

13. Schleiermacher, *The Christian Faith*, vol. 1.

14. Cf. J. T. Beck, *Die Christliche Lehr-Wissenschaft nach den biblischen Urkunden* (Stuttgart: Belser, 1840/41); J. L. S. Lutz, *Biblische Dogmatik,* ed. R. Rüetschi (Pforzheim, 1847); M. Kähler, "Biblische Theologie," in *Realenzyklopädie für protestanische Theologie und Kirche,* vol. 3, ed. A. Hauck, 3rd ed. (Leipzig: Hinrichs, 1898), pp. 192-200; H. Frei, *The Eclipse of Biblical Narrative: A Study in Eighteenth and Nineteenth Century Hermeneutics* (New Haven, Conn.: Yale University Press, 1974).

English-speaking realms,[15] and the other regions of the world as well.[16] This new fundamental orientation, as well as the exemplary systematic fecundity of many thematic contributions by exegetes, and also the efforts to correct the canonical-theoretical demotion of the Old Testament in the systematic and New Testament theologies of the nineteenth and twentieth centuries, and finally the concern to enter (once again) into dialogue with widespread styles of piety — which cannot place themselves in a fruitful relationship with conventional academic theology — have led to two very different expressions of biblical theology.

Common to both is the need constantly to scrutinize and correct the systematic-theological selection of themes and thought forms on the basis of what Schleiermacher called "a large-viewed use of Scripture." They are at different points in the search for a "plain talk of God" which is in proximity to the language of proclamation[17] — in contrast to a systematic theology which constantly approaches faith from outer perspectives — that is, in the search for a "critique of abstraction" which measures systematic-theological and dogmatic forms of thought against the biblical texts to which they refer explicitly or implicitly. In this regard the concern, of course, is not to call into question all models of thought and basic abstractions as such, but to correct reductionistic forms of thought with forms and styles of thought that are both more exegetically grounded and more powerful as well in their time- and cultural-diagnostic capabilities.[18]

15. B. S. Childs, *Biblical Theology in Crisis* (Philadelphia: Westminster Press, 1970); J. D. Smart, *The Past, Present, and Future of Biblical Theology* (Philadelphia: Westminster Press, 1979); R. Morgan, "Biblical Theology," in *A Dictionary of Biblical Interpretation*, ed. R. J. Coggins and J. L. Houlden (Philadelphia: Trinity Press International, 1990), pp. 86-89; H. Seebaß, "Biblische Theologie," *Verkündigung und Forschung* 27 (1982): 28-45; H. Graf Reventlow, *Problems of Biblical Theology in the Twentieth Century* (Philadelphia: Fortress Press, 1986).

16. E. Fahlbusch, J. Mbiti, S. Yagi, U. Schoenborn, L. Schottroff, "Biblische Theologie im Kontext," *Evangelisches Kirchenlexikon*, vol. 1, ed. E. Fahlbusch, 3rd ed. (Göttingen: Vandenhoeck & Ruprecht, 1986), pp. 494-503.

17. F. Mildenberger, "Biblische theologie als kirchliche Schriftauslegung," *Jahrbuch für Biblische Theologie* 1 (1986): 151-62; *idem, Biblische Dogmatik*, vols. 1-3; J. Rohloff and H. G. Ulrich, eds., *Einfach von Gott Reden: Ein theologischer Diskurs. Festschrift für Friedrich Mildenberger zum 65. Geburtstag* (Stuttgart: Verlag W. Kohlhammer, 1994).

18. Cf. Schweiker and Welker, "A New Paradigm of Theological and Biblical Inquiry," in *God the Spirit*, ed. M. Welker, trans. J. F. Hoffmeyer (Minneapolis: Fortress Press, 1994), esp. pp. 40ff.; Welker, *Schöpfung und Wirklichkeit* (Neukirchen-Vluyn: Neukirchener Verlag, 1995), esp. pp. 32ff.; Oberdorfer, "Biblisch-realistische Theologie."

3. Biblical Theology as an
Interdisciplinary Theological Program

On the one hand, the exegetical disciplines work in the name of biblical theology primarily against the disassociation and secularization of their discipline, and search for a unity and *proprium* of the biblical records amidst an explosive fullness of detailed historical and religious-historical research. On the other hand, in the name of biblical theology systematic and practical theological disciplines primarily seek to establish a unique identity in distinction from, for example, specific philosophical or other extra-theological rationalities and forms of systematics that follow their own primary interests — and the religiosity shaped by them. Starting with the achievements of *loci*-structured dogmatics, they work at examining and, if necessary, transforming basic theological ideas and forms of thought that are reductionistic or too wooden and simplistic, with constant reference back to the respective relevant biblical texts and with a concern constantly to refine and intensify these references in conversation with the exegetical research. It is precisely in following these opposite concerns[19] and biblical-theological intentions that the exegetical, systematic, and practical theological disciplines are directed toward and dependent upon each other.[20]

Whereas exegetics, with its historical-critical competency, must protect systematic theology from over-hasty analogies and biblicistic "fusions of horizons," systematic theology has the task to help test those concepts employed by exegetes, such as "unity," "*proprium*," and "middle of the scriptures," that is, in terms of their systematic power in view of the history of doctrine and of contemporary history. The fruit of this critical discussion includes experiential gains, both in view of a variety of inadequate conceptions of unity[21] ("covenant," "the mighty acts of God," "reconcilia-

19. In contrast cf. C. Westermann, "Aufgaben einer zukünftigen Biblischen Theologie," in *idem, Erträge der Forschung am Alten Testament; Gesammelte Studien,* vol. 3, ed. R. Albertz (Munich: Chr. Kaiser Verlag, 1984), pp. 203-11; for a critique of Westermann, cf. Ritschl, "'Wahre,' 'reine' oder 'neue' Biblische Theologie?" Cf. n. 5.

20. K. Haaker et al., *Biblische Theologie heute* (BthSt 1) (Neukirchen: Neukirchener Verlag, 1997); Graf Reventlow, *Problems of Biblical Theology.*

21. H. H. Schmid, "Schöpfung, Gerechtigkeit und Heil," *Zeitschrift für Theologie und Kirche* 70 (1973): 1-19; P. Stuhlmacher, *How to Do Biblical Theology* (Allison Park, Pa.: Pickwick Publishing, 1995).

tion," etc.) and of concepts in need of further examination, but also including a high sensitization for the context-bounded nature of basic biblical-theological ideas and modes of operation.[22] Finally, theological disciplines that adopt the programmatic title of "biblical theology" have the common task of grasping theologically the limits of the canonical records and constantly expressing anew and in a theologically sound manner the continuity of God's revelatory agency in the biblical texts — which ultimately leads toward trinitarian-theological questions.[23]

4. Biblical Theology as a Basic Regulative Idea for a Theology Immanent to and Appropriate to the Biblical Texts, and the Authority of Scripture

In 1951 Ernst Käsemann asked the question, "Does the New Testament canon give the foundation for the unity of the church?" which he answered negatively, with the claim that the canon gives a foundation for the multitude of confessions. Today, however, the dominant conviction is that the living unity of the church is based precisely on the multitude of confessions.[24] Dynamic concepts of unity are sought and developed — not ones set abstractly over against difference, but rather concepts of unity that distinguish between fruitful and creative differences and unfruitful and destructive differences. The "conviction that the divine *Logos,* who comes to speech for believers in the biblical Word, is first heard when the Bible is made accessible as a whole, as an interconnected textual framework,"[25]

22. Cf. Fahlbusch et al., "Biblische Theologie im Kontext"; esp. also the work of leading feminist-theological exegetes as in E. Schlüssler-Fiorenza, ed., *Searching the Scriptures,* vols. 1-2 (New York: Crossroad, 1993-94); P. Trible, *Feminist Approaches to the Bible* (Washington, D.C.: Biblical Archeology Society, 1995).

23. This is well expressed in Ritschl, "'Wahre', 'reine' oder 'neue' Biblische Theologie?"

24. E. Käsemann, "The Canon of the New Testament and the Unity of the Church," in *Essays on New Testament Themes,* trans. W. J. Montague (London: SCM Press, 1964), 95-107; idem, *Das Neue Testament als Kanon: Dokumentation und kritische Analyse zur gegenwärtigen Diskussion* (Göttingen: Vandenhoeck & Ruprecht, 1980); and already in 1948 (German) K. Barth, *Church Dogmatics,* vol. I/2, §§19-21; also H. D. Betz, "Begründet der neutestamentliche Kanon eine Kirche in Fragmenten?" *Concilium* (1997): 322-33.

25. N. Lohfink, *Studien zur biblischen Theologie* (Stuttgart: Verlag Kath. Bibelwerk, 1993), p. 8.

goes along with the insight that this textual framework points to God and God's revelatory agency in a "contrastive"[26] and simultaneously complex and coherent manner.[27] Instead of searching to develop a simple — inevitably reductionistic — "scripture principle," there is the need to develop formal and internally appropriate forms of the "faithfulness to the scriptures,"[28] that is, forms which take the scriptures seriously, not as a mechanical whole, but in reference to the wealth of its internal frames of reference, which for their part point to the living God.[29] In theological-historical perspective, the development of non-monolinear conceptions of "history" appropriate to this understanding of unity,[30] and the exploration of the connection between "faith" and "cultural memory,"[31] especially "living memory," as well as historical, cultural, and ecclesial learning and the development of a clear understanding of the "name" of the trinitarian God, still lie far ahead in the future.

The manifold biblical records, quite blatantly bound together and at the same time latently interwoven on many different levels, build a framework that connects the recognition of God's activity among people,[32] the living memory of this activity, and the anticipation of this activity — a framework that enables historical, cultural, and ecclesial learning and growing in this knowledge, yet keeps it from coming to an end.

Precisely in this respect does the self-referential nature of scripture show itself to be a living whole,[33] in that it points from a variety of perspectives giving witness to God and divine agency in and for the creation,

26. Zenger, *Die Tora als Kanon für Juden und Christen,* p. 18 and *passim.* Cf. n. 10.

27. Schweiker and Welker, "A New Paradigm of Theological and Biblical Inquiry."

28. G. Sauter, *Grundlagen der Theologie* (Göttingen: Vandenhoeck & Ruprecht, 1998), ch. 3.3.

29. H. Haag, "Biblische Theologie," in *Mysterium Salutis: Grundriß heilsgeschichtlicher Dogmatik,* ed. J. Feiner and M. Löhrer (Einsiedeln: Benziger, 1965), pp. 440-59.

30. H. Gese, "Erwägungen zur Einheit der Biblische Theologie," *Zeitschrift für Theologie und Kirche* 67 (1970): 417-36; *idem,* "The Biblical View of Scripture" in *idem, Essays on Biblical Theology,* trans. K. Crim (Minneapolis: Augsburg, 1981), pp. 9-33.

31. J. Assmann, *Das kulturelle Gedächtnis. Schrift, Erinnerung und politische Identität in frühen Hochkulturen,* 2nd ed. (Munich: Beck, 1997).

32. R. Williams, "Der Literalsinn der Heiligen Schrift," *Evangelische Theologie* 50 (1990): 55-71.

33. Cf. P. Walter, E. Haag, K. Kertelge, "Biblische Theologie," in *Lexikon für Theologie und Kirche,* vol. 2, ed. W. Kasper et al., 3rd ed. (Freiburg: Herder, 1994), pp. 426-35; Sauter, *Grundlagen der Theologie.*

through which it itself becomes a source of living water. It is on the basis of this inner constitution and outer certainty that scripture acquires its authority. It is on the basis of this inner constitution and outer certainty that one can say of it: *scriptura "ipsa per sese certissima, facillima, apertissima, sui ipsius interpres, omnium omnia probans, iudicans et illuminans"* (scripture is "in itself the most certain, most easily understood, most plain, is its own interpreter, approving, judging and illuminating all human claims").[34]

34. M. Luther, "*Assertio omnium articulorum* (1520)," in *D. Martin Luthers Werke* (Weimar edition, 1883-), 7.97, 24f. ["Defense of All the Articles of Martin Luther Condemned by the Recent Bull of Leo X"].

The Relation of Historical to Systematic Theology

E. DAVID WILLIS

I. Caveats Concerning Methodology

There is a temptation to think of "systematic theology" and "historical theology" as realities which exist somewhere, perhaps in some transcendent theological encyclopedia and hopefully in the writings of some specialist, which we can identify if only we have the correct spiritual or bibliographical insight. This approach has a remarkable tenacity among us when we concentrate on the discreteness of the various disciplines and confidently say that someone is studying historical theology or biblical theology or that so-and-so has shifted from church history to theology. As descriptions of what people are doing when they work with different materials and do different things they think are appropriate to those materials, such functional discreteness is both legitimate and necessary. There is another temptation: to join the widespread practice of suggesting that methodological questions are prior to fruitful practice in any discipline. Frequently theol-

---

Author's Note: This is the paper I read to the Colloquium of Area II of The Graduate Theological Union, Berkeley, January 12, 1967, soon after my move there from Princeton. I have not updated it, not only because it is a whole piece on its own belonging to that time and place, but also because I find its central argument even more compelling now than I did then. I am sobered, of course, by some of the noninclusive language commonly used then; but I have chosen to leave exposed such arcane practice.

ogy is subsumed under methodology, e.g., the predominance of discussion about pre-understanding for biblical interpretation as compared with actual exegetical practice, or the excitement among systematicians over structure compared with their discernible impatience and loss of nerve when it comes to setting forth specific doctrines. Yet another temptation is to hypostatize into discrete disciplines areas that are merely the results of academic sociology. We find ourselves appointed to a chair that bears the title of some predefined discipline, or admitted to some predefined graduate program, and we naturally tend to ideologize our profession. Identifying these three temptations does not exempt us from vulnerability. But it should help put our convictions about the worth of the disciplines (corresponding to the danger of ascribing to them an eternal character), our efforts to clarify what we are doing (corresponding to the danger of putting methodology before practice), and our desire to work out a useful division of labor (corresponding to the danger of ideologizing our spot in the academic enterprise) in a perspective that will prevent us from taking ourselves too seriously.

Historical theology can refer to systematic theology, whose subject matter is the church's historical consciousness expressed in contemporary faith concepts. Historical theology can also refer to the critical study of the history of theology in relation to other agents in the development of Christianity. In the next two sections we will treat the relation of systematic theology to historical theology defined in these two ways, and in the final section we will suggest some systematic implications of the relation between faith and historical criticism.

II. Systematic Theology as Historical Theology

The task of systematic theology is the articulation, in terms which are cogent for contemporary people, of belief which the church defines as faithful to the witnesses of the Old and New Testaments. It is called dogmatics if it concentrates on the dogmas of church definition, and doctrinal theology if it works with a broader range. In either case its subject matter is the church's expression of faith, and its perpetual task is to reexpress that faith so that it, as far as is humanly possible, continues to refer to the God known in Jesus the Christ and continues to be intelligibly challenging for each generation. Systematic theologians are especially concerned about the congruence among the various distinguishable teachings which are involved in such a contemporary presentation of belief, and the impossible ideal toward which they work is the stating of self-evident connections among the various faith concepts. This ideal is pursued even by those who claim that systematic theology is a misnomer on the grounds that faith statements are paradoxical by nature, since the very affirmation of paradox implies that the whole is a unity. When this congruent presentation is directed not primarily to those who identify themselves as Christian but to those who are indifferent or hostile to the Kerygma, it functions as apologetics. Given the nature of secularization, which has only emphasized the place that doubt always plays in any genuine belief, the sharp distinction between systematics as discourse from faith to faith and apologetics as discourse from faith to unbelief is increasingly untenable.

Historical theology also is concerned with communicating the Kerygma intelligibly and persuasively, but it concentrates on the relation between past events and faith and on the problem of discerning and describing the historical process as medium of revelation. Putting it this way means that "theology" remains the noun and "historical" the adjective. The ultimate subject who is sought is God, the quest is historical interpretation, and the impossible ideal is to describe the manner in which God is related to each historical event. This ideal is pursued even by those who know that each event becomes more, not less, complex the more it is investigated, since the very generalization about the absolute relativity of historical judgment is used as a key to the meaning of the whole. In his historical-critical work to determine connections between events verifiable to anyone willing to examine the same monuments and documents, the historical theologian is indistinguishable from any other historian; he is as exposed to having his ultimate loyalties completely replaced as any historian is. History of doctrine and history of theology can be done as well without specifically Christian commitments as with them, although most historians of doctrine consider themselves Christians.

Both systematic theology and historical theology serve the transition from biblical communication to proclamation. Both are church activities in the sense that they are done from a confessional stance within the community which interprets and proclaims by faith. Both assume that this community has its origins in history in the sense that God makes himself and his claims known through the procession of interpreted happenings in time and place, and both are thereby exposed to the shattering effects and unparalleled opportunities afforded by critical historical science. Both perform a critical, disruptive, questioning function, to destroy man's credulity, in order to edify an examined faith. But historical theology serves systematics as systematics serves proclamation; that is, historical theology critically examines systematic use of historical material as systematics critically examines the internal congruence of proclamation and the external congruence with existential demands. Dogmatics serves historical theology as contemporary political theory serves political history, that is, by raising to explicit and congruent consciousness those ultimate commitments which inform the interpretive task.

The historical theologian is more motivated and better equipped linguistically to bring the past dialogues between Christ and culture to bear on present proclamation. He wants most to know about the continuities of historical process, and will constantly be up against the question of causality. He wants to know the historical basis, or lack of it, for a possible motivating contemporary theological conviction. The risk to the historical theologian's faith is that he will become convinced that other interpretations of historical data make the one of faith superfluous.

The systematic theologian is more motivated and better equipped linguistically to concentrate on keeping that dialogue going in the widest possible range of contemporary dialects. He wants most to know about the continuity among the components in any given presentation of ideas, and will constantly be up against the question of logic. He is not so much interested in the historical foundation for a motivating theological conviction as in achieving its most compelling expression in the contemporary mode. He will engage in more normative assertions than the historical theologian, insofar as he must say a Yes and a No to various proclamations and insofar as value judgments about the good and the true (and not simply the consistent) are inevitably a part of his critical task. The special risk to his faith is that he will find that alternative contemporary modes of thought and expression describe the human situation better than theological ones do.

Thus far we have been speaking of historical theology as theology done in a historical key, not as the historical investigation of theology. In this first sense it is only slightly distinguishable from systematics, so much so that any supposed inherent distinction between them based on subject matter and method remains unconvincing. If anything, systematics is not, in contemporary American practice, even as distinguishable from historical theology as we have been trying to suggest in functional sense. Most of those today who call themselves systematic theologians are actually engaged in historical theology whose history is only the most immediate past. It must be said that instead of being well-done historical theology, what is called systematic theology is only pale, attenuated, popularized historical theology. This is characterized by programmatic language which claims to be descriptive but which is really exhortation and which organizes second-hand historical generalizations and translates them into contemporary media with which it also has only a second-hand knowledge (e.g., especially in the case of sociology in a good deal of recent American Protestant theology).

This is not a condemnation of those of us doing systematic theology; it is rather a recognition of the difficulty of our properly systematic task, which in order to be done must be built on many more years of research in the auxiliary disciplines than we seem presently to realize.

III. Historical Theology as Critical History

If it is difficult to distinguish between systematic theology and historical theology in the first sense of the term, it is difficult to relate them positively when historical theology means the critical-historical study of theology. Indeed it is the tenuous character of the relation between theology and critical-historical study which is still *the* problem facing theology today. It is not a new problem; the classical formulation of it is Lessing's opinion that "accidental truths of history can never become the proof of necessary truths of reason." Applied to theology, the question is: How can faith be based, even in part, on events which the biblical witnesses proclaim to be of saving significance but which we cannot show historically to have happened according to the Scriptures or to have happened at all? Many attempts to solve this problem have been made and are being made, but I think they can finally be grouped under two basic responses: (a) faith is not vulnerable to historical research because its material is of another order than that of historical science, and (b) faith is dependent on historical knowledge and this tells us as much about historical knowledge, positively or negatively, as it does about faith.

The first response is, with many variations, the dominant one in contemporary theology derived from Kierkegaard's view that eternal happiness is based on historical knowledge only if the saving event on which it relies is different from all other kinds of occurrence and only if knowledge of it is different from all other kinds of historical knowledge. According to him, objective data are known by scientific research, existential becoming is known by ordinary faith, and the unique moment of God's historicity is known by eminent faith (the "happy passion"). This scheme gets modified into the argument that history is the sphere in which revelation occurs but that events having saving significance are known as *Geschichte* and not as *Historie*. This distinction in term may simply be that between *assensus* and *fiducia* applied to historical knowledge (and is therefore a distinction in the mind of the historical knower); or it may refer to some supposed ontological difference between two kinds of series of happenings (and is therefore close to being a distinction between ordinary history and metahistory — or to put it another way, between subhistory and "real history"). Barth takes more seriously than Bultmann the corporate and churchly character of this special knowledge of special events, but he suggests that there is a different kind of special knowledge for biblical comments than for other documents. Bultmann and Tillich have taken more seriously than Barth the common anthropology which historical knowledge implies and both have refused to develop a special hermeneutics for biblical documents. Bultmann so single-mindedly ties the eschatological event to the proclaimed Word that he is relatively unperplexed by the question of whether or not the proclaimed Word refers to a happening theoretically verifiable to a nonbeliever; his form of historical knowledge results from a one-sided application of the doctrine of justification by faith alone (an intensely personal one) to an analysis of the knowing subject. Although Tillich is not as good a practicing historian as Barth (Barth's most lasting contribution may very well be his excursus in the history of doctrine, and in intellectual history, which are the fine print of the *Church Dogmatics*), he has provided a better theoretical foundation in his Systematics for a positive relation to historical study. This he has done by his description of event as happening with interpretation (e.g., in the case of the resurrection, the earliest Christian community is remembering something and interpreting a happening, despite the facts that the two can never be separated and that the happening becomes history only through interpretation), by the positive role he gives to the dynamics of corporate memory through the use of symbols, and not least of all by his idealist ontology.

The advantage of the *Geschichte-Historie* distinction is its refusal to solve prematurely the tension between faith and history by reducing the former to the latter as it was the tendency of historicism to do. Moreover, its theological premise is one which seems to be inescapably a part of the Kerygma, namely that faith is a gift of grace which is sovereign over factors already given by nature. It makes room for divine initiative in dealing with a reality, Creation, which is other than the divine nature. The difficulty with too ambitious an acceptance of the *Geschichte-Historie* distinction is that one affirms the historical character of Christianity only by defining history in a way minimally recognizable to historians. Christianity is thus historical only by the Christian's definition of history, just as theology is a science only by the Christian's peculiar use of the term.

The other type of solution is not necessarily more promising. As the *Geschichte-Historie* distinction is undergirded by existentialism, so generally the helpmates of this solution are variously a learned naiveted idealism, a modified romanticism, or a faithful agnosticism. One can use the first helpmate and say that historical reason is able to discern, quite apart from faith, events as revelatory.

Another way of holding faith and history together is to argue that history is revelation; since history is ultimately the outworking of the divine Spirit, history is intrinsically a part of the doctrine of God. The difficulty here is one of identifying any kind of doctrine of *creation*, of distinguishing between God and his creation.

A third approach (that of R. R. Niebuhr) is to argue that historical knowledge and historical fact cannot be defined *a priori* by terms drawn from natural science but that historical knowledge and event in general are to be defined by the resurrection and the interpreting community's knowledge of it. Instead of starting with a general definition of historical knowledge and event and then seeing how saving event and knowledge of it can fit the general definition, the procedure moves from the particularity of the resurrection to the general. One can say this is an effort to apply a *theologia resurrectionis* to historical knowledge as Luther applied a *theologia crucis* to the knowledge of God. What such an examination of the resurrection tells us about historical reason in general is (a) that each event insofar as it is historical is unique; (b) that each unique event becomes history only through the mediation of a witnessing, interpreting, remembering community; and (c) that the analogies between present and past which are implied in any historical judgment are provided by the historian's own participation in the community of which the interpreted event he is investigating is also an expression. I think this line of thought — with some serious modifications — one of the most promising, and I shall return presently to suggest some lines along which to develop it. But here let us note that its weaknesses are (a) that it is an act of faith to accept the resurrection and the community's remembrance of it as paradigms for historical event and reason; (b) that historical science is brought closer to the church's historical knowledge by removing it further from natural science; and (c) that the reason the community is considered to be the medium of historical knowledge is a conviction that the spirit which found expression in an earlier event is the same spirit which finds expression in the historian's contemporary community.

A fourth approach is that of a fiducial agnosticism. God and his faithfulness are taken for granted, but one does not know how the origin of this faith can historically be shown to derive from him. This position (most concisely put by J. Barr) holds that it is confusing to speak about God's revelation in history because (a) one cannot isolate, by a historical examination of the biblical accounts themselves, events which are treated as revelatory acts of God; (b) there is always a previous cultural and religious tradition which creates the situation by which some event is interpreted as divine communication; and (c) divine acts of interference in political matters are only one of the forms of divine communication along with prophetic ecstasy, wisdom sayings, and cultic celebration. We do not know when this revelatory situation first appeared and why. We can only point back further into the dim mists of the religious legends which Israel used and changed, and say that we do not know when the concept of a benevolent and covenanting God occurred. How our faith has as its ground the one who directs history, and not history itself, is left unexplained.

The implication of such a position can either be that (a) one answers the questions of the uniqueness of Christianity, or of Israel, by a leap of faith in which God's gracious election is posited as the ultimate cause of those situations in which God's communication takes place; or (b) one adopts a thoroughgoing relativism in which faith has no absolute claims except for those who happen to have been born into a society which interprets its history in terms of God's faithfulness, in which case sociology, or perhaps ultimately, chance, is posited as the cause behind which we cannot go.

For my own part I think we must attempt again to state more positively than negatively the relation between critical-historical research and whatever faith statements we associate with Christianity. The risk must be run of overstating the connections between systematic theology and historical research more than of overstating the distinction between the two. Ultimately there remains an *extra* to faith, something which is united to but not exhausted by historical research. That such an *extra* should linger in the thinking of a historian can well be ascribed to one's sociological environment. There is, as far as my thinking has gone on this matter, no adequate way to meet this critique; one can only say that each person in a pluralistic society has his choice of expression for the way in which reality as he has experienced it holds together *best*, or makes *most* sense, and that the Christian faith does that best for him. Put differently, one confesses that seeing oneself as a present member of the body of forgiven and forgiving sinners who ascribe their power to persevere through all testing to God's covenantal faithfulness gives one viability for present tasks, i.e., it "works best" for him.

IV. Some Systematic Implications of
Faith's Relation to Historical Criticism

It seems difficult to go behind this very subjective vindication of one's faith orientation. But one must continually investigate the conditions impinging on this faith and examine what the historical conditionedness of the church's consciousness has to say positively about the nature of revelation. Faith seeking understanding should not stop with seeking logical continuity between faith concepts, nor with affirming the paradoxical character of faith almost to the point of suggesting that one believes because faith is absurd. Faith seeks historical understanding. Such seeking is the positive function which critical-historical studies serve for systematic theology. They describe the very complexity of created factors which comprise any interpreted event. What we call grace is really identified as such retrospectively, much as in the Joseph story the ground for forgiveness is that what was meant by the brothers for evil was meant by God for the preservation of many and, *n.b.*, many Egyptians.

It is the situation comprised of tradition (false as well as true) and novelty which is to faith revelatory, and it is revelatory because there was a tradition of expectation, comprised of both acceptance and rejection, to receive the novelty of an event or a person or, ultimately, the Messiah. Christologically this can be expressed by admitting first that the symbol of the virgin birth of the Messiah has validity insofar as it points to the primacy of divine initiative in the fulfillment of the covenant and to the fact that Israel must wait in the lowliness of a handmaiden upon the restoring word of God instead of creating its own instant religion on the high places. But the virgin birth is also a dangerous symbol if it minimizes the variety of things which constituted the humanity of the first-century Jew. Mary's obedience is that of a true representative (along with the others featured in the narrative: Elizabeth, Zechariah, Simeon, Anna, and above all Joseph) of Israel, which God preserved to that moment to receive, nurture, feed, and educate the Messiah in the way of the free obedience which was Israel's unfilled side of the covenant. This means that the religion of the late Jews, indeed of the Pharisees and of Judas, has a part in the creation of the situation of Jesus' victorious obedience. It is not so much the conception without human agent which is important in the birth narratives as the fact that Israel labored to bring forth the Messiah. The Messiah's instruction by the tradition and his novelty beyond it are expressed by the evangelist's story of Jesus' being about his Father's business and his going down to Nazareth to be obedient to his parents.

But in terms of the doctrine of the incarnation, the *assumptio carnis* means that the Word took on not mere flesh but manhood which is a social, linguistic, political, economic, religious, and evolving reality. It is not incidental or embarrassing that the Messiah thought and spoke in the idiom of his day, that he proclaimed the Kingdom in parables drawn from Israel's political history and from rural imagery and from reinterpretations of the law, and that he shared his contemporaries' mythical worldview. He communicated the properties of radically free obedience to all this which he received from the *matrix* of Israel and raised it to universal (of the *oikoumene*) significance through the church's vindicating proclamation of his resurrection. What is not assumed is not healed, and all constituents of historical life are taken up in the Messianic person. To put it still another way, the Eternal Son of God was fully united to the humanity he assumed, but he raised it to new dimensions because he was not limited to that humanity and because the radically free obedience by which he transcended his cultural givens did not merely negate that culture but also affirmed it in raising it to a broader and more universal historical significance. This happened as the covenantal history of the Jews got translated into the covenantal history which God has with the Jews for the sake of his covenantal history with all the nations.

The definitive character of this culture-transforming, radically free obedience which is the coming of the Messiah is set forth in a standard way in the writings which the church, by the habit of hearing God's word when reading and interpreting those writings, canonized by use. But an analogous transforming relation between Christ and culture goes on as the church is led, empowered, startled, forced (i.e., "by the power of the Spirit") time and again into the radical kind of obedience which raises the tradition to new levels of significance (wider missionary impact, if you will). In order to reinterpret the tradition, a knowledge of what factors went into its formation is necessary, a knowledge which is not possible without historical criticism. Historical research is essential to the church's culture-transforming task of correcting, positively and negatively, the church's traditional interpretation of tradition. Historical criticism is a means by which the church transcends its own prevailing historical interpretation after the manner, but not with the authority, of the Messianic critique, "You have heard it said. . . . But I say. . . ."

This process is taking place, for example, where historical research has made the continuity between late Judaism and the New Testament community increasingly clear. The church's contemporary teaching has to undo its antisemitism and indeed assign a positively redemptive role even to the Jewish rejection of the Christ (as for that matter Barth does splendidly in *CD*, II/2). The pressure of historical research has broken down traditional interpretations of the Reformation and Counter-Reformation traditions; movements which for centuries have been dismissed as ironic or compromising or seditious are being re-evaluated. The traditional loudspeakers of the period are being made to carry a message which differs from what they have previously been heard to say. The church needs to reformulate systematically a doctrine of church authority by which it can admit its past errors. Historical study has emphasized the closest possible relation between doctrine and allegedly nontheological factors. Systematic theology must develop safeguards against turning theology into just another ideology against social change which would threaten the church's privileged economic and political position. Historical study has indicated the role of cultic celebration in the continuity of religious institutions and the impact, positive as well as negative, of other religions on Israel and other religions on Christianity. Systematic theology must find a new way to explicate the religious factor in a doctrine of man, and it must describe how the Christian religion relates to other religions in a pluralistic world which Christianity has been largely instrumental in bringing about through its complex relationship to missions, capitalism, and technology. Undoubtedly more areas of impact of historical research could be cited, but these suffice to indicate the excitement and urgency of historical research which must be done today by those who are concerned with the church's contemporary proclamation.

Habitats of Infant Baptism

DAVID F. WRIGHT

No factor is responsible for as much damage in the natural world as the loss or degradation of the habitats of flora and fauna. The effects of direct human intrusion in hunting, poaching, and overfishing, for example, are all too familiar to us. The same goes for atmospheric pollution, with its more indirect consequences. Less obvious often is the deterioration or destruction of habitats through changes such as the draining of marshland, the eradication of hedgerows, deforestation, innovations in agricultural techniques, and the introduction, accidental or deliberate, of competing species.

Conservationists consequently devote great energies to safeguarding, rescuing, reinstating, and improving habitats at risk. Nothing conduces so much to the flourishing of a plant or a mammal as its enjoyment of a healthy and adequate habitat. Conversely, the success of a rescue operation based on a breeding program in captivity may in the long term depend on the restoration of a lost habitat in the wild.

The image of the habitat lends itself to a consideration of the setting or settings within which the baptism of infants most naturally belongs. Such an enquiry is suggested not least by the varied ecological history of the observance. Some of the habitats in which it has from time to time been naturalized have distorted or stunted its identity or viability. It may never have been an endangered species, but perhaps it might not be so widely rejected in some of the fastest growing sectors of world Christianity — the Pentecostal and Baptist, in particular — if it had been more frequently observed growing to its proper dimensions in its native environment.

Family and Parents

Infants do not bring themselves to baptism. That is almost invariably the responsibility of parents whose own Christian faith claims baptism for their newborn. Within the Reformed tradition to a distinctive degree, a set of convictions about the place of the believing family in the gathering of the people of God in accord with his covenant promise has furnished a standard warrant for conferring the sign of the new covenant on babies. We may therefore regard the Christian family as an essential habitat — the essential microhabitat — of infant baptism. From this it follows that if the Christian identity of the family or the integrity of the family itself is insecure, infant baptism will not thrive as it ought.

Ministers have long been used to baptizing the children of parents only one of whom is a believer — or at least is willing publicly to undertake to bring the child up "in the nurture and admonition of the Lord." Much more recent is the complex of pastoral problems presented by the swelling tides eroding the normative unit of the two-married-parents family in much of the western world. Should baptism be expected to bear fruit in the lives of infants of cohabiting unmarried parents? That is to say, is it appropriately given when the context which the Christian tradition has invariably held to be the God-assigned habitat for childbearing — the one-flesh union of marriage — is not operative?

The rapid growth of a massive aversion to marriage in large areas of decaying Christendom in the West has left the family an increasingly elusive entity. Government-led social policy cannot abandon the health of the family as an ideal, yet frequently is found defending it with a studious silence, or perhaps ambivalence, about marriage. It may even flinch from provoking charges of discrimination against single parents by suggesting that children fare best in a stable home made by two parents, even if they are unmarried. That infant baptism has suffered from this multifactorial disturbance of its age-old family habitat is undoubted. The steep decline in the number of babies being brought for baptism (so steep in some Church of Scotland parishes that infant baptism has become so gravely endangered as to be almost extinct) has not a little to do with a sense that "christening" is not for the unmarried mother or for partners living together but uncommitted to each other beyond the visible future. A confusion of popular instincts and traditional sentiments interacts with diverse pastoral policies of congregations and pastors. The outcomes are bound to vary enormously, yet rare will be the local church untouched by the huge waves of disaffection for marriage sweeping across society.

Must infant baptism continue to decline *pari passu* with the decline of the familial habitat? Reflection on the image of the habitat may suggest guidelines for responding to some of the dilemmas thrown up by changing social patterns. What if the overriding consideration in deciding whether baptism should be encouraged or conferred were the identification of a parental habitat in which the tender plant of baptism is most likely to take root and bear the promised fruit — that is, a life within the community of Christian faith? Such an approach might well lead to a responsible child-centered baptismal policy in preference to a formalistic insistence on the standing of the parents. The loving and firmly believing single mother is likely to offer a healthier habitat for her baby's baptism to flourish than married parents whose indifference to their child's Christian upbringing has been overborne only by grandparental pressure.

Habitat-focused questions along these lines encourage a forward-looking perspective on infant baptism, rather than a preoccupation with a baby's antecedents. They foster a proper concern with the future of the baptized child and with the realization of the potential of baptism, with a corresponding lessening of emphasis on the parents' (or parent's) status and the status of the newly baptized.

In fact, the rethinking of infant baptism that the changing face of parenting necessarily requires may contribute constructively to its liberation from its false domestication. Critics within and without the churches fault reactionary defenses of the nuclear family on a number of grounds. One aspect of the historical ecology of paedobaptism in such a traditional context has been its reduction to an event in the life of the family, to the detriment of its locus in gospel and church. Its microhabitat in the family circle has smothered it, so to speak, so that it scarcely seems to belong any longer to the local body of Christ as a sacrament of the gospel. The baptism may still take place in the congregation's normal Sunday worship, but its reception is preponderantly conditioned by accompaniments of family tradition, from the precious christening robe to the party for relatives from far and near. The familial reductionism of baby-baptism is even more marked if the minister is persuaded to administer it in a private gathering in home or hotel, or if parents and child travel back for it to the grandparents' congregation, in preference to the congregation in which the child's baptism must be "improved" (as our forefathers used to say) week in, week out.

Part of the problem can be traced to many a church's bankruptcy of practice and imagination when it comes to celebrating baptism of its members' newborn. Why not a church party afterwards, instead of (or at least before) a family do? Does the congregation offer guidance on the selection of godparents where these have a role, or should it itself designate instead a suitable person to serve as a kind of baptismal guardian? New Testament baptismal vocabulary abounds with the imagery of clothing. Even if the renewed interest in immersion at paedobaptism is not taken on board — with the possibility of unclothing and reclothing in white, according to early church custom — baptism at any age is not a proper occasion for candidates (meaning etymologically "those clothed in white") to be decked out in finery or fashion. Theologically this is wholly incongruous.

Confining infant baptism solely or predominantly to the habitat of the family — essential as that habitat must be — produces a stunted plant devoid of growth potential. Or perhaps more appropriately, baptism is thereby hybridized into a celebration of birth (rather than of new birth in Christ), whose future extrapolation looks forward to other milestones in the child's development with not even a nominal counterpart in the church-grounded pilgrim's progress. The task of clawing back infant baptism from the choking luxuriance of familial custom must struggle against generations of assumption and practice. Paradoxical though it must seem, the task may benefit opportunistically from the demise of the hegemony of the two-married-parents family that the new millennium portends. The inherited shape of family life crumbles on all sides. As far as baptism is concerned, the disintegration may allow (we dare not put it higher than this) some recovery of its essentially ecclesial character. The church is the critical habitat for the vitality of infant baptism — and the family or parental context has significance only within the larger habitat.

Secularization and family decay are interrelated in complex ways. The latter will not provide the fortuitous opportunity hinted at in the previous paragraph if the former is given free rein with baptism. Traditionalism reinforced by secularism will denature baptism, transmuting it into a naming ceremony or a welcome-to-baby celebration or a commitment to responsible parenthood or some other innocent or worthy role — but all bereft of its core identity as incorporation into Christ. As fewer and fewer parents show any interest in this Christian baptism for their offspring, ministers experience the subtle temptation to tailor some lesser baptism to

257

suit sub-Christian tastes. What is incontrovertibly already happening with weddings and funerals (popular songs instead of hymns, readings from any book but the Bible, prayers in theistic terms at best) will surely dumb down baptism too. This secular familial captivity of infant baptism will be resisted only if the indispensable habitat of responsible parenthood is not allowed to take complete possession of the plant. The baptism of newborn children is viable as familial event only when rooted in an unmistakably ecclesial habitat.

The Local Community

Ministers of the Word and sacraments of the gospel rightly sense a threat to their responsibility when tenacious family forces bid to determine how the baptism of its latest progeny shall be conducted. Even more threatening can be the pressure of the wider community's expectations. For baptism is uniquely a point at which popular attitudes to the church or "religion" impinge upon ministerial roles. This is likely to be most true in countries with an established or officially national church, but probably obtains to some degree wherever a paedobaptist church has long had a paramount presence within its neighborhood. In such a situation the custom of baptizing newborn babies commonly gathers around itself a body of widely held understandings, hopes, and fears. Often they will reflect the wisdom of popular religion (in part what an earlier generation called superstition), which may stand at some remove from the teaching of catechism, creed, and confession. It finds expression, for example, in calling infant baptism "christening" and in visceral convictions that without it the new life is somehow vulnerable or at risk, at least of missing out on some of the health, wealth, and happiness that are otherwise everyone's birthright. Most readers will already have in mind local traditions that retail the potential deficit sooner or later of the baby that is not properly "done," as the saying goes.

The vigor of this broader communal take on infant baptism often makes itself felt in the congregation's baptismal ministry through the conduit of the family — not always the parents, or solely the parents — of a newborn baby. In a paedobaptist context, there are solid biblical and theological grounds for reckoning seriously with the family, even if its quest for baptism for its newest member is driven by a somewhat debased notion of what it is all about. Part of the difficulty of dealing with such a situation rests precisely on the fact that the request reflects a generalized populist view of baby-baptism, and that the church's response to the request is likely to be fed back in interaction with it. How infant baptism is handled easily becomes a test case for relations between the church and its feeder community. An unrestrictive provision of baptism on request will help to lubricate smooth church-community harmony, while a more restrictive approach may issue in a clash between inconsistent understandings of baptism, souring relations with more than one family.

Is the wider catchment area of a church one of the habitats in which infant baptism is meant to grow successfully? Among the complicating factors that frustrate a simple answer is the recognition that behind the dissonance between the church's view of baptism — as expressed, for example, in its order of service for baptism — and communal views lies normally a hangover from an earlier age when the majority of the population had their children baptized more or less as a matter of routine. To state the issue thus is not to pass judgment but simply to facilitate understanding. When the civil and the ecclesial communities were virtually coterminous, baptism functioned almost as a mark of belonging to both. Few in the Reformed tradition today would defend the practice of general or indiscriminate baptism, regardless of the parents' overt attachment to the life of the congregation. Most of us find the Swedish experience, in which still some 90 percent of babies are baptized in the Lutheran church but well below 5 percent of the population attend worship, more bemusing than enviable.

From the perspective of this paper, what happens to infant baptism when it is earthed not so much in the community of faith as in the wider community in which it is set? A case for an open baptism policy — allowing baptism for the children of parents with little or no church connection — is sometimes advanced precisely in the interests of a sense of community solidarity which extends even to a feeling that this is "our church." Even though "we" do not belong to it, in some way it belong to "us." Such a case may be made along the following lines for the special circumstances of a parish marked by multiple social deprivation — in UK terms, an "urban priority area" or UPA. In such a world, lone-parent families require all the support a church fellowship can provide, and children at risk from neglect or abuse need the affirmation of childhood that infant baptism expresses. In the bleakness that blights life in many a UPA, every opportunity to celebrate something good and beautiful should be welcomed. In this setting, infant baptism witnesses signally to Jesus' special concern for the marginalized and despised. The last thing that parents struggling to survive against a host of pressures should have to face is rejection by the church — for rejection is how refusal or reluctance to baptize their babies will be received.

An argument of this kind carries considerable emotive force. Nor is there any reason why a parallel case should not be formulated for the distinctive circumstances of a parish community much higher up the socio-economic scale. Yet it is difficult to escape the impression that when infant baptism is cultivated within this communal habitat, its identity as the sacrament of incorporation into Christ in his body is gravely imperiled. In reality, baptism is being made to serve any number of purposes which, however laudable in themselves, are not integral to its distinctive role. Planting infant baptism in this habitat, which is found near the margins of the worshiping congregation, fosters its adulteration. The testing demands of relating church to community are not to be met by the abuse of baptism. It is perhaps a sobering measure of the widespread lack of consensus about the rationale for infant baptism that it has proved so pliable to service such diverse ends.

Consider, for example, the notion that baptism is an affirmation of babyhood or childhood — which might seek support from some of the sayings of Jesus about children. The sacraments of the gospel, however, are not age-specific. That baptism has a defining connection with babyhood — rather than with teenage or adult years — could be concluded only by ignoring the New Testament's witness to baptism. There, if infants are included at all, they are embraced invisibly in baptisms that are determined by the conversion and faith of their parents. That is to say, if baptism bears a special message about young children, it is one that relates to the offspring of believing parents, not to children generically, by virtue of their tender years alone.

One could pursue a fresh line of enquiry at this point, investigating what happens to baptism when the habitat in which it is naturalized is that of babyhood. Fixing baptism in this setting is entirely understandable, for paedobaptism has been the common form of the sacrament for most of the church throughout most of its history. Yet although it has in practice been the norm from some time after Augustine until the present, to assume therefrom that infant reception is integral to baptism may quickly end up with two baptisms, not one (cf. Ephesians 4:5). Treating the passivity of the babe in arms at the font as illustrative of God's — or the parents' — role understands infant baptism in terms that cannot be applied to believers' baptism. Baptism is always done to us, not by us, but the command "Be baptized" (Acts 2:38) implies no less intentional an act than "Take and eat." The same caveat holds for the claim that infant baptism demonstrates "the priority of grace over faith" — where the faith in view is the future faith of the child.

Even more questionable are illustrations that fetch the meaning of baptism from natal or ante-natal experience. The baby in the womb surrounded by protecting and nourishing water is made to speak of the child held within the life-giving waters of God's love. Or baptism may be likened to the breaking of the mother's waters and the child's emergence from the confines of the womb to the new wide world of God's kingdom. Resort to such images may appear harmless enough, but they only too easily so shape conceptions of baptism that faith- or conversion-baptism becomes the problematic exception instead of the norm — as it undoubtedly was in the early centuries. The difficulty can be traced back to siting baptism in the habitat of babyhood instead of the believing family in the worshiping congregation.

The dominical appointment of baptism gives us no authority to turn it into a thanksgiving for birth or a celebration of babyhood — or for that matter into a custom hallowed by communal tradition whose observance is justified in terms of pre-evangelism, building bridges with the unchurched, social cohesiveness, the welfare needs of vulnerable children, the nurture of a sputtering spark of parental faith, or many another such commendable objective. We have no biblical warrant for baptizing except where we can believe that all are being baptized by the one Spirit into the one body of Christ (cf. 1 Corinthians 12:13), and are so baptized into Christ as to die with him to sin and rise with him to newness of life (cf. Romans 6:2-4), to be no less than clothed with him (cf. Galatians 3:27).

The Congregation

One resort of those who seek to defend the baptism of children whose parents cannot credibly be received as believing Christians is to shift the locus of faith in the baptismal service to the congregation. The shift may be invoked sometimes in terms of a quasi-parental or adoptive role for the congregation in cases of a parent or parents felt to be inadequate in more than the spiritual care of the child. At work here is a wider tendency, observable also in changing attitudes towards confirmation or admission to the Lord's supper. In an age when teenagers and young adults shy away from any kind of life-commitment and frequently lack the decisiveness to make a public profession of faith, the spotlight focuses instead on the faith of the receiving congregation. The persons being confirmed or admitted are viewed not so much as enlisting to be Christ's faithful soldiers and servants unto their lives' ends but rather as setting out on a journey in the first faltering steps of faith.

Much might be said about this broader tendency to soft-pedal the call to pledge oneself openly and irrevocably to Christ, but our subject is infant baptism. Placing baptism centrally in the local congregation is to plant it in its native habitat, apart from which it cannot truly thrive. It has been a healthy Reformed insistence that baptism be administered in the face of the congregation. It is there with unequaled appropriateness that the essential ecclesial lineaments of baptism are evident. Only there do the people of Christ recognizably welcome a new member in his name. And beyond doubt the congregation's role is that of participants, not spectators, for which role faith is indispensable. Furthermore, this is a faith that believes for the parents and the child, that the promises of God in Christ in the covenant of grace are fulfilled for them here and now, no less than it believes for the congregation in its vocation of welcome and integration of the baptized, and for each member severally in reaffirming afresh his or her own baptismal pledge.

But it is a false step to imagine that the corporate faith of the church can do duty, vicariously as it were, for the parents' absent or uncertain faith. Neglecting the vital habitat of the believing family cannot be compensated for by overtaxing the habitat of the believing congregation. Both are essential for the flourishing of baptism, the former within the latter, neither one without the other. Unless the conditions exist for the healthy growth of the seed of the Spirit in the baptized in that environment where the new person is reared and trained, there can be little hope that the church can provide that habitat on its own. Most baptismal theology in the Reformed tradition would recognize no normal grounds for believing that it is meant to do so — for believing, that is, in the propriety of baptizing the child of unbelieving parents in the confidence that the congregation's faith and nurture of the child will suffice.

What emerges at this point is the essential correlation between the habitat of the Christian family or parent(s) and the habitat of the Christian congregation. The health of one safeguards the other. Together they contribute to the proper planting and successful growth of infant baptism. In particular they together serve to protect the integrity of baptism as an apostolic ordinance. For example, if baptism is viewed as part of the children's program of a church, its necessary rootedness in the soil of parental faith may well be played down in favor of its value as the church's contact with a new child in the community as early as may be in the child's life. Something very similar happens when infant baptism in dubious cases or worse is justified in terms of the evangelistic opportunity it offers when many nonchurch folk are present on this special occasion. This way of squaring the ministerial conscience has been not uncommon in both the Church of England and the Church of Scotland on the part of those uncomfortable with their Church's lax (as they see it) baptismal discipline.

But baptism is intended to be neither an instrument of congregational outreach nor a slot within the church's ministry to children — although when allowed to be itself, it may well be of value to both. The indispensability of baptism may also need defending when some other activity of the church minimizes it. In recent years within the Church of Scotland, pressure from the Christian Education department to promote the admission of children to the Lord's table led to a move to extend admission even to unbaptized children who attended the Sunday School. Had it succeeded it would have sanctioned action somewhat similar to a possibility discussed above, in which the congregation's faith would stand as surety in the baptism of children whose parent or parents could not responsibly speak for them at the font — but were concerned enough to send them to Sunday School. On the other hand, there is some evidence of an increasing tendency for parents who are active church members to decline baptism for their infants — and some Reformed churches in different parts of the world have recognized this choice as a proper baptismal option.

It is surely a critical test of a satisfactory baptismal theology that it can encompass both infant and believers' baptism within a single understanding. As I see it, baptism as the sign of the covenant is appropriately given by Christ's ministers whenever there are grounds for believing that God is calling persons into his covenant people which is the body of Christ. These grounds are of two kinds: for those able to speak for them-

263

selves, it is their faith, professed (cf. Acts 8:12, 37-38; 11:16-17; 16:31-33, etc.); for those not so able, it is their birth to parents whose faith enables them to speak on their children's behalf.

In the church of the early Fathers, these two patterns were held more closely together than is generally apparent today. This happened partly in the baptism of children jointly with their parents following the latter's conversion. It happened also in the manner in which the earliest known adaptation of the baptismal liturgy to cater for infants preserved the requirement of faith professed. Just as candidates of sufficient years answered "I believe" to the creedal questions, so the baptizing ministers asked of parents sponsoring those too young to answer for themselves "Does he/she believe?"

The family of faith and the congregation of faith — these then are the two key habitats for infant baptism's flourishing. Like concentric circles, the smaller habitat and the larger mutually enrich each other. As the child develops, nurtured as a plant is within a habitat that escapes degradation and pollution and thus provides the right conditions of sturdy growth, so he or she progressively spreads out and takes his or her rightful and independent place within the congregation. The movement from dependence on parental faith to self-owned faith in the worshiping community may be a seamless one, especially if the minihabitat is firmly integrated in the macrohabitat and each strengthens the other.

Nor must the wider community be forgotten, for this is the church's primary field of service and witness, and baptism is like the door into the church. If the two essential markers in a baptismal ecology are faith and the church, it is an ecology that is open to the world beyond these, for baptism is a sacrament of the gospel. It is no less true of it than of the Eucharist, that in it God's people proclaim the Lord's death and resurrection until he comes. Baptism best serves the town or neighborhood when it is true to its evangelical, that is, its kerygmatic nature, not when it is dispensed according to communal expectations or the requirements of the church's social welfare program.

We probably should not expect sacraments of the gospel to thrive in an ecclesial context where the gospel itself is stunted or impoverished. Sacraments testify to the gospel in a secondary sense also, that the form and style of their presentation disclose the gospel by which a particular pastor or congregation lives. A test that I would like to see applied to all ordinands in their final church assessment is simply this: Do they show credible evidence of having a gospel to live by and die for? Not of course an idiosyncratic gospel of their own devising but the apostolic gospel of Christ which they have so made their own that with Paul they can truly call it "my gospel" (cf. Romans 2:16; 16:25; 2 Timothy 2:8). Where the gospel of God's grace in Jesus Christ is robustly nurtured in church ministry, there the sacraments of that gospel may be expected to thrive in their native soil.

Social Science and Public Theology

ROBERT WUTHNOW

A woman who participated in a recent research project of mine remembered the exact moment she decided to leave the church. "I was sixteen and our youth group was having a rap session with the minister. I was
doing a lot of thinking about the Trinity and asked him about it, especially
to tell me about the Holy Spirit. He said he really didn't think there was
any way to answer my question. I guess every teenager needs a ticket out
the church door. That was mine."

If theology is using the human mind in service to God, this is a trou-
bling anecdote. Why was the minister unable to answer this young woman's
question? Was she, as another study suggested, one of the millions of baby
boomers who left church in late adolescence because it failed to answer their
questions? Is the minister's response indicative of some larger shift that
makes it hard to formulate theological answers to life's enduring questions?

Social scientists can sit back, safe in the security of empirical relativism, and pose such questions about theology. But a good definition of theology does not limit theological reflection to theologians. It suggests that
any mind may be used in the service of God.[1] What then might we expect
of social science?

One answer that has gained popularity in the past half century is to
say that social science can pretty well accommodate anyone's theological
views, as long as those views remain private. Someone with deep interests

---

1. I have greatly appreciated Tom Gillespie's understanding of theology in these
terms and have benefited from his leadership at Princeton Theological Seminary.

in Christianity, following this perspective, might devote personal time to those interests, much as to a hobby, but check them at the door each morning before leaving for work. This approach should not be dismissed too easily, especially in a society where few people spend any time thinking seriously about their faith. But it differs from theology that is somehow public, which is what I want to focus on here.

Social science is relevant to public theology — or, we might say, becomes a form of public theology — in widely varying ways, as a recent study of Catholic and evangelical social scientists and journalists suggests.[2] At the risk of oversimplification, I want to consider three of these approaches: social science and advocacy, social science and apologetics, and social science and practice. Each describes an approach that has genuine appeal to some contemporary social scientists and, in my view, has strengths and weaknesses that warrant careful consideration.

Social Science and Advocacy

For someone aiming to bring Christian theology into a specific relationship with social science, I have in mind as advocacy an approach that essentially derives certain first principles from Christianity about what is right and good, and uses social science as a means of identifying social conditions that fall short of those ideals or social programs that aim to bring them more fully into realization. Examples might include teaching and research about racial discrimination that social scientists might pursue because they believe racial discrimination violates biblical standards of love, equality, or justice; studies of divorce that might be motivated by social scientists' conviction that Christianity favors lasting marriages and loving commitment of spouses to each other and their children; or research comparing faith-based and nonreligious social service agencies in hopes of identifying models that people of faith could use to better serve the needy.[3]

2. John Schmalzbauer, "Living Between Athens and Jerusalem: Catholics and Evangelicals in the Culture-Producing Professions" (Ph.D. Dissertation, Princeton University, Department of Sociology, 1997).

3. See for example, J. Philip Wogaman, *Christian Perspectives on Politics* (Philadelphia: Fortress Press, 1988); Anthony Campolo, *Ideas for Social Action* (Grand Rapids: Zondervan, 1985).

In many respects, social science is ideally situated to facilitate this kind of advocacy and thus to make a genuine contribution to public theology by addressing social issues in these ways. Complex social problems in an era of highly specialized knowledge and social institutions require scholarly engagement of this sort. Had the woman who left church at sixteen been puzzled about how to bring her Christian convictions to bear on social problems in the wider community, the minister might well have counseled her to seek advice from a specialist in the social sciences or consider a career in those fields. Indeed, it is difficult to imagine serious objections being voiced against such counsel. Yet there are some thorny questions needing to be addressed.

Mentioning specialized knowledge raises the question of how much a specialist in social science needs to think about the intellectual assumptions surrounding those first principles that motivate specific programs of research. Does one, for instance, need to have an elaborate intellectual justification for assuming that racial discrimination is contrary to biblical principles, or is it sufficient to take that assumption as a starting point and devote one's intellectual energies to the study of racial discrimination? The answer can only be that "it depends." But on what?

Certainly the context in which one chooses to work is critical. There is no reason to insist that every social scientist who decides to work on racial discrimination must develop an elaborate theological justification for choosing this topic, any more than one would insist that everyone who drives an automobile knows how to build one. Time is scarce and intellectual energy is sometimes even scarcer. I am glad some social scientists who are people of faith have chosen to devote their energy to studying racial discrimination, rather than pouring themselves into questions of general theory and methodology.

I know many social scientists who take a stance like this. One would scarcely know they have been influenced by any faith tradition. They are good at what they do, specializing in research and teaching about social problems that trouble them. Their work has a clear normative or prescriptive focus. They are not simply engaged in theory building or in contributing to the discipline. They write about human rights, social justice, ethics, law, poverty, inequality, discrimination, economic development, political participation, and so on. Often it is only in private conversations that they describe the religious influences that shaped these interests.

Nonsectarian public or private research universities and liberal arts colleges are hospitable environments for this kind of work. Social scientists in these settings are generally rewarded for doing careful scholarship that informs public debate about current problems. These are religiously pluralistic settings, so scholars are often uncomfortable about linking their studies too closely to a particular tradition. But the advantage of the advocacy stance is that most of the problems one might study are assumed to bear on humanitarian conditions about which there would be little disagreement among various religious traditions. Thus, scholars might debate the seriousness of racial discrimination or the best ways of overcoming it, but would agree that it is a problem.

How then might religion be relevant to such work? For the scholar in a nonsectarian setting, religious convictions may be relevant mostly at the point of identifying problems on which to focus. Rather than choosing a topic that may result in a best-selling book, scholars may focus on problems that arouse their convictions about justice or about helping the needy. Once an investigation is under way, it is likely to be guided mainly by the canons of research that govern the discipline. But the results may also emphasize practical steps that can be taken to correct the problem. To the extent that this kind of "public theology" has any specific religious content, therefore, it is likely to come as a result of other scholars, such as theologians and religious educators, incorporating it into their own teaching and writing.

I suspect there may be more opportunity for religious convictions to be linked publicly with this kind of scholarship than was the case a generation or two ago. In the 1950s and early 1960s, the social sciences in the United States were increasingly rooted in philosophical assumptions that reflected European influences and provided an ostensibly universalistic foundation (one thinks of the work of Talcott Parsons, for example), more so than an earlier generation of American social scientists had offered. These assumptions were never as wedded to Enlightenment thought as later critics would suggest. But they regarded the social sciences as a special kind of knowledge that did not depend on particular religious traditions. Social science could usefully mimic the natural sciences in its quest for objective generalizations about human behavior, but it also recognized the historical and cultural particularities of human behavior. The late 1960s did much to unsettle the assumption that this kind of scholarship was necessarily conducive to the public good. As social advocacy emerged in the civil rights movement and in protests against the Vietnam war, it was often linked more explicitly to Marxist and politically populist arguments than in the past. Yet in the 1970s and 1980s, as these arguments receded in popularity, the social sciences also became more heavily influenced by constructivist arguments (sometimes associated with postmodernism) that challenged the validity of all efforts to arrive at objective generalizations about human behavior. It is against this backdrop that new calls have been heard for scholarship to be grounded in specific cultural traditions, including religious ones. Advocacy can thus be advanced in the name of Christian tradition, just as it can in terms of feminist theory or Marxist theory.

The rediscovery of tradition as a useful element of advocacy has, however, raised new questions about the social settings in which effective advocacy can take place. While many social scientists are content with the freedom and resources available in nonsectarian colleges and universities, there appears to be growing interest in alternative settings as well. For some, theological seminaries and divinity schools are attractive because of possibilities for speaking from a particular faith tradition. For others, independent think tanks and institutes or private advocacy groups are attractive for the same reasons.

If social science is to be a kind of theology that engages in public advocacy, it will probably need to rely increasingly on linkages and partnerships between the research universities that provide ample resources for high-quality scholarship and other organizations that give greater opportunities for reaching particular constituencies. Whether these other organizations are clearly identified with a particular theological tradition or not, their role may be to interpret scholarship for leaders in religious organizations and for government officials and community activists who can implement new social programs.

Social Science and Apologetics

I mean "apologetics," not in a technical or formal sense, but as scholarship that is strongly concerned with furthering a particular faith tradition, perhaps even by demonstrating that this faith tradition is uniquely true, or at least by showing that it offers special or distinctive insights. One thinks of recent efforts to defend the idea of Christian scholarship, for example.[4] Interest has also been expressed in the idea of integrating faith and learning.[5]

These approaches are, in my view (and probably in the view of their proponents), harder to reconcile with the social sciences than the advocacy stance. They more explicitly question the value of standard practice in the social sciences and make stronger claims about the influence of worldviews on scholarly knowledge. Apart from these intellectual assumptions, they often appear to be concerned with legitimating work at Christian colleges or seminaries over against that which takes place in nonsectarian institutions.

Over the past three decades there have been many efforts to bring Christianity and the social sciences together in ways that demonstrated the unique value of doing so. For example, scholars have questioned the naturalistic assumptions of the social sciences, suggesting that Christianity implies a need to recognize God in all discussions of human behavior.[6] Some discussions have focused specifically on deterministic assumptions, such as those in Marxism or in scientific positivism, and have argued that a faith perspective requires greater recognition of the voluntaristic character of human behavior. Other discussions question optimistic assumptions about the possibilities of bringing about social change (such as those implicit in the advocacy stance) and argue that Christianity requires scholars to think of the human condition in more negative terms.[7]

In my view, these are helpful criticisms, but not ones that point to the necessity — or even to the distinctive value — of doing social science from a uniquely Christian perspective. They are not a necessity because the social sciences are sufficiently complex and diverse in their own assumptions about human behavior that they readily concede most points (such as those about the limits of naturalism, or the need for voluntaristic and crit-

4. George M. Marsden, *The Outrageous Idea of Christian Scholarship* (New York: Oxford University Press, 1997).

5. Michael Beaty, Todd Buras, and Larry Lyon, "Baptist Higher Education: A Conflict in Terms?" *Baylor Line* (Winter 1997): 43-51; Mark A. Noll, *The Scandal of the Evangelical Mind* (Grand Rapids: Eerdmans, 1995).

6. John Milbank, *Theology and Social Theory: Beyond Secular Reason* (London: Blackwell, 1993).

7. For example, see the essays in Stephen A. Grunlan and Milton Reimer, eds., *Christian Perspectives on Sociology* (Grand Rapids: Zondervan, 1982); and Stan D. Gaede, *Where Gods May Dwell: Understanding the Human Condition* (Grand Rapids: Zondervan, 1985).

ical views of human nature); moreover, it is unclear that substantive studies are as guided by general philosophical assumptions as these criticisms suggest. Such criticisms therefore are not distinctive either because the same sorts of questioning can and do occur as a result of other theoretical orientations within the social sciences themselves. While useful in the same way that other debates about theory and methods are useful, these arguments are for this reason less than compelling as a form of Christian apologetics.

But with a weaker agenda in mind, social scientists can contribute valuably to apologetics. One role that social scientists have played in recent years has been to bring their distinctive methods and concepts to bear on questions about the origins of Christianity, its growth, and the history of the church. While these studies may be unwelcome to adherents who attribute the origins and development of Christianity only to God, they have been received favorably by scholars who recognize the inevitability of social influences on faith. To show, then, that Christianity grew because its early followers took special care of one another or because they weeded out heresies that would have weakened apostolic authority is simply to expand understanding of the processes involved.

This is only one example, however, of a larger role that the social sciences can play. Let me offer an analogy. Many social scientists believe their work makes its greatest contribution when it is directed toward building and extending the theoretical core of their discipline (it is for this reason that research studies that often appear trivial to outsiders seem worthwhile to scholars themselves). Such studies may challenge a hypothesis that has been central to a particular theoretical interpretation, for instance, or show that a proposition from one research domain is helpful in another domain. Such scholarship is seldom content to simply report findings; rather, these findings are linked explicitly with "the literature," meaning that their relevance to previous work is acknowledged, and they are generally couched in a "discussion" of possibly fruitful suggestions for further research. In similar fashion, social science research could be oriented toward extending the faith tradition, instead of a particular social science field. To do so would require situating findings in a different literature, especially one that emphasized church history or theology or Christian education.

Some scholars have been calling for greater attention to the idea of Christian studies as a way of promoting such scholarship. Christian studies departments or programs, they argue, might be established in the same way that Jewish studies, East Asian studies, or women's studies programs have been initiated. This suggestion, it seems to me, has considerable merit. It provides a space within the academy for scholarship that differs in intent from that occurring in sociology or political science or history departments. There are nevertheless costs. Whereas Christian perspectives sometimes dominate scholarship simply because of their prominence in Western history, a distinct Christian studies emphasis would necessarily relativize Christianity, making it simply one among a number of possible perspectives (perhaps a good development in the long run, of course, but not one that some institutions would welcome). For those who might wish to orient Christian studies toward demonstrating the unique truth of Christianity, there would also be strains because Christian studies departments would probably need to differentiate themselves from theological schools, on the one hand, and demonstrate that they could uphold the same norms of critical or dispassionate investigation that pertain in other scholarly fields, on the other hand. Doing so would require a clear understanding of the purposes of Christian studies.

To this point, nonsectarian institutions have shown relatively little interest in Christian studies programs, perhaps for the same reasons that they have been disinclined to initiate men's studies or white Anglo studies programs. But, whatever the reasons for this disinterest, it has given church-related colleges an opportunity to launch such programs, especially in contexts where there may be little competition from theological seminaries or where seminary programs focus on the professional training of clergy. Indeed, some church-related colleges have adopted the Christian studies approach to such an extent that efforts are made to orient the entire curriculum around a tighter integration of faith and learning.

The problem in doing so is that curricula at most church-related colleges are themselves increasingly diverse, especially because of the growing popularity of degree-completion, fast-track, and other adult-learner programs. While some interaction between faith concerns and these programs is inevitable, models that derive from a single philosophical orientation are likely to be overly restrictive. In such settings, care must be taken to administer integration of faith and learning requirements fairly, with appropriate input from all segments of the campuses, and with procedures that preserve academic freedom and encourage open deliberation. These precautions are particularly important because Christian traditions are them-

273

Robert Wuthnow

selves highly diverse and have resulted in many different understandings of the role of faith in church-related higher education.[8]

Because of the priority that most social scientists give to the scholarly standards of their disciplines, another precaution needing to be included in discussions of Christian studies or other efforts to integrate faith and learning is to retain some distinction between religious faith *as faith* and religious faith as a focus of intellectual inquiry. The impetus for recent discussions of "integration" has been the perception that this distinction was often too sharp. Yet it is possible to err in the direction of obviating it as well. For example, assertions that a social scientist is "not doing Christian scholarship" may mean only that such a scholar's work is oriented more toward his or her discipline or toward the general understanding and amelioration of social problems than to the advancement of Christian studies. But if there is a normative component to such assertions, such that a person of this kind is somehow under suspicion as not genuinely being a person of faith or that this approach to scholarship is intrinsically less valuable than some other approach, then there are reasons to reject such assertions.

Social Science and Practice

A third alternative that has received increasing attention in recent years derives from the idea of "social practices," as developed in the work of Alasdair MacIntyre and others.[9] For MacIntyre, the central problem of contemporary moral philosophy is that it has irretrievably lost touch with some pre-Kantian, unified theological outlook that once provided clear and authoritative principles of moral action. Although there is much more to MacIntyre's argument than this, he entertains the idea that social practices in the absence of a unifying theoretical perspective may yet be a valuable way of learning and teaching moral behavior. As an example, he suggests that the game of chess is a social practice through which chess players can develop not only technical skill but such virtues as cooperation, courage, playing by the rules, and perseverance.

8. Richard T. Hughes and William B. Adrian, eds., *Models for Christian Higher Education: Strategies for Success in the Twenty-First Century* (Grand Rapids: Eerdmans, 1997).

9. Alasdair MacIntyre, *After Virtue: A Study in Moral Theory*, 2nd ed. (Notre Dame: University of Notre Dame Press, 1984); and Jeffrey Stout, *Ethics After Babel: The Languages of Morals and Their Discontents* (Boston: Beacon, 1988).

Social scientists have been drawn to the idea of social practices (albeit from sources other than MacIntyre) because they emphasize the lived realities and implicit norms that seem to govern most human behavior to a greater extent than abstract philosophical systems or worldviews. Practical theologians have also emphasized practices as a way of revitalizing religious teachings and congregational life by linking theology more closely to such activities as service and hospitality, daily decision-making, worship experiences, hymn singing, work, and devotions.[10] Some attention has also been given to the possibility that practice may provide a helpful way of thinking about the role of religion in higher education.

A key contribution of the idea of practice is its emphasis on the routine activities of scholars and teachers. Unlike the advocacy approach, where the role of faith is most evident at the start of a project or after it is finished, practice suggests that being true to one's faith consists in the details of a project as well: for example, in the courage it may take to keep working on a project that seems to be getting nowhere or in the diligence and ethical integrity one displays in the classroom. Practice, in this sense, has public implications but less through work having explicit religious content and more through the ethical behavior evident in scholars' professional lives. Whereas the apologetics approach emphasizes the intellectual integration of faith and learning, a practice-oriented approach attempts to be more inclusive of the whole person: for example, by recognizing that scholarly creativity may be an intuitive process that cannot be fully articulated in propositional theological knowledge or that time devoted to prayer and meditation may be as important as writing a paper about doctrine.

The greatest difficulty with the practice approach, in my view, is finding anything in it that is distinctive to a particular faith tradition. Much of the research that emerged in the 1960s and 1970s on the so-called sociology of science, as well as some work in the history and philosophy of science, could easily be reinterpreted to suggest that it regarded science as a practice. For instance, such virtues (norms) as cooperation in the scientific enterprise by sharing research results, applying universalistic standards of

10. Craig Dykstra, "Reconceiving Practice," in *Shifting Boundaries: Contextual Approaches to the Structure of Theological Education*, ed. Barbara G. Wheeler and Edward Farley (Louisville: Westminster/John Knox, 1991), pp. 35-66; Dorothy C. Bass, ed., *Practicing Our Faith: A Way of Life for a Searching People* (San Francisco: Jossey-Bass, 1997).

evaluation to these results, and imposing a kind of skeptical neutrality on one's own work were emphasized.[11] Indeed, it was suggested that these norms were an important reason why science had been so successful, and other research showed that scientists were human enough that organized efforts were also needed to detect fraud and to discover those occasions on which objectivity was more of an appearance than a reality. The implication is that good science is unlikely to differ very much if it is conducted from a faith perspective or from a secular one. Of course the fact that scientists can choose to violate norms of good science may leave open possibilities for faith to reinforce good behavior. But the idea of a practice is that the rules of good behavior are *internal* to the practice, not simply ones received from some other practice, and the thrust of research on science has in fact been to suggest that these rules are institutionalized rather than depending only on the choices of individual scientists.

Approaching the idea of practices from a theological perspective leads to a comparable difficulty. When Christian theologians are asked what makes practices *Christian,* the typical response is that they are activities done by Christians or done within the Christian community or tradition. For instance, being hospitable is a Christian practice when Christians do it and when they interpret it within some understanding of Christian tradition; otherwise, or strictly in terms of the number of times someone shows hospitality by inviting neighbors to dinner or giving directions to lost motorists, there are no discernible differences between Christian practices and non-Christian practices. So, for social scientists' work to count as a Christian practice, they would have to do it within a Christian community or interpret it within the Christian tradition — which may mean that there is little difference between the practice approach and the apologetics approach after all.

An additional difficulty with the practice approach derives from its reliance on words like community and tradition. These words have clearer meanings with respect to Christianity if they are associated with Dutch towns or Swiss villages in the sixteenth century than they do today. At present, they make sense to theologians whose lives are spent in Christian seminaries and to clergy whose energies revolve around Christian congregations, but they make less sense to ordinary people who live among (and

11. Robert K. Merton, *The Sociology of Science: Theoretical and Empirical Investigations* (Chicago: University of Chicago Press, 1973).

often between) many different communities and traditions. Especially in the social sciences, where scholarly work problematizes the very meaning of community and tradition, and where there is keen sensitivity to the pluralistic complexity of contemporary society, the idea of a practice being Christian by virtue of its embeddedness in a single community or tradition may seem peculiar.

What then can be salvaged from the idea of practice? In my view, the term needs to be defined more narrowly for it to be meaningful. One way of restricting its definition is by emphasizing spiritual practice or devotional practice — that is, intentional activities focusing specifically on extending one's relationship to God and one's awareness of that relationship.[12] The emphasis on intentionality is meant to indicate that the practice is a focus of attention, rather than being activities that may implicitly or inadvertently derive in some way from a person's spirituality. Playing chess is a practice because people spend time learning the game and playing it, not because they happen to be among chess players; similarly, a developing awareness of one's spiritual aims and aspirations is likely to require time set aside for doing so, rather than simply assuming that doing research (or being hospitable) within a certain tradition is sufficient.

I doubt that practical theologians would object to this refocusing of the issue, particularly because any spiritual practice of this kind is likely to be related to a religious tradition and understood better by reflecting on that tradition. Yet there is an openness about a practice's focus on God or on a comparable approach to spirituality that differs from one that emphasizes tradition and community. In a pluralistic world, people may live more in one tradition or community than others, but they are also full participants in the wider world and are likely to benefit by taking serious account of its pluralism.

The other concern with community, however, is that practices may be difficult to sustain without being part of a community or, even when they are sustained, may be relegated almost exclusively to private life rather than becoming a part of one's public identity. One response to this concern is to say that spiritual practices, even when they are largely private, seldom take place without participation in some community. But these

12. My book *After Heaven: Spirituality in America Since the 1950s* (Berkeley and Los Angeles: University of California Press, 1998), esp. ch. 7, discusses spiritual practice in more detail.

communities may not be rooted in a particular tradition or resemble religious congregations; for example, they may be support groups, or virtual communities of people who interact by e-mail, or task-oriented groups, such as research teams or academic seminars. The other response is simply to question whether practices that deeply influence someone's private life are, after all, such a bad thing if they do not result in distinctively religious public behavior. Given the diversity of contemporary higher education, it may be desirable to adopt a public identity that stems from spiritual depth but permits participation in a variety of venues.

Encouraging Reflection

As I write this, it has been my good fortune to have participated for the past two years in a seminar on religion and higher education that brings approximately forty scholars together from across the country twice a year for wide-ranging discussions about teaching, research, administration, and other aspects of the scholarly life. The seminar, as far as I have been able to determine, has no particular agenda other than promoting discussions that probably would not happen in other settings. The participants are from universities, church-related institutions, and seminaries, and they represent several religious traditions as well as many different disciplines.

What has impressed me most about these discussions is how much the participants' views reflect the settings in which they work, and how different these views are. Those of scholars in seminaries are quite different from those of scholars at church-related colleges, for example. The social scientists' views are different from those of religious studies faculty, and additional differences can be traced to particular denominational traditions or to the battles people have fought at their institutions.[13] Thus, there is seldom any agreement on such encompassing questions as how to integrate faith and learning or how to enhance the teaching of religion in higher education.

But disagreement prompts further reflection. It heightens awareness of the enormous diversity of American higher education — and of the vast

---

13. How disciplinary norms in philosophy and religious studies departments shape these debates is illustrated in the essays in William J. Wainwright, ed., *God, Philosophy, and Academic Culture* (Atlanta: Scholars Press, 1996).

resources that permit scholars to work in interesting ways and from different perspectives. Recognizing the abundance of these resources does not eliminate the need to make wise choices about their use. However, it does reduce some of the urgency that pervades discussions about which way is the right way to engage in scholarship. Indeed, we can be grateful that scholars are inclined to pursue the life of the mind in different ways.

Whether social scientists choose to emphasize advocacy, apologetics, or practice, they can benefit from the fact that others choose differently. American higher education will be challenged as never before in the next few decades by the needs of an increasingly diverse population and by new technologies and their ethical implications. Faculty and administrators who focus only on whether their particular discipline, institution, or style of research is flourishing or declining are unlikely to be the major contributors in facing these new challenges. Those who can recognize the benefits of working together, of specializing, and of creating new structures are likely to contribute more. Deep commitment to a religious faith need not be inimical to those possibilities.

Contributors

Robert M. Adams   Yale University, New Haven, Connecticut

Wallace M. Alston, Jr.   Center of Theological Inquiry, Princeton, New Jersey

H. Russel Botman   University of Western Cape, Cape Town Province, South Africa

Don Browning   The Divinity School, University of Chicago, Chicago, Illinois

Edward Idris Cardinal Cassidy   Pontifical Council for Promoting Christian Unity, The Vatican, Rome, Italy

Ellen T. Charry   Princeton Theological Seminary, Princeton, New Jersey

Yasuo Carl Furuya   International Christian University, Mitaka, Tokyo, Japan

Peter J. Gomes   The Memorial Church, Harvard University, Cambridge, Massachusetts

Gustavo Gutiérrez   Instituto Bartolomé de Las Casas-Rimac, Lima, Peru

William O. Harris   Princeton Theological Seminary, Princeton, New Jersey

Robert W. Jenson   Center of Theological Inquiry, Princeton, New Jersey

John H. Leith   Union Theological Seminary in Virginia (ret.), Richmond, Virginia

Contributors

Bruce L. McCormack   Princeton Theological Seminary, Princeton, New Jersey

Patrick D. Miller   Princeton Theological Seminary, Princeton, New Jersey

Jong Sung Rhee   Institute of Advanced Christian Studies, Seoul, Korea

Gerhard Sauter   Ökumenisches Institüt der Evangelisch-Theologie, Bonn, Germany

Eduard Schweizer   University of Zurich (ret.), Zurich, Switzerland

Thomas F. Torrance   New College, University of Edinburgh (ret.), Edinburgh, Scotland

Károly Tóth   Ecumenical Study Center, Budapest, Hungary

Leanne Van Dyk   Western Theological Seminary, Holland, Michigan

David B. Watermulder   Bryn Mawr Presbyterian Church (ret.), Bryn Mawr, Pennsylvania

Michael Welker   University of Heidelberg, Heidelberg, Germany

E. David Willis   Princeton Theological Seminary (ret.), Princeton, New Jersey

David F. Wright   New College, University of Edinburgh, Edinburgh, Scotland

Robert Wuthnow   Princeton University, Princeton, New Jersey